AROUND THE
WORLD ON
50 BUCKS

AROUND THE WORLD ON 50 BUCKS

How I Left with Little
and Returned a Rich Man

Christopher Schacht

W PUBLISHING GROUP

AN IMPRINT OF THOMAS NELSON

Original German publication © 2018 by adeo Verlag in der Gerth Medien GmbH: *Mit 50 Euro um die Welt*

Published in Nashville, Tennessee, by W Publishing Group, an imprint of Thomas Nelson.

English translation, Christopher Schacht, *Around the World on 50 Bucks*, by Janet Gesme.

Thomas Nelson titles may be purchased in bulk for educational, business, fund-raising, or sales promotional use. For information, please e-mail SpecialMarkets@ThomasNelson.com.

ISBN 978-0-7852-2942-1 (eBook)

Library of Congress Cataloging-in-Publication Data

Names: Schacht, Christopher, 1993- author. | Gesme, Janet Leigh, 1971- translator.
Title: Around the world on 50 bucks : how I left with little and returned a rich man / Christopher Schacht ; [English translation by Janet Gesme].
Other titles: Mit 50 Euro um die Welt. English | Around the world on fifty bucks
Description: English language edition. | Nashville, Tennessee : W Publishing Group, an imprint of Thomas Nelson, [2019] | "English translation, Christopher Schacht, Around the World on 50 Bucks, by Janet Gesme"—T.p. verso. | Description based on print version record and CIP data provided by publisher; resource not viewed.
Identifiers: LCCN 2019009747 (print) | LCCN 2019021593 (ebook) | ISBN 9780785229421 (E-book) | ISBN 9780785229407 | ISBN 9780785229407 (Softcover) | ISBN 9780785229421 (eBook)
Subjects: LCSH: Schacht, Christopher, 1993—Travel. | Voyages around the world—Biography. | Tourism.
Classification: LCC G440 (ebook) | LCC G440 .S2313 2019 (print) | DDC 910.4092 [B] —dc23
LC record available at https://lccn.loc.gov/2019009747

Printed in the United States of America

19 20 21 22 23 LSC 10 9 8 7 6 5 4 3 2 1

For my mother, who almost worried herself
to death during those four years.
Mom, you should probably stop reading here ;-).

"It's a dangerous business, Frodo, going out
your door. You step onto the road, and if you
don't keep your feet, there's no knowing where
you might be swept off to."
—J.R.R. Tolkien, *The Fellowship of the Ring*

Life
awaits
you.

CONTENTS

FOURTH LEG: ASIA AND THE MIDDLE EAST

A QUICK OVERVIEW

I OBVIOUSLY EXPERIENCED MUCH more than can fit between the covers of this book during the four years I spent traveling around the world, and yet I want to share the most hilarious, exhilarating, utterly surreal, and ludicrous of my adventures with you. Who knows, maybe it will leave you wanting more!

A rough overview:

- Forty-five countries
- 1,512 days
- More than sixty-five thousand miles over water and land
- Five of the Seven Wonders of the World
- Four new languages
- Four fewer wisdom teeth
- Hilarious encounters
- Intense new friendships
- Pictures to make you jealous (?)
- Disgusting food
- Life-changing insights
- A ton of adventure
- And more . . .

And now—let's go!

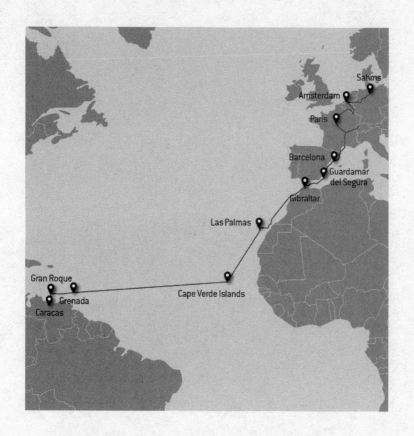

Sahms
Amsterdam
Paris
Barcelona
Guardamar
del Segura
Gibraltar
Las Palmas
Gran Roque
Grenada
Caracas
Cape Verde Islands

EUROPE, THE ATLANTIC OCEAN, AND THE CARIBBEAN ISLES

1

A NEW ADVENTURE

CLICK. **THE LOCK TURNED.** *Clack.* The deadbolt slid home. *That's it!* I threw the key through the mail slot next to the door, turned around, and tried to capture this moment in my memory. The sun shone warm on my face, and the gentle breeze carried the scent of pine trees and freshly mowed meadows. What a dreamy first day of July. I blinked into the sunlight, smiling ear to ear—I had been waiting for this moment for a year and a half!

Behind me lay a stressful year full of final exams, more than two hundred hours of work for a computer programing competition, a part-time job in Hamburg, Germany, and an overpacked schedule constantly filled at least three weeks in advance. I had just checked off the last few items on my calendar, and all that lay in front of me was . . . freedom!

I shouldered my backpack, hopped down the stairs, sprang

out onto the sidewalk, and strode about one mile out of our tiny German village to the bus stop along the highway. I waved to our elderly neighbors, who were taking advantage of a glorious Monday morning to do some gardening, and started daydreaming, reliving the past week.

We had celebrated my grandfather's ninetieth birthday the previous weekend. At the party I said farewell to my relatives, happy that I did not know if this was goodbye for months or for years. My little sister and mother cried, but my father and twin brother were more relaxed about the whole thing. Then my family left for vacation in Denmark. This was the first time in ten years they left without me.

"You are really crazy," my friend said, shaking his head as the party ended. "I have no idea how the heck you expect to do it with so little money!"

By "it" he meant my plan: I wanted to travel around the world. Literally. With only fifty euros (about sixty dollars) in my pocket and no solid plans. In fact, the plan was *not* to have a plan. Just take off and see where life would lead me. If I liked a place, I would stay as long as I wanted and then leave whenever I felt like it. No deadlines. No appointments. No goals. A complete contrast to my previous life. Pure freedom!

"Don't you want to go to college? And where will you sleep? Who will wash your clothes?" Some of the questions were downright humorous. As if my life depended on a washing machine. . . .

Of course I had taken a few precautions. I read up on what a backpacker should bring. (There are a lot of blogs and vlogs about it.) I bought a decent-quality tent, got my immunizations, and applied for a passport. I also had to get my parents used to the idea, a task that I accomplished little by little over the course of several weeks ;-).

Above all I was prepared *not* to be prepared—you simply can't predict all the potential problems. So my preparation consisted of being open to all possibilities. For example, a tent means you are not dependent on organized sleeping arrangements, a map gives you alternative routes, and learning the basics of the prevalent language and using a translating app make communication easier. Medicines, immunizations, and good nutrition can stave off sickness. If you have a lot of time, good connections, or very low standards for comfort, then a plethora of unimaginable possibilities open up before you. When problems arise you can usually find a quicker solution by knowing what you want and having a positive attitude.

The bus pulled over at the bus stop, coming to a halt with a little squeak. The passengers stared at me curiously as I heaved my over-stuffed backpack up the stairs and lugged it down the aisle to an open seat.

At the next major stop in a commercial district, I got off and walked to a moderately busy on-ramp leading to the A1 autobahn. With my right arm stretched out, thumb in the air, and a winning smile on my face (at least I thought so), I waited for someone to react to the cardboard sign in my left hand. On it I had written in black Sharpie: "A1—toward Bremen." I drew a smiley face at the bottom.

For the first half hour, cars drove by, not giving me any notice. I kept waiting. Still nothing.

Patience!

Nothing.

My smile started to cramp up and my arm got tired. Instead of the smell of freedom, exhaust fumes blew in my face. The midday sun, which had seemed so friendly that morning, blazed down on me mercilessly. No shade in sight. A quiet voice in my head started to get nervous. Louder and louder, it demanded my attention: *Hitchhiking days are over. No one hitchhikes anymore! No one will pick you up. By tonight you will already have turned back before you really even started—*

"Why don't you try a little farther down by the Burger King?" The voice of a passerby interrupted the voice in my head.

"Uh . . . yeah, thanks," I stuttered and had to laugh at myself. I had started off on a trip around the world, and all it took was a half-hour wait on an on-ramp to plant seeds of doubt. The laughter chased away the negative thoughts. Newly motivated, I shouldered my backpack and followed the stranger's advice.

Moments later I found myself sitting between two grade-school kids in the back seat of a dark-blue Opel Corsa. We rolled over the asphalt and, outside the windows, the green undergrowth turned into blurry stripes.

A Swedish couple picked me up in Osnabrück. Even though I was new to hitchhiking, it did not feel awkward. Quite the opposite. The atmosphere in the car was warm and open. After all, you only ride with people who want to pick you up. I never forced myself on anyone.

When you are hitchhiking, even though you are riding with people you have never met before and you will probably never meet again, conversation does not feel as strange as might be expected. You start with the obvious questions: "Where are you from?" and "Where are you going?" From there, depending on the length of the trip, the discussions often lead to laughter and, at other times, to deeply meaningful conversations.

Hitchhiking gave me a peek into the lives of others—people who, because of age, diverse interests, or social circles, I otherwise would have never met. On the highway you really do meet all kinds: doctors, housewives, convicts, construction workers, people who own crocodile farms, and even members of the Mafia. It's almost like flipping through the channels on TV, randomly watching a program for ten minutes and then switching to another, again and again. You gather little snippets of a story, but you don't know what led up to it or how it will end. It is fascinating how much you can learn about careers, countries, and how people approach life differently.

As the sun set that first day, we reached the outskirts of Amsterdam. My first destination. After that I would travel to Paris and Barcelona.

"We have to celebrate tonight," my new Swedish friends and I decided. We stowed our belongings in a cheap hotel room they had rented and went out on the strip.

In the narrow streets and canals that wind through downtown Amsterdam, we ran into a large group of people. When we asked them where they were going, a young man in a red T-shirt invited us to join them. Written in white letters on his shirt was: "Pub Crawl—a night you won't remember but you'll never forget!" Moments later we squeezed into a dirty bar with red lighting and dancing.

"Paradise!" exclaimed one of the Swedes when he read the flyer on the door: "1 Euro Beer Special!"

I blinked. Sunshine flooded the car. I ran my hand over my head, feeling a bit foggy. Whether it was from sleep, the weed, or the drinks was hard to say. Probably all of the above. We had taken a taxi back to the hotel four hours ago, and the Swedes let me sleep in their car.

My mouth was dry. I grabbed a water bottle from the dashboard, took a few big gulps, and opened the door. The breeze felt cool and pleasant. As my gaze drifted over the hotel parking lot, I put my hand in my pocket and took out my cash, an old piece of chewing gum, and a tattered note. One of the guys in a red T-shirt had given it to me when we were sitting on the sidewalk in front of a bar, chatting.

I pushed the note back in my pocket and started counting my money. *Nooooo!* I had blown thirty-five of my fifty euros in the very first night!

"Well done!" I congratulated myself sarcastically on my spectacular failure.

One thing was clear: I was in desperate need of a job and a place to sleep. The best (and only) option at the moment was the scribbled note from the man who had invited us to the *pub crawl.* I decided to look for him first thing.

My search for him took me through Amsterdam's largest city park, Vondelpark, whose green expanses and relaxing atmosphere lure its visitors, especially students and artists, into a state of idleness. A guy with long blond hair sat on a bench, gently strumming his guitar and singing. His guitar case was open, inviting money to be thrown inside. Behind him a thin young woman sat watching their two big backpacks. Her hair was short, unlike his, and she had a nose piercing.

"Where are you from?" I asked them.

They were from Slovenia and were traveling around Europe for a few weeks, earning money by playing street music along the way. We talked a little and hit it off immediately. I asked them if they would watch my stuff while I looked for a job. They seemed trustworthy. They were happy to help out and said they would be there late into the night, since it was such a good location.

A few hours later I came back to the park, exhilarated—I had actually landed a job as a party tour guide! But then I couldn't believe what I saw. Or rather, what I didn't see. There was the park bench, lit up by the pale yellow glow of streetlights. At sunset, right here in this exact spot, I had left my backpack with the Slovenian couple.

And now, *nothing!*

I frantically looked around and scanned the silhouettes of the bushes. Not a soul in sight.

No, no, NO! My heart beat faster. I couldn't believe it! The raindrops pitter-pattered sympathetically on my shoulders. *What now?* My documents were in that backpack. The little money I had left. My camping gear. I had been away from home just one day, and not only had I blown all my money, but I lost everything else as well! How could I have been so naïve to trust two strangers just like that? I was apparently not as good a judge of character as I had hoped.

"Chris!"

Two figures emerged from the shadow cast by a group of trees. *Could it be?* I ran toward them, breathing an enormous sigh of relief.

"Sorry if we scared you," the guy with long hair explained. "But it suddenly started to rain, so we went to find shelter under a tree."

I was so relieved that I hugged him! He was slightly surprised, but he returned the gesture anyway. My instincts had not failed me after all.

I spent that July as a party tour guide in Amsterdam, and then it was time to set off for Paris with my cardboard sign. Getting to Paris took longer than I had planned, but circumstances that seem negative at first can turn into unique opportunities.

As in this case: I ended up in a car driving around the Arc de Triomphe at 4:00 a.m. The rest of Paris was sleeping, and the traffic circle that was usually jam-packed was completely deserted. It was so incredible that the driver took a couple of extra victory laps just for me.

Back in Amsterdam I had made contact with a host for couch surfers who described his apartment as having a view of the Eiffel Tower and Montmartre. In spite of the early hour, my friendly host opened his door for me. The members of this guest-friendly network use the website Couch Surfing (www.couchsurfing.com) to find free lodging on trips or to offer it to others. The idea is that the host not only offers a couch to sleep on but shows the guest their city as well. The network has more than ten million members. I think the idea is awesome, but in the end I used it less than ten times during my entire journey. My traveling style turned out to be too spontaneous. (To use it you need reliable Internet access, which I did not often have. But if you want to "calculate" your travels, then I highly recommend it!)

To live within my means in one of Europe's most expensive cities, I gave myself a budget of five euros a day: two for food and three for other things. It was hard, but doable. In other countries where the cost of living is lower, I often spent only one euro a day or even less. Believe it or not, I spent only thirty-three euros during the entire week I was in Paris and was still able to see all of the big attractions.

Next stop: Spain.

2

MORE LUCK THAN SENSE

I STRODE QUICKLY THROUGH BARCELONA. I had heard about a block party and was hoping to find a place to stay. The temperature was a mild 82 degrees, but lugging my heavy backpack as I sped through the city made it anything but a relaxing stroll.

"Dónde Saints? Fiesta?" I asked the only person I met using my—at that time—still rudimentary Spanish. She was a small, olive-skinned, middle-aged woman with black hair and a kind face. She laughed and said something in Spanish or Catalonian— whatever it was, I didn't understand—and then, using English as rudimentary as my Spanish, she said, "Follow me."

Her unending patience and genuine interest in me made it possible for us to communicate. It turned out she was from Colombia but had lived in Barcelona for many years. She taught preschoolers. In broken phrases, I told her about my trip.

"Dónde duermas?" she asked, simulating a pillow by pressing her hands together and laying her head on them. I pointed to the sleeping mat tied to my backpack and shrugged my shoulders. She laughed and pointed at me. *"Tú. Dormir."* She then pointed to herself. *"Mi casa."*

I understood and laughed while exclaiming, *"Gracias! Gracias!"*

She was a single mother with two boys about my age. Over the next few days her sons showed me the city. At first I didn't know much Spanish, but the experience of not being able to make myself understood made me want to improve my language skills as quickly as possible. The Colombian lady had two weeks off for vacation and seemed to enjoy helping me with Spanish. We also polished her English a little bit along the way.

Although it seemed like she would have been happy to adopt me, I took my leave after a week and set off. I grew up with horses and had a childhood dream to fulfill: I wanted to work on a horse ranch in Spain. Years ago my father had purchased an Andalusian stallion from a ranch east of Murcia on the Costa Blanca. That ranch was my next destination.

Hitchhiking out of Barcelona, however, was very difficult, due to the widespread belief in Spain that only beggars and criminals would do such a thing. That's why you usually get picked up by people on vacation in Spain, rather than by the locals.

Fortunately things changed when I finally arrived at my destination. The ranch owner remembered both the stallion and my father. I got hired!

El Refugio is on a hill above La Mata and Parque Natural de Torrevieja (Torrevieja Salt Lake National Park). Beyond the outstretched dunes lies the sea with a long, deserted beach. Farther inland are arid evergreen forests and orange plantations.

Along with taking care of horses, mucking stalls, gardening, slaughtering pigs, and handiwork, I got to lead trail rides for tourists, which I loved doing. Regulars at the ranch included locals who had immigrated to Spain. One was a former architect from Germany. He was eighty-three years old and had his own horse at the ranch.

During a trail ride I told the German about my plans to travel around the world. "Why would your parents let you take a trip like that at your age?" he said, holding his chestnut gelding back a little to be at my level. Both the horse and the man were in great shape for their ages, which became obvious during the ride.

"Well, at first they were against it. They probably hoped it was just some obsession I would soon forget about." I laughed. "But when I started getting serious about my equipment and immunizations, it slowly dawned on them: *The boy really means it.*"

"And then?" he asked. "Did they try to talk you out of it?"

"They sat me down and tried to appeal to my conscience: *Do you know that you could die?* I said I knew that was a possibility and wanted to do it anyway. I would rather die doing something I love than just sit in some office for fifteen years thinking, *If only I had . . .*"

He nodded. "That's exactly what happened to me. That's why I came here. What are you planning next?"

"Conquer the whole world," I winked at him.

The old man shook his head. "Only fools want to conquer the world. A wise man wants to conquer himself."

I had to smile. He had apparently not understood that I was joking with him, and yet there was a lot to be learned from what he said. I silently repeated his words to myself and committed them to memory.

"And what will you do when you have to fly?" he asked.

"I don't plan to fly. If you fly very far, you lose all sense of distances. You board at point X and get off a couple of hours later at point Y, and you missed the whole journey. I'd rather help out on a sailing yacht and cross the sea that way."

He lifted an eyebrow. "Can you sail?"

I had to admit that I had practically no clue. He grinned. "Well, then, you're in luck! I used to be a sailing teacher. We won't let this get in your way."

"What do you think my chances are of getting picked up?"

"Not bad I should think, if you are well prepared. A good skipper values attitude as much as experience. The season for crossing the Atlantic starts at the end of November and lasts through February. That's when they take on crewmembers in exchange for room and board—that is, you can sail for free, as long as you pitch in. If I were you, I would try Gibraltar. A lot of people ship out over the big pond from there."

I am deeply indebted to this man. It felt like providence had somehow planned for us to meet right before the sailing season.

In the coming days he brought me his sailing manual, a sailing knife, and sailor clothes. "What is an old man like me going to do with these things?" he said. "I hope they'll come in handy."

And that they did. For my entire journey, in fact.

3

HITCHHIKING OVER
THE ATLANTIC

I LEFT EL REFUGIO in the first week of November, three days before my twentieth birthday, and headed south.

Through the big front windshield of the semitruck that had picked me up, I caught my first glance of a gigantic cliff towering on the blue horizon: *Gibraltar! The gate to the Atlantic!* I hoped this gate would open up for me.

At noon I walked over the border where, to my surprise, I had to wait for an airplane to take off. On the other side of *la línea*, the English had built an airport. Anyone commuting back and forth had to cross the airstrip. Gibraltar, with typical British architecture, monkeys living in the cliffs, and a fascinating history, is a great weekend destination for travelers.

"Hang your flyer on the bulletin board with the others," said the port office attendant. "If you can find room."

I turned around and gasped. The board was crammed with notes from people like me who were looking for a boat to travel across the Atlantic. Quite a few of the applicants had experience and even documented qualifications. I left the office downcast. My chances were pretty slim against that kind of competition! Impossible, actually, if I wanted to cross the Atlantic that same year.

However, I started to gain confidence walking down the quays, making as many contacts as possible. The people who wrote and posted ads on that board seemed to put all their confidence in their flyers. I, however, could make a personal impression—even if I did have to share this tactic with two Polish guys, a young woman from England, and an Australian man.

I spent my birthday with sunshine, squawking seagulls, and a little whiskey in the cockpit of a French sailboat in the port. Its crewmembers covered their expenses by playing street music and planned to stay in the Mediterranean. That evening I went dumpster diving with a guy from the Czech Republic. That's when you take usable stuff out of trash cans. The Czech had lived off of it for four years and had never had any health problems. In Paris he once found a brand-new Armani suit in the trash. His friends had collected laptops, tablets, and smartphones from the dumpsters around US military bases. The devices were not broken but had been thrown away because they did not have converters for the electrical outlets. It's unbelievable how much stuff gets thrown away! In Germany alone approximately twenty million tons of food ends up in the trash each year. That's 550 pounds per person!

That evening we celebrated my birthday with something special we found on our trash-to-treasure hunt: a (formerly) frozen pizza! We heated it up in a microwave. On my way back I called my twin brother to wish him a happy birthday. At that time I still had a cell phone, which I later lost in Argentina. After that I ended up traveling for two years without technology, other than my mother's old digital camera. It took nice pictures, but you had to smack it a couple of times to turn it on.

Three days later I had a wonderful surprise: an Italian man and his Thai wife were planning to cross the Atlantic on a beautiful cutter that he had made himself. Two of his friends who were supposed to help him sail didn't show up, and his unfortunate predicament ended up saving me. A few days earlier he had heard about me through casual conversations. After going on a test sail, and with no further ado, he offered to take me to the Canary Islands. If all went well, I could help sail all the way to the Caribbean.

I was bursting with joy! My new captain would never have looked at the ads on the bulletin board. Well, maybe he did, but he barely knew any English, so he certainly couldn't read the countless offers from experienced skippers. I could hardly believe my luck.

Less than a week later I put out to sea with the fifty-eight-year-old Italian and his wife on board a forty-two-by-thirteen-foot sailing yacht. They wanted to sail to the Caribbean first, and then maybe later to Thailand. His wife got seasick easily, which was another reason he wanted at least one more person on board for safety and assistance.

We set sail in the Strait of Gibraltar late in the afternoon. I was finally striking out on the first really big stage of my journey. I had already been traveling in Europe for four months, but crossing the Atlantic felt like the most important step "out into the world" that I had made up till then. Indescribable freedom lay in front of me. Words simply cannot capture this feeling. The only thing visible on the western horizon was the endless expanse of deep blue ocean.

This was my first day at sea and I would soon witness my first sunset on board!

"When the sun is just about to go below the horizon, keep your eye on it!" the Italian advised me in a secretive voice and looked at me knowingly. "Only once in a sailor's life will he, exactly at this moment, see a green flash. It is a special moment when the souls of the drowned gather at that place."

I was riveted. *Would I be able to experience such a moment in my short life as a sailor?* Together we watched the sun set, and, in fact, the very last sunrays suddenly turned green.

"Was that the light you were talking about?" I asked. But he did not answer.

My captain's jaw had fallen open.

Although we had good weather, the waves tossed the boat from side to side. Seawater washed across the deck regularly and flowed over my feet. Due to a headwind, we could go only six or seven knots with the genoa (a large headsail), but we were happy to be on our way—thank goodness I did not feel even a hint of seasickness. Unfortunately this was not true for everyone; the captain's wife lay with her eyes closed on a couch in the center of the boat where the motion was the least noticeable. She threw up every couple of minutes into a soup pot.

The Italian wore a gray jogging suit and a blue beanie almost all the time. You could tell he had managed an electromechanics company for years—unlike most Italians, he valued German precision and punctuality, ranting about most Italians' poor work ethic. Plus, as the boss, he was always right and could get riled up pretty quickly. Nevertheless, he was still a nice companion with a great sense of humor.

His rotund wife had much more influence over him than he would admit. She laughed a lot, spoke of herself in the third person, and amused me day after day with her hilarious grammar mistakes. She often came across as childish, but then again, in critical moments she surprised me with her sensitivity and keen insights into human nature. When she was not suffering from seasickness, she fell victim to snack attacks, which explained her full figure. I was almost jealous because my meager rations often left me hungry.

Neither of them spoke English, but Italian and Spanish are similar enough that we could roughly understand each other. They spoke Italian and I spoke Spanish until I gradually adapted to their Italian. Since it was mostly the Thai lady who talked with me, my Italian developed with Asian idiosyncrasies, which must have sounded very funny. In retrospect, I think that explains the weird looks I often got from Italian sailors I met in harbor towns.

After five days and nights we reached the Canary Islands. The crossing had been brutal. With no autopilot, we had to steer into headwinds and waves the entire time. Theoretically, it meant twelve hours for the Italian and twelve hours for me each day. However, since he was responsible for the radio, trimming the sails, and navigating, as well as being older and not as fit as me, in reality I spent fifteen hours a day at the helm. Plus we swapped every two hours— hardly enough time to get any deep sleep. I lost all orientation due to the rocking of the boat and had to rely completely on the tiny red LED light on the compass to keep my bearings. Dreams and reality blurred together. It took every ounce of willpower to keep my burning eyes glued to the little compass needle pointing the way.

However, I was richly rewarded. At night I often saw luminous milky seas. Tiny organisms in the water release beaming light signals under certain conditions. In the dark, it looked like neon-blue underwater fire showers scattering away from underneath the boat. Sassy dolphins often met us, playing boisterously in the waves and, curious about our boat, swam beside us for long stretches. The glow of each sunrise and sunset was magical. This was more than mere eye candy; it filled me with a deep sense of awe.

Our last stop before setting off on the same route that Christopher Columbus had taken five hundred years earlier was Gran Canaria. Along with amassing provisions for the journey, we took on a new crewmember: a young Italian man. There was no lack of labor being offered at this port either. At least fifty young adults were looking for a free spot on a yacht to cross the Atlantic. I was happy I had already found mine.

December 2013–January 2014

On December 24, we stopped for a couple of days at the Cape Verde Islands west of Senegal. It was the first Christmas I had spent away from home and without my family. *Gulp!* It took me a while to get over how much I missed them, but then again, it was so warm. Here I was, on Christmas Eve, in swim trunks. That was a first.

Yippee! I thought while jumping out of the boat into the turquoise-blue water. In rainy, Northern Germany my family was probably wearing rubber boots and down jackets, freezing on their way home from the Christmas Eve church service.

The rest of the crossing went smoothly with no major complications. Just small issues, such as a few ripped lines, having a jury-rigged rudder, and interpersonal tensions. In such close quarters there are no secrets, and you have no chance of avoiding one another. Our perception of time changed as well. Twenty-four-hour days shrank into three-hour shifts. The days of the week lost all meaning. What was Monday? Or Wednesday or Thursday? No clue.

One night, thousands of miles from solid ground and cruising over twenty thousand feet of deep water, an exhausted bird came gliding up and flew into the cockpit. He rested for about two hours, drank some water I offered him, and then took off, swaying into the air again. I had not expected an encounter like that in the middle of the Atlantic. Flying fish, however, were a normal occurrence. At least once a day, especially at night, we were sure to see one land on deck. Flying squid or octopi came less frequently.

Two and a half weeks after leaving the last landmass, we saw the outline of an island on the pale blue horizon. A turtle had alerted us of its presence the day before. Not long after that, we set our feet on solid ground again, finally landing on the Caribbean Island of Grenada.

Instead of the long beaches I had expected, the coast consisted primarily of cliffs that rose up into overgrown mountains full of tropical vegetation. The dark-skinned inhabitants speak English peppered with Caribbean slang. They greet each other with an amusing ritual called Pong: they bump fists and then hit their chests twice while saying a catchword, like *respect*, *yo*, or *love*. About 60 percent of the population smokes marijuana regularly and another 20 percent occasionally. They get most of their herbal refreshment from the Island of St. Vincent, where it sells for about one euro per gram. That's ten times cheaper than in Amsterdam.

My hosts wanted to sail to Martinique, fly home, and ship their boat back to Italy. Because the shipping fee proved to be exorbitant, he offered me two thousand euros to sail back to Italy with him. I turned him down. Money held little allure, but South America was another story.

I spent a month and a half in Grenada boat-sitting for a man from Ireland. That is, while he was away, I stayed on his anchored boat for free in exchange for maintaining the rig and keeping an eye on things. Since I wanted to take my responsibilities seriously, I did my duty by cranking up some Bob Marley and singing, "Don't rob my boat."

"Any weed you find in the boat is yours," my Irish boss told me. (I found quite a bit.)

I also practiced spear fishing and spent a lot of time with the island residents. Meanwhile, I was on the hunt for a boat to take me toward South America. Few vessels were sailing in that direction both because of pirate attacks north of Venezuela and because the season to sail that stretch hadn't yet arrived.

Eventually I met a Swiss family looking for help with their two kids. Together we sailed to the beautiful, lonely Blanquilla Island, which greeted us with its colorful reefs, clear water, blindingly white sand beaches, and flocks of pelicans.

March 2014

My first few days on the island were paradise, but the Swiss couple seemed increasingly dissatisfied with me. Sensing negative vibes, I buckled down to work even harder. But the more I helped out, the more disgruntled they became.

Upon our arrival at Los Roques, they finally decided to give it to me straight: On the one side, the family couldn't relax on vacation if I was working so hard. On the other, my work would never be enough to match what they had given me—namely, a trip to paradise. They considered the work I had done on the boat's wood paneling to be of as little value as my help sailing, constant babysitting of their children, and the chores I did. I had stuck to all of our agreements and went above and beyond what I was asked. I couldn't have cost them more than a hundred bucks during our ten days together.

Still, in spite of my efforts to mitigate the situation, a solution could not be found. So we parted ways. One of their criticisms stuck in my mind: "You'll only create problems with your style of travel. Without money you always take more than you give."

I had to ask myself: *Am I a freeloader? Am I living and traveling at other people's expense?*

In no way did I want to do that! I tried to never shirk my

responsibilities. I was happy to work either for free or for very little money to help out. I never begged for anything. The only things I requested in return were water and to be taken along for the ride.

Nevertheless, I continually received things from people I met throughout my journeys. I often turned down such offers unless they politely insisted. Although the givers helped me of their own free will and seemed happy to do it, was I living on their dime? For example, the family in Barcelona. Didn't I receive far more than I could have given?

In the end I decided such things are not about a calculated, price-performance ratio, as in business. I am certain the people who helped me along the way did not feel they got the short end of the stick. Those who rarely left their villages or cities and had not experienced much diversity were especially enthusiastic about our time together. The cultural exchange, the joy they took in entertaining me, and the friendships we created were definitely worth it.

In extremely poor countries I gave as much food and clothing to the people as I could afford. Now and then I was able to directly return a favor—for example, I had the opportunity to help the daughter of my host family in Peru get admitted to medical school in Germany.

Many of the people I met became close friends, and we still keep in contact. Several of them even came to my wedding—priceless!

The sun was high in the sky. Colorful wooden boats lay on the beach. A fisher sat next to his radio, mending his nets. It truly was paradise! The Los Roques islands are also known as the Pearl of the Caribbean. I breathed deeply and then sighed, digging my feet into the hot sand. On the inside I was still struggling with the unpleasant memories of the past few days, but I tried to have a positive attitude and look on the bright side.

"*Busco una barca a Venezuela?*" My Spanish and Italian mingled together into one question. My Spanish had been drowned out by weeks of speaking only Italian.

"La Posada," said the fisherman, pointing over his shoulder. I thanked him and headed off in the direction he had pointed. It led me to a long, wide, sandy path. For them, this path counts as a road. There were practically no cars because the island is too small. An inviting house was marked with a sign that said *Posada,* and underneath was a silver plaque that boasted: *Trip Advisor Winner 2013.* As it turns out, *posada* means *inn.*

"*Hola!*" I called through the open door just as a friendly-looking lady in her midfifties appeared. I asked for the captain and she laughed.

"There's no captain here. Whenever someone needs help, they always send them to me. Are you German or Italian?"

She's good! I told her about my trip, and less than fifteen minutes later, she had arranged for me to have a free spot on a freighter, assigned me a room, and ordered some food to be prepared for me. The contrast could not have been greater: a half hour earlier I had felt totally rejected by the Swiss family, and now I was being lovingly cared for by this amazing woman.

She had a cookbook that featured dishes from all over Venezuela, as well as pictures of the landscape and locals. One of the pictures electrified me. "I want to go there!" It was a photo of a wooden house with no walls, built on stilts in the water. The people in the picture were small and had shiny, black hair.

"They are the Warao, indigenous people," my hostess explained. I later learned that they live in eastern Venezuela on the Orinoco in a gigantic river delta. The Orinoco is the second-largest river in

South America after the Amazon. It was in the middle of the jungle, far from civilization and organized infrastructure.

The idea of living among real indigenous people in the jungle was tremendously exciting. In Europe we are the indigenous people, but we no longer have a direct dependence on nature or a connection to prehistoric times. Therefore, I was very curious. I wanted to learn about a way of life that was completely independent of industrial advancements. My explorer-spirit, which had known only the forests of Northern Germany, was drawn to the flora and fauna of the Amazon rain forest like metal to a magnet! In the Warao it all came together: the adventure of a lifestyle completely dependent on nature in the middle of a rain forest *and* it was on the water, which was always a draw for me. *Jackpot!*

I gathered tips for how to get to Caracas, the capital of Venezuela, and from there to Ciudad Bolívar, which was nearer to the Orinoco Delta. It was a safe place in comparison with other parts of the country that were best avoided due to political unrest. I had a new goal: the Warao!

Second Leg

Cartagena

Caracas

Euriapo

Panama

Cuyuni River

Georgetown
Bartica

Parai-Tepui

Chimborazo

Manaus

Lima

Cuzco

La Paz
Cochabamba

Santa Cruz

Uyuni

São Paulo

Rio de Janeiro

Salta

SOUTH AMERICA

4

LIFE IN THE JUNGLE

◯ March–April 2014

I HITCHED A RIDE onboard a steamboat transporting food and arrived at Caracas in the middle of the night. Even at that late hour Gato Negro station was teeming with activity. Peddlers were selling food from pots or grills, and others were hocking their wares off of blankets spread on the ground. The people were clean and well dressed, but aside from the buses and subways, Caracas looked tattered and run-down. Many parts of the suburbs were full of rubble, rocks, and dilapidated houses. There were not many high-rises, and I didn't see a single tourist. Long lines formed at various businesses. For the first time, live and in color, I was witnessing a *Wartegemeinschaft*.[1]

In spite of this, the infrastructure was completely intact, even modern and comfortable. Inside a train car a label reading "Made

---

1 This is a play on words in German: *Wertegemeinschaft* is a society of shared values. *Wartegemeinschaft* changes the meaning to a society of waiting. Socialist countries often experience a lack of goods available for purchase. When items become available, lines form immediately, and people will wait hours even though they may not know what they are waiting to buy.

in France" hung next to socialist party propaganda supporting
President Nicolás Maduro. In 2013, Maduro had been working as a
bus driver. After President Hugo Chávez passed away, Maduro was
elevated to the highest rank in the country without any experience
or qualifications. A man of the people!

I decided to take the bus this time. For one thing, I had
been strictly warned not to hitchhike for safety reasons, and, for
another, a ticket for the 375-mile trip from La Guaira to Ciudad
Bolívar cost me only four dollars. This included subways, a bus,
and a taxi. Risk my life for four bucks? I simply couldn't do that
to my parents.

Traveling by bus was cheap because gas costs next to nothing in Venezuela. I mean that literally—if you do the math, it's
about one dollar for one thousand gallons of gas! Additionally, the
inflation rate in Venezuela is dizzying, despite numerous currency
reform measures. When I was there, one US dollar was worth seventy bolívares fuertes. In December 2018, one US dollar was worth
approximately thirty million bolívares fuertes.

Because gas is so cheap, people are wasteful with it. I witnessed
how boats fill up in the harbor: The gas nozzle was attached to a
long hose, which they would pass from boat to boat without turning off the spigot. They simply passed the nozzle, spraying full
throttle, to the neighboring boat. Each time gallons of gas spilled
into the river, turning large expanses of the surface into a shimmery,
rainbow-colored sheen. Environmental protection is an unknown
concept, and there is little thought given to trash disposal.

I was on the lookout to find possible ways of reaching the natives
in the delta. It was a daunting challenge because there are no
streets—and therefore no traffic—that lead to them. Few people

have a reason to travel into that region. I finally found a missionary willing to take me with him. I made a mental note: the three professions most likely to travel to remote locations are missionaries, doctors, and tradesmen (i.e., smugglers). Anthropologists should, theoretically, be useful as well, but the silly thing is that there are so few of them.

The sun had not yet come up as the missionary and I climbed into a metal motorboat. We sped along the Orinoco for six hours, about one hundred miles as the crow flies.

In the river delta there were many flat islands, and the ocean was close enough to cause ebb and flow in the water's surface, but not close enough to make the water salty. Thick jungle vegetation, watered by regular flooding, sprung up to the right and the left.

The Warao village, Arature, was located in a large branch of the river. It looked just like what I had seen in the cookbook: the houses were built over the water on stilts and had no walls, so you could look right in. Between the houses, boards were laid out, creating partial bridges. It required a bit of balance not to fall off. All along the river children were jumping in the water, playing, and paddling kayaks. It is no exaggeration to say that these children grow up in the water. Since water is so important for daily life, the word for it in Warao is short: *ho*. The same is true for the hammocks, made of dried, woven palm leaves. These hammocks are almost sacred, and out of respect for the owner, you do not even touch another person's hammock. They are called *ha*.

The language is easy to learn because verbs are not conjugated, and there is hardly any grammar. At least that's what it seemed like to me because people understood me when I simply strung words together. Surprisingly, I found that there is no word for "love" in Warao. There is also no word for "please," and to say "thank you," you simply describe the situation as good: *yakera*. The Warao do not talk a lot. Simply being together is more important than conversation.

After the initial shyness passed, the Warao proved to be happy, untroubled, and hospitable. Although they are small in stature, they are very athletic and have an astounding sense of balance. Most of them are only thirteen to fifteen years old when they choose their life partner, and they have children shortly thereafter. Before a missionary told them about God, they believed they used to live in the clouds. When they had eaten up all the food there, they slid down a rainbow to earth, which offered food in abundance. In fact, the river was teeming with fish, and, thanks to the yams and manioc roots that the Warao had planted, two hours of work was more than enough to spend the rest of the day eating and lying in the hammocks.

What a life!

I was allowed to sleep in an empty hut. The nights were filled with the shrieks of terrifying beasts. At least, that's what it sounded like. In reality, they were the sounds of amphibians. (I later met two Argentinians who had been scared to death by these noises. They thought there were giant jaguars nearby, stalking around, hungrily looking for their next victim to maul. In fear they crept deeper and deeper into their sleeping bags and almost melted from the heat. When I explained that the noise was not bloodthirsty predators but harmless little toads, they were embarrassed but also relieved.)

The days were eventful. I had many culinary experiences, including the national animal, the capybara—a kind of water pig that tastes like fish. Iguana meat is another favorite. The Warao told me that iguana orient themselves primarily by smell. If you catch one of these lizards, tie up its legs, and rub it under your armpits, it will take on a human smell. They say that it makes them tame and calm. While gutting the iguanas, we found eggs inside—more than twenty-five per female—which proved to be a delicious side dish. House pigs were seen running about all over the village. They once ate my soap while I was showering with brown river water. The artificial cherry scent was apparently quite enticing to their little noses.

The nastiest part of life in the village was the swarm of triangle-shaped horseflies, whose bite not only hurt but itched like the dickens. There were also countless mosquitoes, which I heard were even worse during the rainy season. I had to regularly pick the eggs of a flea-like creature called a nigua out of the soles of my feet with a needle. Thanks to that little creature I continually fought infections and a badly swollen foot.

I planted manioc and yams with the Warao people, and I even helped build a canoe. After carving the canoe, they use a quick, hot straw-fire to widen the wood into the right shape. I often went hunting and fishing with them as well.

The Warao impressed me time and again with their extremely sharp senses and keen instincts. Once, I was riding with a Warao pastor and his eight-year-old son along a branch of the river. The vegetation to the right and left of the water was as impenetrable as a wall. Grass as tall as a person, leaves, vines, ferns . . .

Suddenly the pastor raised his hand to indicate silence. I quietly lifted the rudder out of the water, resting it on the side of the kayak, and carefully watched the man, who was listening without breathing. I didn't hear or see anything aside from the plethora of green leaves. A moment later he pointed to the other side of the river. With long strokes, we moved to the other shore. He silently picked up his bow and arrows and sprang just as silently out of the kayak, hardly even rocking it. He disappeared into the green thicket. A few moments passed in absolute silence.

"Machete!" came his shrill cry. His son jumped up, grabbing the long bushwhacker, and disappeared into the green wall. Apparently he knew exactly where his father was—I hadn't the foggiest notion even in which direction the man was located. A few moments later the plants on the shore parted and the pastor appeared with a broad grin on his face. Over his shoulder hung a kind of tapir with a grayish-brown pelt, striped tail, and short snout. A three-pronged arrow was sticking out of its neck.

Another time, we took the kayak deep in the jungle through a small, remote side branch of the river. I pushed hanging vines aside and looked in wonder. Past the large, luminous blue butterflies, big, colorful macaws flew and screeched overhead. The impression of being in a fairy tale was made complete by the pink river dolphins curiously poking their heads out of the water.

I was abruptly jerked back into reality when the alert Warao pointed out an electric eel, more than three feet long and as thick as a man's arm. In the murky water I had mistaken it for a log. The thought of accidentally coming near enough for it to shock me was sobering. A jolt from an electric eel paralyzes you, and you sink to the bottom of the river and drown. I decided not to go swimming alone in those parts.

I remember one time when we waited until the river was almost at its highest point. Then we filled the kayaks up to the brim with water. I didn't know why we were doing this, but I decided to just follow directions and see what would happen. Then my native friends broke up a stick they had brought along and wrung its sap out into the water in the kayaks. The liquid from the stick mixed with the river water, turning it milky-white.

A questioning look, a mutual nod, and all at once they turned the boats over, grabbed their spears and knives, and followed the slow-moving white liquid as it flowed downstream. When this liquid came in contact with a fish, the fish lost its orientation and floated belly-up to the surface, where the hunters could just pick them out with a spear. It took about twenty minutes for the liquid to disperse and lose its effect, which was enough time to collect dozens of sedated fish. The other animals in the river woke up after a little nap and continued swimming.

Very clever, these Warao.

5

DRUGS, MURDERERS, AND SEX

ABOUT THREE WEEKS AFTER arriving in Arature, I had the opportunity to ride in a motorboat to the trading village of Curiapo. I said goodbye to my new friends. The Warao pastor gave me his wooden hunting bow, which I carried, unstrung, from that day forward. It later proved to be helpful for climbing steep paths, as a support when waiting and holding a heavy backpack—and for fending off persistent dogs.

British Guiana was my next goal. Many people traveled there from Curiapo to smuggle gasoline, and it is also only a few miles from the route Colombian cocaine takes before crossing the Atlantic to Europe. I traveled in a gas-smuggling boat to Northern Guiana and then in a steamboat carrying food to Georgetown, the capital city.

British Guiana's landmass is similar in size to England. However, only about 135,000 people live in Georgetown, which has approximately one-fifth of the country's entire population. Most of the inhabitants have ethnic roots in India. The second-largest group have African roots, and third-largest are indigenous people, followed by Chinese. There are so few white people in British Guiana that I did not meet any others during my visit.

I wanted to travel from Georgetown to the gold-mining region on the Cuyuni River and then back into Venezuela. The World Cup was about to start in Brazil. If I went fast enough, I could perhaps make it there for the final match.

The little, run-down city of Bartica was my next stop. Bartica lies at the river's conflux, creating a traffic hub that leads to various mining areas. The traders who organize supplies and labor are as busy as the traffic. They recruit workers for mining operations who, upon returning to town, blow all their money on prostitutes and drugs or spend their time recuperating from malaria.

I went to the office of a mining company first. There I learned that military trucks occasionally traveled over the unpaved roads to mining areas to deliver fuel for their pumps and excavators. My plan was to catch a ride with one of them.

Shortly after my arrival, I made friends with two ladies in their early twenties, who offered a place for me to stay that night. "But we live in the middle of the ghetto," they warned. I casually said it didn't matter.

As we walked down the tarred streets, the houses became more and more run-down. The ditches on the sides of the cracked and jagged asphalt reeked of sewage, and we passed a few free-roaming donkeys. Next to a red food cart, we turned abruptly into a small side alley that led to a sandy courtyard. In the middle stood a dismal wooden house, enthroned on stilts. Underneath, between the pillars, were moldy sofas on which dark figures were taking rattling drags off of metal pipes. Crack pipes.

"We'd better put your stuff in our neighbor's apartment. Just take your hammock," they advised me. "Things get stolen here."

There was another little house in the back corner of the courtyard that belonged to a prostitute everyone called Black Woman. Sad, strung-out figures huddled there on a bench. We had barely arrived when a fight broke out between one of the ladies who brought me and the father of her child. I decided to keep my distance.

I went back to the red food cart and sat down on a plastic chair. A muezzin could be heard singing over the speakers from a mosque on a hill. It reminded me of the gaudy, brightly colored Hindu temple a few streets away.

"Those monkeys make that racket every night!" said a man sporting a thin dreadlock hanging off the side of his otherwise-buzz-cut head. He leaned, arms crossed, on the counter of the food cart. Although his haircut made him look silly, he was otherwise good-looking and well-dressed. "To what do I owe the honor, Goldilocks?"

We started talking. He was originally from Barbados, the son of doctors—or so he said. I later found out it was hard to tell when he was making up stories and when he was telling the truth. However, he was well educated and had a sharp, albeit slightly muddled, wit that made his origins believable.

"What do you sell here?" I asked him. It didn't look like the kind of cart that sold burgers or hot dogs—or anything that should be in a food cart, for that matter.

He looked around carefully and smacked a baggie with little white cubes and a pipe on the table. He pushed one of the little cubes through a kwind of grate in the pipe and lit it up. When it was smoldering, he put the other end in his mouth and inhaled. He scrutinized me for about a minute, holding his breath before he exhaled. "I sell tickets to wonderland. Haven't the others told you what this is?"

"A ghetto?" I guessed.

"Err! A branch of a cartel!" he corrected me. "You remember the girl who brought you here, right? Her brother is one of the big drug lords from Guiana, and little sister here peddles his treasures on his behalf."

"And you?"

"I bang her best friend's mother, and I'm the watchdog." He pointed with two fingers to his eyes and then to the street. "Nothing gets past me. When the cops come, I make ten times the racket of those Muslims up in their little tower. And the others disappear out the back way."

"The police don't arrest you?"

"Of course they do. But I know the laws of the land better than any of their big shots. Besides, I have bribed them all and got it on tape too. If they put me in the slammer, they might as well lock themselves up with me. Money talks, B.S. walks."

I finally went back into the courtyard where the zombie-like figures had spread out. This is where I was to hang my hammock and sleep for the next few nights. Every now and then the wheel spun on a lighter and a flame flared up, followed by the sound of puffing on a little metal pipe. If I had stretched out my arm, I could have touched the junkie nearest to my hammock. But that is not why I couldn't sleep. It was the swarm of mosquitoes that, although they didn't seem to be interested in the others, were determined to eat me alive. My mosquito spray was in my backpack, locked in the neighbor's apartment.

Out of necessity, I took a sheet from Black Woman's clothesline and wrapped myself in it. *Peace at last!* Lucky for me, the next day

Black Woman did not seem to mind me helping myself. The ladies even gave me a sheet to take with me when I left. Later, when people asked why I traveled with a pink, flowery sheet, I told them it was a gift from the drug cartel!

When I told my new friends about meeting the Watchdog, they warned me, "That guy is a psychopath. He might pull out his pistol at any minute and hold it up to your head, just because he feels like it. When he was only thirteen years old, he spent time in jail for murder."

As it turned out, the Watchdog and I got along marvelously. The members of the drug cartel quickly became like a second family for me. The situation was ridiculous but also exciting: everyone in the cartel stuck together and took care of each other. There were also a few minors in their group who didn't have any family. An interesting twist of fate had formed this community, and the cartel offered these children the only support they had. The drug boss was certainly grooming them for his employment, but, even so, their lives were probably better than if they had been left alone to live on the streets.

Nevertheless, on a daily basis I witnessed an up-close-and-personal view of what the drugs that my new friends sold did to their customers. Users quickly became like zombies, more dead than alive. They would probably never escape this vicious circle. If it were not already clear to me that drugs can ruin your life, now there remained no doubt.

"Come on, White Boy, tonight we're going to show you the town!" one of the women said, and took me out partying.

I had not planned to get drunk, but since I hadn't consumed

alcohol in weeks, I misjudged. Without really wanting to, I ended up in bed with an attractive Guianese-Brazilian girl about my age. Since blue-eyed blonds are not common in Latin America and usually associated with Hollywood movie stars, the girl had come on to me from the start. I didn't want to hurt her feelings, so at first I refused her advances, making it clear I would soon leave Bartica and she would never see me again. She said it didn't matter, and the evening took its course.

A classic one-night stand. Or so I thought.

Later, in the middle of the night, I was startled awake while sleeping in my hammock back by the yellow house. I blinked drowsily into a pair of brown eyes floating in the darkness above me. I tried to get a grip.

"I loves you so much!"

This wasn't a junkie—it was the girl from last night! But how did she know where I was staying?

"I loves you so much. I want to be with you! I want to come with you!"

Aye yai yai, now it's getting complicated, I thought. And after I had been so clear up front. "I'll walk you home. We can discuss it on the way." I felt lousy.

That experience led me to an important realization: there is no such thing as safe, consequence-free sex. The chances of hurting someone are far too high: yourself, the other person, a jealous partner, parents, a reputation. Of course you can imagine many different scenarios, but there will always be consequences and there are no guarantees. I never wanted to be so selfish again that I would willingly hurt someone else just because I lacked self-control. This experience convinced me that you should only share such a thing with *one* person in life. From then on I decided to wait until I had found that person.

6

GOLD RUSH, THE WORLD CUP, SAVED BY A DONKEY

I WAS FINALLY ON MY WAY to the gold-mining region. It was only 4:00 a.m. when I went out to wait for a military truck that someone in the city had told me about. The driver was friendly and kind enough to give me a lift.

We drove almost nonstop for more than eighteen hours. I was sitting on greasy diesel barrels on the flatbed truck, and the oily fuel quickly soaked through my pants and rubbed my backside raw. Even so, the first rays of warm sunshine and the mysterious, foggy views into the rain forest simply blew me away. Some of the muddy craters and creeks that we drove through were deeper than the shallow end of an indoor swimming pool. Again and again I jumped off the truck and clambered up steep, slippery embankments to help the driver

haul a cable from his winch to a big tree. With the wire cable he could
pull the truck up and over otherwise-impassable stretches of road.

It was night when we finally reached the Brazilian mining
camp. I felt like I would not be able to sit for weeks. I was dirty,
drenched in sweat, and hungry since I hadn't eaten all day. The
Brazilians only spoke Portuguese, but they were incredibly welcoming. They led me to a rain barrel where I could wash and showed
me where I could hang my hammock under the barracks. I was also
warned not to move about at night without a flashlight.

The next morning I found out why: about ten feet from my
hammock was a snake on a stump.

"One bite and in about two hours you will meet your Maker,"
one of the men advised me. "We have a flare to signal for help, but
don't count on being found alive." He took a long stick and hit the
two-foot-long, gray-and-brown-striped snake on the head. "You'd
best wear rubber boots. These snakes almost always strike at ankle
level, and they slide right off the rubber. If you get bit anyway, stay
calm. Remember what the snake looked like and keep your pulse
low. That will increase your chances of survival."

The next morning I walked through the ravaged, strip-mining
region looking for work. There were no tunnels here like you might
imagine in a typical mining operation. Instead, the hills were
sprayed down with fire hoses. The slurry then washes over a kind
of carpet that traps the gold, since it is heavier than the mud and
rocks. This method of mining turned a previously blossoming landscape into a wasteland of brown lakes and piles of red earth. A lone,
broken tree could be seen here and there in between the stumps.

It will take forever for nature to even halfway recover from
this abuse.

Still, I needed cash in a big way, and there were no other options.
After a bit of searching, I found a friendly man with dreadlocks who
was happy to employ me for a week. I was assigned to one of the

barracks for workers and given a bed with a mosquito net. As a part of the accommodations, there was a cook to provide three meals a day. The people here did not get days off, aside from Christmas and Sunday afternoons.

I worked with a crew spraying down masses of clay-filled soil with a fire hose, clearing branches, and pushing bigger stones off to the side. Some of the others operated a machine they called "the crusher," which smashed stones with a big iron hammer. The gold inside would then be washed out of the residue.

"Next," the boss barked out the order. Two men hauled a couple of artificial green carpets over, heaved them up on the wooden ramp, and unrolled them. Gently flowing water washed the mud from the planks again and again. A crossbeam sealed with banana leaves stopped the water at the bottom. The two most-experienced workers mixed the slush with side strokes, like they were painting in the water, sloshing it around. They pushed the remaining sediment side to side and up and down, allowing only the water to flow over and out.

The supervisor, who was sitting at the upper end of the ramp, pulled a little bottle of mercury out of his pocket and mixed a few drops of the heavy, liquid metal into the mud. It looked like little pearls flowing down with the water. A silver border formed on the masses too heavy for the water to wash down to the workers' hands. It was the gold being held together by the mercury.

When the debris had been removed from the carpets, the gold was scooped with a spoon into a plastic container. The supervisor brought it back to camp with his four-wheeler. He washed it thoroughly, evaporated the mercury off with a burner, and, with the help of some acid, made the pure gold shine. That evening they weighed out the shares for us workers.

We were all in luck! Our wage was twice as much as normal due to the unusually high yield. My part ended up being about thirteen pennyweight (approximately twenty grams of gold). Much more than I had hoped for.

June 2014

Content but still suffering from a few festering wounds on my backside and a throbbing toe infected by the dirty mud, I looked for a ride back to Venezuela. A group of young Venezuelan diesel smugglers assured me that I could ride with them after they had traded the remaining forty of their one hundred barrels of diesel for gold. The demand was apparently great, because just one and a half days later we cast off in the long, tin boats full of empty, blue, hard-plastic barrels.

I ended up in the middle of nowhere on a boat bridge when a skinny Guianese man with short hair and sunglasses perched on the top of his head asked me, "What are you doing here?" He wore Adidas shoes with white socks pulled up over his calves and had a black duffle bag hanging from his shoulder.

"I'm looking for a boat to Venezuela."

The stranger nodded. He was from Guiana, but he lived and worked in New York as a precious-metals consultant. "If you like, you can come with me to Kaikan. It's much farther south and will bring you closer to your destination. There's a supply helicopter there that can take you to Venezuela."

I didn't have a map and didn't know how to get there, but "helicopter" sounded exciting. "Okay, when do we take off?"

"Now." The man pointed at an approaching boat.

An hour and a few bends in the river later, we stopped at a big, steel, dark-red pontoon. The New York consultant's workers had been using an excavator to search for gold on this shore and were shipping the heavy machine elsewhere. They loaded it on the boat using a powerful hydraulic crane. We prepared for the ride by stretching out a tarp and hanging our hammocks underneath. For the next twenty-four hours the motorboat slowly pulled us upstream. Now and then we saw caimans and other animals on the shore. Once, I saw an anaconda that was so big, I thought I was imagining things. However, the workers confirmed that large specimens of this constrictor are common in that region, often many feet long and as thick as the post of a streetlight.

We reached the foot of the Arau Mountains the next morning. I climbed up onto the high, savanna-grass-covered plateau with the consultant, some of his workers, and a few natives. The views of the rain forest below, as well as the contrasting landscape at the higher altitude, were breathtaking. The consultant, however, did not notice such things. To him only one thing was important: he had invested more than one million dollars to bring the first excavator to Kaikan, where gold is found in such high concentrations that even the most rudimentary tools, such as shovels and spades, can be used for mining. How much more could he get with his excavator? He also wanted to build a road so he could increase traffic and become the main supplier for other gold prospectors.

There was only one thing standing in his way: the local citizens. They were planning to stay there, and they did not want mining in their community. "With gold comes crime, alcohol, and prostitution," they said. "We don't want any of that here. Within a few years you'll destroy our land and then disappear, leaving us to live in a wasteland for years to come."

This reminded me of what happened to the Native Americans during the westward expansion of the United States. However, the indigenous people of Guiana have many rights, so the chances are good that they can spoil the plans of the rich New Yorker.

"Tomorrow is Father's Day," a friendly villager told me after a short conversation. "Stay for a while."

Accepting his invitation was like deserting: I went to the other side. But some of the villagers were suspicious that I was a spy sent by the rich consultant. Although I was interested in the proceedings, I do not know if or how the conflict was resolved.

I was impressed to find out that the villagers spoke not only their native language of Arecuna but also a dialect of English, Spanish, and even a little Portuguese. This is because they often traveled many days' journey from their hometown.

Their homes were simple, small huts built out of wood and twigs with sandy floors. In the middle of the village stood a white-painted, wooden church that had been built seventy years ago by missionaries. I was invited to a special meal in the church to celebrate with the fathers of the town.

I objected to joining them since I am not a father. They replied, "But you are planning to be a father someday, or maybe not?" My objection was overruled by hospitality, and my half-full plate was filled up to the brim again and again.

The festive cuisine was a unique experience, including red juice produced from potatoes and cooked banana porridge, which were new to me. In addition, there were the unavoidable dried farina manioc balls. These balls were eaten with literally everything. They didn't thrill me at first, but later they became the nourishment I missed the most.

I repaid them over the next few days by giving their children pieces of rope and teaching them how to tie sailor's knots, and by helping the adults prospect for gold.

One of the chiefs from another village came to a community meeting to discuss the consultant's plans. On his return trip he would pass through St. Juan—the place where helicopters landed from time to time. I asked if I could join him.

The chief was in his midfifties, dressed from head to toe in camouflage, and sported a Salvador Dali mustache. Despite his age, he walked so fast through the mountainous terrain that I could barely keep up. I could say that my heavy backpack was weighing me down, but he, too, was carrying a machete and a two-gallon diesel canister.

"Are we in a hurry?" I gasped, when I realized that I was having trouble.

"Yes," he said. "That's why." He pointed to rainclouds that covered the mountain overhead. "The rain will make it too dangerous to cross the river and we will have to wait for days. Come on, let's go!"

I gritted my teeth and hurried on, following the chief. I was pretty sure I couldn't keep up that pace much longer, but I didn't want to make the chief late to cross the river. Staying behind in the wilderness with no orientation was not an option either. So I pushed myself to my physical limits as never before. As hard as it may be to believe, we put ten miles behind us in two and a half hours, nonstop, and I was carrying a seventy-five-pound backpack.

When we finally reached the river that we would cross with a boat to St. Juan, I fell to my knees and put my head in the water like a camel. The water was dark from plants but clear, and it tasted gloriously refreshing. It was ten times better on my dry throat than any cold soda could have been!

I made my way through the jungle to find the municipal administrator in St. Juan and asked him about the helicopter. He gave me hope: "The pilot brings fuel, food, and other products on the way here. On the way back he sometimes takes people with him."

"When is the next time he will be here?"

"He's actually overdue. Keep your stuff ready, because when he comes, he won't stay more than a couple of minutes."

Although I was constantly ready, days went by without the helicopter's arrival. Along with many conversations with the locals, whom I helped with various activities, I used the time waiting to read the little pocket Bible I had brought on my trip. My plan was to read the entire thing during my journey. I was interested in finding out why the Bible is the most-read book in the world. I felt that it must be part of a well-rounded education to know what's inside. Why did famous thinkers such as Immanuel Kant find "infinitely more clarity and deeper truth [in the Bible] than in all of the other scriptures and philosophers put together"?

I started with the New Testament because it seemed easier to understand. But either Kant's and the other philosophers' thinking were superior to mine, or I was not ready yet. Instead of deeper truths, all I got were bits of wisdom and contradictions—but above all, questions, which I wrote down.

After eight days the pitter-patter of the morning rain was joined by the sound of spinning blades. "Is that . . . ?"

"Yes!" said the man from Colombia who had invited me to breakfast. I had been helping him search for gold for the past few days. "That's the helicopter! Hurry!" He gave me a quick hug and I ran to the landing pad.

In spite of the rain, the views of the untouched jungle from above were unbelievably beautiful. My euphoric cries of "oh!" and "ah!"—although drowned out by the noise of the rotors—lasted the entire twenty-minute flight until we landed in a small village in Venezuela.

"Take care of yourself. There are dangerous people in these parts," the helicopter pilot warned me.

The wide grin plastered on my face may have seemed inappropriate in light of his warning, but flying in a helicopter over such amazing landscape was just too awesome! Plus, I had gotten used to warnings like this. In almost every place I visited, the locals had explained to me that the people in the neighboring area were "very dangerous." In Venezuela I was warned not to travel to Brazil. They covered their faces with their hands in Brazil because I wanted to go to Bolivia. In Bolivia, they were convinced that traveling to Peru was a death wish. But, in fact, during my whole journey, I was never seriously threatened, robbed, or assaulted.

"Everything out of your pockets and on the table, gringo!" barked the border inspector after taking me into a small side room. As in Venezuela, I had decided to take the bus because it was so ridiculously cheap. But on the way to Santa Elena, a little town on Brazil's border, I got pulled off the bus by an officer and brought into the guardhouse.

Without even glancing at my other stuff, he grabbed my wallet and counted the contents. "Don't you have any more?!"

"Do I need more?" I dodged the question. I was ready for this kind of stunt and had sewn my larger bills into my underwear.

Grumbling, the officer flipped through my passport. My heart sank. I had hitched a ride with a helicopter to the middle of Venezuela where there was no border office to get my passport stamped. A victim of circumstance, I was in the country illegally. Depending on the officer's mood, things could have been very bleak for me. I could get charged a high fine or be deported back to Germany!

Then I noticed the officer was holding my passport upside-down, only pretending to read it. My terror turned into amusement, but I kept a straight face. I was released with an abrupt, "Good, that's all!"

I could hardly believe my luck!

My next destination was Roraima, the mesa that inspired Arthur Conan Doyle to write *The Lost World*. (Sherlock Holmes is also his brainchild.) Isolated from the rest of the world for thousands of years on a high plateau, unique plant and animal life has developed in that region. The descriptions of this mountain were so impressive that it made me give up my original idea to watch the World Cup in Brazil.

I stocked up on several pounds of oatmeal and lentils and took off for Roraima. In Parrai-tepui, the last major stop before climbing the mountain, I found a tour guide. Then a young Brazilian man named Felipe, who also wanted to go to Roraima, joined us.

To be able to spend three days on the mountain, we traveled what would normally be a two-day journey all in one day. It rained a lot. Whatever wasn't drenched by rain showers got soaked through by the overflowing rivers we had to cross.

Despite all this, the landscape was glorious. Once, when I was enjoying the high-altitude view, an anteater walked past me, only inches away. I was excited to see this animal up close, but equally confused because its head looked almost exactly like its other end.

"Brazil is playing Germany today," Felipe said, panting as we walked up the hill toward the mountain.

I turned to him and said, "Who do you think will win?"

"If it's Germany, then you won't be getting off this mountain!" he joked while grinning at me.

Along the way we saw a group of people and asked them for the latest news on the World Cup. "Seven to one, Germany," was the response.

Felipe and I burst out laughing. "No, really. Seriously. How did it come out?"

"Seven to one, Germany," they repeated.

I peered over at my Brazilian friend who stood looking at me, mouth hanging open as if he were trying to figure out a difficult math problem. I topped off the crushing result by singing, "Always look on the bright side of life!" and patted him reassuringly on the shoulder.

Felipe and our guide had not brought nearly enough provisions. Luckily I could offer them bags of oatmeal to provide some relief. I had practically lived off of lentils cooked with spicy ant-sauce before climbing up the mountain, but now we had no means of cooking the lentils. Instead we ate oatmeal three times a day with some tuna fish or sardine flavor for dessert, thanks to Felipe. Luckily, there were more than enough opportunities to fill our water bottles.

The rain kept coming, but we scrambled onward in good humor. It kept getting cooler the higher we climbed. The hand-holds and footholds provided by the thin brush made our ascent over the steep, slippery path known as "the ramp" possible. We crossed through strange, marshy vegetation covered with pale, moss-covered trees and hanging plants.

When we reached the edge of the plateau, the sun shone for a few minutes as if welcoming us. The view was simply unbelievable—as if we had landed on another planet! The plateau was wild, with high cliffs and deep crevasses in strange formations, through which little brooks made their way to the clouds lurking in the abyss below. The sunbeams illuminated the dark-yet-brilliant grasses and flowers tucked among the crevasses, clothed in greenish yellow, orange, red, and black.

It was dead silent as we made our way to a high-altitude cave that would shelter our campsite from the rain. We were occasionally met by tiny, solitary frogs and scorpions. Freezing and soaked to the bone, we spent a restless night trying to dry our stuff and warm up.

Despite the weather, Felipe and I hiked the long trek to Punto Triple, where the borders of Brazil, Guiana, and Venezuela converge. We were not disappointed!

In addition to the rain, thick fog limited our field of vision to about one hundred feet on all sides. As we walked, brooks, craters, grottos, and white, shimmering mountain-crystal gardens appeared as if out of nowhere. It was off the charts! And to think: this was all happening at more than eight thousand feet above sea level.

❖

"I have a little surprise for you." My friend Felipe laughed as a little group of townsfolk dispersed.

We had gotten back to Parrai-tepui the night before and watched the World Cup final on the only television in the village, pressed into a room with fifteen locals. Although all of the others were rooting for Argentina, I had cheered for my home team at the top of my lungs. Luckily no one took offense.

"No! No! Go away!" Felipe shot past me down the hill yelling, chasing away the dogs that were ripping into his backpack. "The beautiful bread! I bought it from the townsfolk as a surprise for you!"

He did not seem concerned about the fist-sized hole in his bag, just the chewed-up loaf of bread. Cursing, he collected the pieces from the ground.

"It's still better than nothing," I said, and grabbed a water bottle to rinse off the dog slobber. The manioc bread was a bit bland, but after five days of oatmeal and water three times a day, I wouldn't have dreamed of throwing it away.

"Just get it all wet," Felipe suggested. "Then we won't know what was in the dogs' mouth and what wasn't." Chewing the soggy cuisine, we sat down next to each other and discussed what to do next.

Inspired by my stories, Felipe was planning to hitchhike to Mexico and look for a boat to sail to the Caribbean. (Three months later he was successful.) I wanted to take off toward the Amazon River and then travel south. Starting in Northeast Brazil, I would make my way to Bolivia, then on to Peru by the end of October. I had kept in contact with Wilfried, the couch-surfer from Paris, and he wanted to hang out with me there for two and a half weeks.

"If you go to São Paulo, you can stay with my family!" Felipe offered on their behalf. "My mother loves cooking for people."

"Then it's a done deal!" I laughed, sticking the last piece of bread in my mouth and shaking the crumbs from my hands.

○ August 2014

In Manaus, the Amazon River was much different than I had imagined. Here, instead of untouched rain forest as in Venezuela and Guiana, there was just one predominate feature everywhere you looked: water. There was so much water that the banks sometimes disappeared and you felt like you were out at sea. In certain areas a river of a different color joined in, and a distinct border formed between the two. It looked like a rip on the surface.

The tropical climate was stiflingly muggy. You had a choice: you either sweated underneath long pants and sleeves, or you let the swarms of mosquitoes give you a full-body tattoo. Thank goodness I had received a pink mosquito net as a present. It may not have matched my camouflage hammock, but I slept all the better with my flowery sheet holding the plague at bay.

I had many fascinating experiences with food in South America, including my first time eating armadillo and manatee. But it was the unending variety of bizarre fruits in all colors and shapes that amazed me the most—fruits I had never seen before and would likely never see again. They could be enjoyed out of season as ice cream flavors as well. It is incredible what the earth has to offer. I had no idea!

I did not learn about culinary matters only. South America took my concept of hospitality to a whole new level, particularly in Brazil. Due to urban influence, city dwellers were a little less open to strangers than what I experienced in the countryside. However, they remained warmhearted in their own way, still inviting foreigners into their homes.

A sentence I heard often was: "*Não vai não rapaz. Fica um pouco mais!*" ("Don't go, boy, stay a little longer!") With that, my hosts would convince me to stay another week. Then another and another, until I had spent a whole month there, even though my original plan was to stay for just three days.

In northern Brazil, it is simply a part of the culture to be trusting and open—definitely a practice I want to emulate. We Germans tend to be reserved and mistrust anything foreign. While traveling through South America, it finally became clear to me that most people in the world are nice, and they just want to have a good life. Of course, there are also scoundrels, but they are in the minority. This realization was confirmed throughout the rest of my journey.

In short, the lesson is this: if you reject strangers, the probability is much higher that you have missed an amazing encounter with a nice person, rather than an unfortunate encounter with a mean person.

Of course, that does not mean you shouldn't be careful. I can count on one hand the number of times that something didn't feel right during my four-year journey. When that happened, I usually just talked to the person, asking them targeted questions to see if they were up to something.

For example, one stranger on the street asked me, "Where are you from?" as the door to the drug store closed behind me. I had

just stocked up on mosquito spray because the malaria prophy-
laxis protected against only one of five different kinds of malaria.
Mosquito nets, long clothing, and mosquito spray are much more
effective. If you don't get bit, then you have nothing to worry
about.

Even though the stranger's question sounded like a sales pitch,
I let him pull me into a conversation.

"Oh, Germany," he said, giving me a cigarette. "I have a friend
from Germany."

"Really? Where in Germany?"

"From . . . the capital . . ."

"Frankfurt?" I was testing him.

"Yes, from Frankfurt."

"What's your friend's name?"

"What was his name exactly . . . ," he mumbled, and it became
clear that his my-friend-from-your-country number was a shoddy
attempt to lure me in.

He tried to change the subject. "It's dangerous here. You'd better not let yourself get mugged."

A yellow warning light went off inside me. That was the second attempt to seem trustworthy. He just needed to pretend to be
religious to cover all the standard moves.

"I'll take you to my sister," he said. "You can stay there. We'll
show you around and watch out for you."

At this point my warning light turned from yellow to red. He
demanded that I follow him, emphasizing that my safety was in his
hands. But I didn't buy it. "Where does your sister live?"

"Just a couple of blocks away. Come on."

When I turned him down again, he got more forceful and
aggressive. Finally he grabbed my arm and tried to drag me with
him. I remained polite but started talking loudly until he let go. He
took off, swearing as he stormed away.

Following a tip from a local, I went to check out the famous Jericoacoara beach. Due to limited rainfall, it was not the palm-tree, coconut paradise I had expected, but its surroundings made it absolutely unique. Rows of lagoons, one after the other, were full of seahorses and puffer fish. Beyond that were spectacular hiking dunes. From the highest dunes you could slide more than three hundred feet on a snowboard. From there I hitchhiked down the coast for six days, arriving in the suburbs of Rio de Janeiro early one morning.

Many months had gone by with no contact with the outside world. This was the second time that my mother was afraid she would never see me alive again. To calm her fears, she gave a Brazilian acquaintance a GPS tracker that I could use to let my family know I was okay or if I needed help. He brought it to Brazil, and I picked it up along with an extra pair of socks.

They don't show much of Rio de Janeiro on television—usually only the shimmering bay front view of the city. In reality, it is a thickly populated city about twice the size of New Jersey. It consists mostly of *favelas*, poor districts, where dilapidated huts are usually equipped with a TV, refrigerator, stove, and quite often air-conditioning. The first favelas were reportedly built in the mid- to late nineteenth century when the slaves were set free and they populated the uninhabitable steep slopes.

The national team from Germany had engaged in social projects during their stay for the World Cup. They had left a good impression. Since Brazilians and Argentines can't stand each other, everyone told me without exception, once Brazil was out of the running, the Brazilians all rooted for Germany.

The evening of my arrival, I located the residential community where I could stay during my time in Rio de Janeiro. From there I explored the city up close and personal. I had wanted to visit since

I was a kid. The view of the ocean was priceless, and the myriad little staircases and alleys bubbled with life. Day and night there was music, dancing, wine, beer, and the local favorite, super cheap Cachaca 51, an alcoholic beverage distilled from fermented sugarcane juice.

October 2014

Although I had gotten an early start on my journey to São Paulo, I ended up waiting at a gas station on Expressway 116 for ten hours before a truck picked me up. This would have discouraged me at the beginning of my travels, but I had practiced a lot of patience in the meantime and was sure of the outcome: *sooner or later someone will come.* And they did.

In São Paulo Felipe's family did, indeed, take me in. After we had climbed Roraima, Felipe confessed his fear to me: "I bet my family will let you take my place!" He was right. They did. But only his seat at the kitchen table. Felipe was also right about his mother's love of cooking for people. In the end, my reputation for being a bottomless pit had to surrender unconditionally to her hospitality!

Loaded down with a ton of provisions, I finally started off on the single largest stretch of hitchhiking that I undertook throughout my travels. I was supposed to meet my Parisian friend, Wilfried, in Peru, and I had eleven days to put the 2,300 miles from São Paulo to Cuzco behind me. That's about a tenth of the earth's circumference and a third of the distance back to Germany.

There were only nine days left until my rendezvous with Wilfried.

"You can shower at my house," the driver of the compact car offered. I glanced at myself. There was no doubt that I was in desperate need of a shower! My snazzy-looking travel partner, dressed in a light-blue polo shirt, stared at me lasciviously. His ulterior motives were plain as day.

"That's okay. No thanks."

"Are you sure? My bathroom has more to offer . . ." Before I could answer, his hand shot down toward my crotch. But just as fast, I slapped his hand away.

"Hey!"

Unfortunately it was not the first time something like that had happened to me in Brazil. In the past I would have clocked this man for his shameless advance without thinking twice. But lately I had been thinking about matters of faith, and I was pretty sure that hitting him would not be an example of "loving your neighbor." That was the principle I was now trying to live by. The next time I had a chance, I left the car with some polite parting words and started looking for another vehicle.

A big blue street sign reading "Bienvenido en Bolivia" greeted me. I hung my hammock between two trees about a hundred yards past the sign and refreshed myself with oatmeal and water, as usual. The people there looked totally different than in Brazil. *Almost like the Warao*, I thought. This is no big surprise, since more than 60 percent of the population in Bolivia has indigenous ancestry. I couldn't help but notice how many of the people were walking around with badly swollen cheeks. I felt sorry for them. The dental care in Bolivia must be truly awful!

I staked out a place that lots of vehicles were using as a rest stop. The distances in South America are so huge that people rarely drive personal cars. Instead, they take a tour bus or, for longer stretches, an airplane. There are only a few highways, and the regular traffic consists almost exclusively of semitrucks. That was my best chance to find a ride.

I tried to take a nap in the heat of the day, since most of the trucks wouldn't show up until evening. As I was dozing off, a forty-foot white moving truck stopped right next to me to change drivers. I seized the opportunity to ask for a ride to Santa Cruz. They said yes. So I took off down the 450-mile stretch with Paulo, a Brazilian in his midforties. He had thrown his stuff in the moving truck and taken over the job from the other man.

The landscape was scarcely populated and overgrown with bushes. Rocky plateaus jutted up here and there.

"The coca farmers have their plantations here," Paulo gestured to some fields protected by green thickets. Even though the plants and leaves are legal in this country, selling the cocaine that you extract from them is not. But, due to corruption, it is hard to control. The drug is so cheap that the Brazilian side of Bolivia is a pilgrim destination for junkies. Addicts that have totally lost their minds and go around screaming are a part of normal, everyday life there.

The coca plantations were followed by hours of flat, monotonous steppe. Giant billboards by the side of the road advertised soy seed and manure fertilizer. After what felt like an eternity, we stopped at a gas station where I had an encounter I will never forget.

A young man sat waiting on a wall. He was very white and wore long gray pants, a red-and-white plaid shirt, and suspenders sporting a Hamburg soccer team logo. I had to blink several times; I felt like I had been transported to a village in Northern Germany. To top it off, he greeted me with the familiar Plattdeutsch: "*Moin, moin!*" (hello), making the situation all the more surreal. His dialect, which has since died out in Germany, sounded a little strange.

He told me that his great-grandparents had moved to Mexico, along with several other agriculture workers, sometime around

World War II. From there they immigrated to Bolivia, where they maintained the traditions of their farming colony. They still wear North German clothing, usually marry among themselves, drive around with horses and buggies, and even strive to maintain the German style of farmyard architecture. I associated them with the Amish, but the young man explained to me that for them, it had nothing to do with religion.

I still think they may have some connection with the Mennonites. It is so unbelievable to me that today, in the middle of South America, there are fully functional North German cities! I was astonished that he was, in some ways, more North German than I am. They speak much better Plattdeutsch and wear traditional North German clothing. They just live on the wrong continent, far from dikes, lighthouses, and mud flats.

Ah, Northern Germany, I'll see you again someday.

About sixty miles from our destination, we took a break to sleep and then drove on and on in the dark from 2:00 to 5:00 a.m. The headlights were getting weaker and weaker, for some reason, until finally we had to stop by the side of the road and wait until morning.

When Paulo went to start the truck, nothing happened. "I can't believe it! *It's easy. You just have to sit down and drive,*" Paulo sarcastically imitated the other driver for whom he had taken over.

We waved down another truck. They gave us a jump-start, and we happily drove on for another fifteen minutes before a police officer pulled us over. "Looks good," he said, checking out our papers. Peering through the window he said, "That will be seventy bolivianos" (about ten dollars).

That's so nice of him to name the exact bribery price, I thought, even though he had added on a foreigner markup. After all, in

Brazil the traffic cops could be bought for twenty real (about eight dollars), sometimes even cheaper.

After we paid, Paulo drove off, and within moments the motor sputtered and died. We had to wait for half an hour for a big rig equipped with flat-nosed pliers to give us a jump.

The fun started all over again twenty miles down the road at a construction site. Luckily an excavator was there to help us out. Then we got pulled over again. "It's not like we have a deadline or anything," Paulo grumbled through gritted teeth.

"Where is your first aid kit?" this police officer asked.

We couldn't find it.

"Come with me." The Bolivian traffic cop led us quickly to the guardhouse. I noted how Paulo hid behind me, fumbling around in his pocket. "This is a serious violation of traffic codes. Your fine is two thousand bolivianos, and I'm doing you a favor!"

"Two thousand?" my driver wailed before explaining that he was just filling in for someone who was sick. He told about the other time he had been pulled over, and by the time he got around to the problems with the battery, he almost had tears in his eyes. "I only have enough money left over for lunch!"

"And what about him?" The cop pointed gruffly at me.

I stuck my fingers through some holes in my shirt as an answer.

"He sleeps on the street. You won't get anything out of him," Paulo answered, protecting me. "And I only have enough left over for lunch . . ."

Had. The officer grabbed his wallet and confiscated everything inside. Then he released us. No receipt, no evidence.

"If you like oatmeal, I—"

"Keep your food," Paulo interrupted me as we climbed back into the truck. He dug in his back pocket. There was no trace of sadness on his face as he put the bills back in his wallet. *What a sly guy!*

After circling around strategically for quite some time, we finally reached our goal in Santa Cruz.

"What took you so long?" complained the recipient, an extremely effeminate Brazilian man in his late thirties.

"Long story," Paulo sighed. "Who will unload the shipment?"

"You are going to bring it in my house! Your company contract clearly states that—"

"*Calma, calma*—keep calm. I'll get it taken care of." Paulo distanced himself, taking out his cell phone.

The Brazilian, still upset, came over to me and started flirting. Even though I was not interested, I tried to be nice and polite.

"I told the boss. He will come and take care of everything tomorrow." Paulo turned to me. "Do you think you could keep an eye on the moving truck until then? I have to be at work in Brazil in twelve hours."

"Sure thing." I stayed behind with the keys and the truck, and made myself comfortable with my hammock hanging between the running board and a streetlight. Next to me stood a tall, red wall protecting a private housing complex. The guarded entrance was a little more than fifty yards away. The watchman had a plastic baggie with green leaves in it, which he stuck in his mouth from time to time. He pushed the leaves into his cheeks, puffing them out quite a bit. *Aha! So the people here don't have dental problems after all!*

"What kind of plant is that?" I asked the man who, like most Bolivians, had straight, shiny, black hair.

"It's coca leaves," he mumbled, rubbing a white powder on the leaves in his open mouth with his pinky. "The baking soda draws out the cocaine and makes you alert and energetic. It hardly works without baking soda or some other catalyst, but older people eat the leaves to help with stomach problems."

Later I was told that cocaine is good for altitude sickness, good for your teeth, and has tons of positive effects and no negative side effects—it almost makes you skeptical. Incan priests originally used it for religious purposes, and it is still a standard component of shaman rituals in Peru and Bolivia. Some people read coca leaves like the psychics who read tarot cards at fairs. Others offer tourists the opportunity to experience ancient rituals, such as *salla huaska*, in combination with illegal "organic drug trips," using substances like *San Pedro* extracted from cacti. In youth hostels, harmless coca-tea is always a big hit.

I was told that coca plants were first introduced into daily life by slave owners who discovered that the slaves worked longer and complained less when they chewed on coca. To me it seemed a little bit like the coffee and energy drinks we use to boost our productivity in the West. At this point I must confess to having a full-blown coffee addiction. *Nectar of the gods!*

Two days passed and the boss had still not appeared, so I decided to leave the truck and go on my way.

Since neither the guard nor the recipient of the goods wanted to take the keys, I wrote a note in Portuguese and stuck it to the inside of the window. It said that the keys were located "under the truck's problem." I was hoping the Spanish-speaking Bolivians were not smart enough to deduce the note's meaning and that the Brazilian man responsible for the truck was clever enough to figure out that the keys were under the truck's defective battery.

I didn't feel quite right as I shouldered my backpack and headed off, but I was supposed to meet Wilfried soon. How the story with the moving truck ended I'll probably never know.

In the outskirts of Santa Cruz, I boarded a bus to Cochabamba, Bolivia. After a few hours of driving, the first ascent began, and the dusty steppe turned into tropical forests. We slowly wound up the switchbacks, ever higher into the mountains, and were suddenly plunged into the foggy, rainy regions of the Andes. Here, short grass and evergreens decorated the sparse, rocky landscape. The scenery was magical. I couldn't tear myself away from the window!

From Cochabamba it was on to La Paz. By the time we arrived, the sky had turned from black to cobalt blue. I helped a woman packed in wool clothes pull her bulky, white plastic sacks out of the baggage area of the bus. She wore a little bowler hat over her pigtails as a status symbol. The taller the hat and the finer the material, the better. The countrywomen who wore this headdress were called cholitas—little cholas. In downtown city districts the people who dressed in Western clothing looked down on the bowler hats, known as a *borsalino*.

Underneath her wide skirt she wore long socks that ended in shoes with buckles. She thanked me with a smile, gold teeth sparkling. I picked up my backpack and started looking for the best way to cross into Peru.

Without noticing at first, my breath had become shallow and quick. The cool, high-altitude air tasted like stone and smoke. At twelve thousand feet La Paz is the highest capital city in the world—even though the city of Sucre, where most of the government buildings are located, claims to be the capital as well.

La Paz's historical district is located in a sinkhole surrounded by the modern areas of the city, which are situated on higher ground. These are called *El Alto*. The colorful, funny-shaped façades reminded me of a mixture between architecture from the seventies and *Star Wars*. I had never seen anything like it! This architecture is certainly unique, not found in other parts of the world. On top of the flat-roofed commercial buildings, the owners built Western-style houses, which do not fit in at all.

The next stretch of road led me on from La Paz toward Peru. Fields of potatoes, corn, and quinoa glided past. The Spanish conquerors had considered the ancient grain of quinoa to be "poor people food" and fed it to their animals. This caused many natives to bristle at the idea of including it in their diets. For decades this delicious, nutrient-packed grain was all but rejected until North Americans and Europeans discovered it as a "health food" and started selling it at marked-up prices. Now, mysteriously, quinoa is an accepted part of the locals' diets once again.

Lake Titicaca spread out silently to the right, and bright, snow-peaked mountains punctuated the horizon. The streets were muddy and no one followed the traffic rules. Whoever brakes first, usually inches away from impact, yields the right of way.

Like the tuk-tuks in Thailand, the taxis here were large, covered tricycles or motorcycles with three wheels. The people looked very similar to the Bolivians although the women did not wear bowler hats. They did, however, wear brightly colored, striped blankets called *aguayos*, which they used to carry groceries or children on their backs.

In the morning a trucker gave me a lift through the breathtaking landscape of Peru and dropped me off just sixty miles from Cuzco. The landscape there was barren and treeless. Llamas and alpacas grazed in the wide-open meadows. Advertisements for political parties were painted on the houses and walls in the little villages. Here and there, large firing ovens were available for the people to make their own bricks.

I made it on time for my meeting with Wilfried. He had only two and a half weeks to travel with me, but we planned to make the most of it!

Cuzco is a popular launching site for people who want to visit the ancient Incan city of Machu Picchu. Of course, we wanted to see this Incan citadel, too, but I had another special mission to complete. While in Manaus, I had met a Brazilian street artist. When I described my plans to her, she said, "Oh, an old friend of mine, Volver, lives in Cuzco. I haven't seen him in years. If you go there, please give him my regards." I promised that I would.

There was one small problem, however. Cuzco has a population of about 350,000 people, and the only thing I knew about the man was his first name: *Volver*. Still, I had given her my word, and I love a good challenge. Is it possible to track down a person without the help of social media? I wanted to find out.

I had one clue: he was probably a street artist or a hippie like the young woman. Wilfried and I left our backpacks in a tourist office in the *Plaza de Armas* (Weapons Square). Interestingly, the central square in almost all South American cities is called *Plaza de Armas*. We headed off for San Blas, the city's alternative district. I made my way around, questioning everyone who looked like they knew the scene.

"Do you mean Golber? The guy with two huskies?" one art vendor suggested.

Hmm—at least it sounds similar. Given the accent, she may not have been able to differentiate between a *B* and a *V*, and I could have misunderstood a *G* as a *V*. "Maybe. Where can I find him?"

"He lives in the ruins of Sacsayhuaman. But he comes down here regularly to work in the store *Maracuyea*. Try there this evening."

I did just that. In the store, which smelled like incense, there were a few African drums and a didgeridoo, colorful T-shirts and pants hanging on the walls, and jewelry made of bones and semi-precious stones displayed on low-lying tables. And, much faster than expected, I ran into the aforementioned Golber. He turned out to be a young trapeze artist. I relayed the greetings from his friend.

"Hey, thanks! That's so rad!" said Golber, winking at me. "You're a chaski, right?"

"A chaski?"

"That's what the Incan messengers were called. They used to trek around on two legs, like you. They also carried backpacks like yours!"

For some reason I found the idea appealing.

Along with sightseeing at Machu Picchu, Wilfried and I climbed Chachani, a twenty-thousand-foot-high inactive volcano. The frigid air had so little oxygen at that altitude that every motion took five times as much effort as usual. But it was worth it. From the peak, the land rolled out like a tapestry beneath us, extending for hundreds of miles.

It was truly a once-in-a-lifetime experience.

After Wilfried flew back to Europe, I worked in Bolivia for a while as a tour guide in the world's biggest salt flat, *Uyuni*. From saguaro cacti to flamingos, and bubbling geysers to baby llamas, the salt flat never ceased to amaze me.

A few days before Christmas, I started off for Salta in Northern Argentina, where I would spend the holidays with friends of Wilfried.

The trucker stepped on the brakes, and we rattled to a stop. He glanced out the dusty window and said, "We're here. Atocha." It was just after midnight, and the little Bolivian city was dark and deserted. "Are you sure you want to get out here?"

"Yep. Here is great. Thanks!" I grabbed my backpack, swung the door open, and jumped out. "Have a nice drive," I said, tapping the hood twice to say goodbye.

It was cold as I walked down the wide, sandy path. The pale moonlight shone eerily on the mud houses. A crouching figure slowly materialized out of a dark alley.

"Good evening." I made my presence known. The man turned around. He was a full head shorter than I am and was wearing an old bike helmet wrapped in several feet of yarn and plastic trash. *That's not normal*, I thought, but it was still worth a try. "Excuse me, do you know a place where I can sleep?"

The man stared at me for a full minute without saying a word. I repeated my question. "Ari, ari!" he said and nodded, wobbling his trash-mobile and helmet back and forth. It was quite possible that this was the result of long-term drug abuse.

We went on a nocturnal walk together through the little town. After a while, we reached a big, paved square. Dirty streetlights bathed their surroundings in a pale, yellow glow.

"Is here good?" I asked.

The helmet man nodded and wobbled onward until he disappeared behind a house. I was standing in front of what looked like a corrugated sheet-metal structure full of trash bags. *Not exactly five-star, but it should do for a few hours' sleep.*

I spread out my camping mat and sleeping bag at an angle to block off a corner. After placing my backpack in one of my black plastic bags, I set it in the corner so no one could get it without going over me first. The trash bag would serve as further thievery-prevention. Not only did it make my luggage look worthless, but the bag would crinkle loudly if anyone tried anything.

Okay then, good night.

I had just fallen asleep when a rustling noise woke me. *The helmet man?* I sat up and blinked into almost a dozen pairs of eyes. *Street dogs!* An icy chill went up my spine. The mutt nearest to me lowered his head and gave a low growl. The others immediately chimed in. They bared their teeth, canines glittering in the dim light. The dogs were haggard and emaciated. They were missing patches of fur here and there. *Hunting dogs*, I guessed based on their build. Barring a couple of rats, they had no hope of finding prey in this desert. They must have been starving.

In Bolivia they tell stories about stray dogs attacking children at night. I may not have been a child, but sitting in my sleeping bag, I was about the same height. I quickly surveyed the situation. There wasn't a lot I could do. I couldn't make a run for it with my feet stuck in my sleeping bag. Even if I could, the dogs are three times as fast. I was also way outnumbered. If the pack attacked me, I wouldn't stand a chance.

Considering the circumstances, I wasn't as freaked out as I could have been. I shot a prayer toward heaven and hoped that God would take care of me again. By that time I had become convinced that a far better life after death awaited me in heaven although I was embarrassed that I was obviously still attached to my measly earthly existence.

A few other dogs that had been rummaging around in the trash came over and filled in the gaps of the quarter circle. There was no way out. But for some reason they didn't attack. Maybe they were intimidated.

"*Sale!*" I yelled loudly in Spanish, trying to sound as authoritative as possible. A couple of dogs actually cowered, and three of them even retreated a little. But then they barked and growled and came closer than before. Clearly, trying to scare them was not such a good idea.

Strangely, though they looked ready to attack, none of the stray dogs dared to come closer than six feet. *Are they unsure?* Possible. It was probably the first time they had met a white guy in a sleeping bag.

Clank! Clank! Clank!

The dogs spun around. A free-roaming donkey had bit a plastic bag on the pile of trash and shook it up and down, scattering the contents all over the ground. The strays immediately forgot about me and ran at the newcomer, barking furiously. Instead of bolting, he pinned his ears back and lowered his head, countering their attack. With my mouth hanging open, I watched the pack animal chase the dogs away through the square. I had to pinch myself to make sure I was awake. It was just too crazy! The donkey fought off the pack until dawn, keeping the dogs away from me.

What a bizarre night! Saved by a donkey! No one is going to believe this.

7

THE MOST EMBARRASSING MOMENT OF MY LIFE (SO FAR)

January 2015

I MANAGED TO GET THROUGH northern Chile and back to Cuzco, Peru. But there I had to deal with a problem of a different kind.

After I left home in Germany, my family moved to a new place, leaving the house where I had grown up. I had spent my whole life in that house, playing in the garden with the bleating of nearby sheep and goats. I simply could not picture another house as ever being my home. That alone was a lot to process.

Unfortunately this move created an even bigger problem for me: I had to reregister at our new address to stay legal in my home country. My parents had been told by legal council that this registration could only be done in person. Vacation travels did not qualify as sufficient reason to be represented by someone with power of attorney. Disregarding this notice would result in a fine of several thousand euros. The worst part was that it could ruin my dream to travel around the world without using an airplane.

My parents had phoned the courthouse and asked if there was any way to reregister without requiring me to travel home. The answer was a solid no. For special cases it was possible with power of attorney, but that was only for extended hospitalizations or absences required by work.

The situation seemed hopeless—for me, anyway. My mother was rather looking forward to having me home for Christmas.

Amazingly, I was not really worried. I had a strong feeling that it would somehow work out. The countless times that I had been so lucky, bringing me as far as I had come—this couldn't just be coincidence.

On a whim, I mailed my ID and permission for power of attorney to my family. I called them and explained, "Somehow I just have this feeling that it will work out. Just go to the registration office and try."

At the other end of the line, my mother countered, "But they said you have to do it in person."

"Yes, I know, but—just try." I begged her until she gave in.

When my package arrived, my father immediately brought the documents to the registration office. He was firmly convinced this was a useless endeavor and that his request would be denied. When it was his turn to go in the office, however, a tech worker burst into the room with a box. "I have the solution to all your problems," he said, smiling at the clerks.

It turned out that the office printer and copier had gone down the previous day, and both women were eagerly awaiting a repair. The tech worker carried on an animated conversation with them while he fixed the copier. Their attention was on him while one of them absent-mindedly typed my reregistration into the system. She didn't notice that it wasn't exactly valid. Then she stamped it and handed it back to my father, no questions asked.

I was reregistered!

An enormous weight lifted off of my shoulders. The IT worker had solved my problems too! I was free to continue hitchhiking up the west coast of South America to Lima, the capital of Peru. Friends of friends that I had met in Rio de Janeiro provided a place to sleep and showed me around.

When my hostess, a middle-aged woman, took me to the wake of a recently deceased colleague, I stumbled into possibly the most embarrassing moment of my entire life.

The coffin was crafted out of light-colored wood, and the lid was open. It was decorated with ribbons and vases, and about seventy visitors had added cards and flowers. Other than that, the room, located on the third floor of a funeral home, was sparse. The bare walls were lined with plastic chairs, and the dark tile floor had a matte shine. In the entrance were three tables offering snacks and coffee, but the mood was glum and heavy-hearted.

"Let's go talk to the family," my hostess said and introduced me to the widower and his grown children. I shook their hands and offered my condolences.

"My wife would have loved to talk with you," the widower smiled painfully. Then he pointed to the open coffin. "Please."

With lowered gazes we approached the coffin and looked inside. Embedded in red velvet lay a woman in her fifties. Her straight, black hair was combed, and her eyes were closed. Her red lips had a hint of a smile, and her hands were lying peacefully on her lap.

"Heart attack," murmured my escort. I held my chest sympathetically and then sat down on a chair at the edge of the room. I felt helpless and miserable, surrounded by so much sorrow and

suffering and unable to do anything about it. Out of pure embar-
rassment I took out a Spanish pocket Bible—a gift from a Bolivian
friend—and started reading.

"Excuse me?"

I looked up. The widower was standing in front of me. "Do you
perhaps have a few words for us?" He pointed to the Bible.

"Um, sure, of course," I answered and flipped to a part that
I thought might be appropriate for the situation. I was somehow
happy to be of use. After I read, he nodded his satisfaction and
gave his children a signal. They immediately started gathering the
people together. I anxiously watched as the visitors made a half
circle around the coffin.

*What is going on? Is someone going to make a speech? Wait a
minute—he doesn't think that . . .*

Unsure, I looked at the widower, and he looked back at me
expectantly. *Gulp!*

Upon realizing the extent of the misunderstanding, I went pale.
The people thought I was a missionary or someone who could offi-
ciate the spiritual part of the ceremony! But I couldn't do that.
Impossible! In desperation I looked into the widower's eyes yet
again.

Oh no! I can't bring myself to disappoint them. I gave myself an
internal pep talk: *Come on! A couple of verses from the Bible and a
prayer—what could possibly go wrong?*

I stood up. It got quiet. My heart was pounding. *There's no
going back now.* I welcomed everyone. To show who I was, I opened
my Bible and read out loud the verses that I had just read to the
widower. *So far, so good. And now?* My hands shook. *Shouldn't you
actually have some kind of relationship with the deceased? Say a couple
of things about her life?*

I awkwardly cleared my throat and then pressed on: "It is
always sad when someone dies." *Yes, keep going!* "And we are all sad

that . . ." *Yikes! What was her name again?* "that . . . the . . . uh . . ." In panic, I looked from person to person. *Help!* No one knew what I was looking for. ". . . are all sad that the dead person . . . died."

I could have smacked myself on the forehead. *Ouch!* I couldn't think of any appropriate Spanish vocabulary, so I fell back on the most boring words possible. With my heart pounding wildly, I stuttered on: "Many of you have memories of a very personal nature with . . ." I looked desperately at the cards and flowers. *Surely there is a name somewhere!* ". . . with . . ." *Nothing. Nothing, and still nothing.* ". . . with the dead person."

What a catastrophe! I had to stop! "Let us fold our hands in prayer. Lord, please give . . . uh . . . the dead person's family . . . and her friends . . . comfort . . ." *How utterly pathetic!* "We ask you to receive . . . the dead person . . . and give her your peace. Amen."

The mourners stared at me in horror. I felt like the helmsman who had just rammed the *Titanic* against an iceberg. *Why doesn't the ground just open up and swallow me?* Stunned, I walked through the room and took a place next to my hostess in the crowd.

"You forgot her name!" she whispered the obvious to me in a shocked tone. The widower tried to halfway rescue the situation by making a little speech of his own. He was visibly embarrassed by my babbling. When he finished, my escort pulled me out of the room. I should have said goodbye to be polite, but it was apparently better to avoid confrontation.

At least one thing was sure: those people will never forget me!

I rode the bus to the north side of Lima and positioned myself at a gas station, ready to hitchhike to Ecuador. There was not a lot of traffic going in my direction. No one offered me a ride, so I walked along a row of semitrucks that were parked on the sandy median, asking questions. One driver said, "We have to load first, but if you help, then we'll give you a ride!"

Sounds fair. The load was made up of all sorts of potted plants, bags, and bundles that were on the median. I grabbed two little bushes and heaved them with one swing onto the truck. Then the next two. "The quicker we finish, the quicker we'll get moving!" said one of the workers, grabbing a bunch of flowers. We worked at a steady pace. The sun blazed down on us. Bit by bit, we filled the truck bed.

Dusk was falling by the time we closed the latch on the semi. I took off my T-shirt and fanned myself. *Done.* A couple of people climbed into the truck and the wheels started rolling.

They don't mean to leave without me?! I sprinted after the truck as it slowly rolled away, and caught up to the cab. "Hey, wait! You forgot me!" I shouted.

The driver stopped for a second and stuck his head out of the window. "Sorry. There's no room now."

I stood there speechless, watching the semi drive away.

"That's a part of life too," my father would have said in this situation. "Let it be a lesson." He was right, of course; I should actually be happy that it was only one afternoon of work and not more. But that piece of wisdom still didn't make me feel better. It put my painful experience in perspective, but it didn't make it go away.

Then something I had read in the Bible came to mind: you are supposed to bless your enemies. The driver wasn't exactly my enemy, but he had been mean to me. However, if I were to hold it against him, I would be the one stuck dragging a grudge around. It wouldn't bother him a bit.

So instead of staying upset, I decided to let it go and wish the driver well. It wasn't easy at first, but gradually a contented smile spread across my face, and I went off in high spirits to look for another ride.

I only spent a week in Ecuador, but it was packed to the brim with great experiences and new friendships. In retrospect, I can't believe that my time there was so short. One of the highlights was climbing up Chimborazo, an inactive volcano, with some students and having a snowball fight right on the equator! How cool is that? Come on!

I would have loved to stay longer, but I had to get to Panama as quickly as possible, otherwise I would miss the season to sail across the Pacific. The most direct path to Panama was through Colombia. I had been warned about guerilla warfare in Colombia, and was, in fact, affected by it on my second day there—a troop of rebels had blown up a bridge on my route. No one was hurt, but it brought everything to a standstill for several hours.

The reason for such attacks is supposedly political, but in reality, it is about cocaine. That's why you have nothing to worry about traveling in Colombia as long as you avoid the farming regions in the backcountry. You risk your life by going there. One gram of Colombian cocaine is worth about five dollars in Colombia, but in Europe or the United States it sells for more than one hundred dollars. The drug business is worth millions, and dealers are willing to go over dead bodies to maintain it.

Other than that, Colombians are just as welcoming as the people in Venezuela or Ecuador. They enjoy an overwhelmingly happy, relaxed Latino lifestyle.

There were no roads through the jungle between Panama and Colombia, so I went to the historic port town of Cartagena to look for a yacht to Panama.

After several months of overland travel, I was back to boat hunting. The yacht club would not allow me access to the docks, so I posted myself next to a white wall at the entrance. There, sooner or later, I would be able to talk with each of the boat owners.

"So, my boy, any news about finding a ride to Panama?" asked a bald Canadian who was out walking his bull terrier. Since he lived on his boat, he was a regular at the club. I had already met him several times when he went for walks. He had been the manager of a strip club in Quebec for many years but was now in real estate. Although he had a great sense of humor, I suspected he could be very unpleasant if you caused him any trouble.

"Not yet," I said hopefully, "but I've only been trying since yesterday."

"Where did you sleep last night?"

"Over there." I pointed along the walkway. "I hung my hammock in a construction site between an excavator and a palm tree. The night watchman said I could."

"A suite with an ocean view, eh?" The Canadian chuckled and offered a place to sleep on his boat if I would help out. I was all too eager to crash with him.

On the docks the following day, I found myself in a conversation with a tall Swede. After I had explained that I was looking for a boat, his first question was, "Can you cook?"

I raised an eyebrow. *Me? Cook? Well . . .*

"My cook didn't pass the cooking test. She even burned the rice . . . in a Teflon pot!"

Not long ago I had done the exact same thing! I had since learned how to do it right, but work as a professional chef? I said evasively, "Well, I can cook rice."

"Very good. The charter trip to the San Bas Islands on to Panama takes a week. Here is the menu. There are six of us."

The Swede gave me a long list. I quickly looked it over. Most of the dishes I had never cooked before. *Thai Chicken Curry. Pasta Puttanesca. Lobster. Roasted Chicken.* I got hungry just reading it!

"How long do I have to decide?"

"One hour. I need your passport by then. We're setting sail tomorrow morning." He was already hurrying off and added over his shoulder, "We'll meet here in an hour!"

Torn, I ran my fingers through my hair. *It was such a good opportunity! If only I could cook a little better. What now?* I needed a miracle to pass a whole week's worth of "cooking tests" on that boat. I walked briskly back to my Canadian host and burst into the cabin.

"I have the chance to sail to Panama tomorrow with a charter yacht," I babbled. The bald boat owner looked up from his smartphone. "But I think I'd better turn him down."

"Why? Isn't that exactly what you want?"

"Yes, but the position is as a cook, and I can't cook very well."

"YOU WILL ACCEPT IT!" the Canadian roared and slapped his palm on the table. Shocked, I recoiled. "I used to be a cook," he said. "Is that the menu there?"

I gave him the list.

"Ha! No reason to freak out! This is all child's play. Sit down, and we'll go over it together. It will be a great week!"

He explained a few things to me, and then, overjoyed, I brought my passport to the Swede. I sat with the Canadian late into the night, learning everything he knew about cooking. Most important were his top three rules of cooking: "First, always taste the food while cooking. Second, you eat with your eyes too. Third, serve the food hot."

We went over everything from cooking to decorating to how to arrange the food on the plate. To top it off, he mixed some spices together and gave them to me. I was secretly still hesitant, even after this crash-course. But it turned out that the Canadian was right: I can cook!

"Oh my goodness, this tastes better than at Grandma's house!" one of the tourists declared during the first week. At the end of our voyage, the Swede told me that if anyone was looking for a recommendation for crossing the Pacific, they should call him and he would recommend me.

I was indebted to the Canadian—not only for the successful voyage, on which everyone was satisfied with my cooking, but also for teaching me an important life lesson: from now on I wanted to be a positive "enabler" as much as possible, just as he had been for me. In most circumstances it is quite easy to help someone move forward when they would not have done it alone. Providing good advice, connecting people, or sometimes just saying a few encouraging words—it doesn't have to take a lot of time and effort to invest in the future of another person. And yet with a few little rocks you can start an avalanche of blessings.

February 2015

The San Blas Islands, located between Colombia and Panama, are exactly how you would imagine the Caribbean: lots of small, dreamy, idyllic islands with light-colored, fine-sand beaches and hundreds of palm trees. The islands are surrounded by turquoise-blue water, colorful reefs, and shipwrecks here and there that you can explore while snorkeling. Just like the postcards!

The islands are populated by the Guna, an indigenous people who lead a traditional fishing life but have also become dependent on trade with tourists. Coconuts and mola embroidery are among the items they trade. I found it interesting that some of the most sought-after molas are made by transvestites.

I also found it interesting that Guna Indians do not become transvestites due to sexual orientation but because they were raised as girls in a matriarchal society. If no girls are born in a Guna family for a long period of time, then they choose a little boy to raise as a girl. They dress him in girls' clothes, teach him to talk in a high voice, and give him chores traditionally assigned to girls.

Later I ran into this same custom on the island of Samoa in the Pacific Ocean, as well as in the French Polynesian Islands. However, the Polynesians choose the biggest, strongest boy in the family to be raised as a girl. He then helps the mother maintain the household. These guys are usually well over six feet tall, burly, and often poorly shaved—but they wear traditional women's clothing and lipstick, and they speak in a high voice. In Polynesia they are called rae-raes.

To be chosen as a rae-rae is a great honor in the community. Since most rae-raes are not homosexuals, they often spend their lives without a partner, whether male or female. Tourists who think they can score some easy sex with a rae-rae, like with the Ladyboys in Thailand, risk losing their front teeth. The Polynesians, with or without flowers in their hair, are always ready to dole out a swift punch.

"Oh, wie schön ist Panama!" (*Oh, How Beautiful Is Panama!*) When I was just a little squirt, I loved that book by Janosch.[1] The two main characters, a bear and a tiger, find a wooden banana crate in the river that has *Panama* stamped on the side. They are overcome by the desire to travel to this place, so they set out on a journey to find it. But, without knowing it, they just walk in circles. After a long time they reach their home again, but they don't recognize it. The plants have grown wild, and the house has fallen in. When the two find the remains of the banana crate on the ground and read the word *Panama* on the side, they are overjoyed; they think that they have finally reached their destination! And so the tiger and

---

1　This is one of the most popular children's books in Germany. The English version is called *The Trip to Panama*, trans. Anthea Bell (New York: Little Brown, 1981).

the bear rebuild their crumbled house, and from then on they live happily ever after in their dream location.

It's a very sweet story. Like most good children's books, it offers something valuable for adults as well: the tiger and the bear needed only one thing to be happy—namely, to be in Panama. Of course, at the end of the story they weren't in Panama, but in their own home where they had always lived. It wasn't a change in their outer circumstances that had made them happy, but a change in their inner perspective. Seeing the old with new eyes.

Author Nikolaus Lenau has a wise saying: "Many search for happiness as we look for a hat we wear on our heads." We often try to convince ourselves: *If I made more money, if I could lose a few pounds, if I could find a more loving partner, then I would be happy!* What we already have may be good—but still not good enough.

Today even the poorest people in Europe and North America live in greater luxury than most people throughout history. We can choose from thousands of products in the corner supermarket: cordon bleu along with chocolate ice cream and add a banana from overseas. A hundred years ago even kings would have been jealous of us! Televisions, smartphones, heat and air-conditioning, running water, electricity, cars, sports clubs, medicine, washing machines. Life has never been so easy and comfortable as it is now!

With so many advancements shouldn't we be happier than people used to be? And what about the countless people in other countries who don't have these things? On the contrary: on my journey I met lots of people who were happier and more content in their bamboo huts than most Porsche drivers in Germany.

Even a trip around the world like mine doesn't automatically make me happy—but I learned anew to see the world with thankful eyes and treasure my experiences. Indeed, in this way I found quite a bit of happiness.

Oh, How Beautiful Is Panama!

Turns out, Panama really is beautiful!

I debarked the charter boat at Portobelo (the Beautiful Port), a small historical city in the bay of Panama. With its mossy ruins carved out of stones, old cannons standing around, and dilapidated colonial buildings, I had the feeling of discovering a pirate's secret hideout. It is completely surrounded by mountains and a rich green rainforest. Yet again I found it hard to believe that I was actually there!

As a child I thought Panama was so unimaginably far away that I wasn't even sure if it really existed. Wasn't Panama somewhere near Timbuktu? That's where it was in my naïve, childish imagination. I later found out that Timbuktu, that mythical place that everyone has heard about but no one has actually been to, is an African city on the edge of the Sahara desert. This, of course, is only about a third of the earth's circumference away from Panama. So they were *almost* next to each other.

From Portobelo I walked and hitchhiked to Shelter Bay, a remote port at the northern entrance of the Panama Canal. Every year hundreds of sailboats pass by to exit the canal and cross the ocean. Surely there was one for me! The best time to start a journey across the Pacific is late February or March. The eastern trade winds are relatively stable in those weeks, and if you set sail then, you can spend the most time on the South Pacific Islands without worrying about getting caught in a tropical storm.

That first night I slept nearby on a lonely beach. Little crabs scurried here and there across the sand in search of food. The breeze wafted the smell of the Caribbean Sea over my face and, right there where the night sky touched the water, dozens of lights from cargo ships glittered and sparkled. They were all waiting to pass through the canal's lock. Countless stars shone down on me from the clear sky.

I was, yet again, caught up in reverent amazement over the greatness and complexity of our universe! *How much further does it go on, beyond what we are aware of here on earth? And to think, we already know about one hundred billion more galaxies in our universe. To say that it must be the work of a genius is a huge understatement.*

My little, earthly life was truly wonderful and I was confident that I would find a ride for the next leg of my journey. After all, there were so many boats and not very much competition. I was so excited about crossing the Pacific and, to top it off, I had found a place to sleep that made me feel just like Robinson Crusoe!

At daybreak I hid my backpack in the bushes and headed up the docks wearing my best clothes and carrying a notebook. I kept track of which boats' crews I had spoken with and which ones I still needed to connect with. The more people who had my contact information, the higher the chances that someone knew someone who was looking for help, or that they could give me a recommendation.

When talking with people I didn't just ask about a ride but also enjoyed building relationships with those I met. My mode of travel was completely dependent on relationships. Just like, by the way, all of life is for everyone—even if we are not always aware of it.

On the first day of my search, I found a boat scheduled to cross the Pacific that was looking for crewmembers: a married couple and their young son were planning to sail to Australia. Because the mother was scheduled for a medical procedure before the trip, they wouldn't set sail for another month. No problem for me. I was not under any time constraints. We made an agreement and it seemed like a done deal. It was almost too easy!

During the next month, I helped a friend of mine whom I had

met in the Canary Islands. She managed an agency in Panama, providing services for yachts crossing through the canal. I was allowed to stay in a room at her place and even earned a little money by working as a line handler, bringing boats safely through the canal. When water is let into or out of the locks, the sailboats have to be kept in the middle with four lines. Otherwise, the maelstrom produced by water rushing in and out of the locks would push the boat against the wall and cause serious damage. It was my job to prevent that from happening, and by doing so, I got to cross the Panama Canal six times. I also swam in it three times and sailed through twice with special permission.

The Panama Canal is considered one of the seven wonders of the modern world. It was one of the biggest construction projects in all of human history and took the lives of more than thirty thousand people while it was being built. The overwhelming majority did not die from accidents but from tropical sicknesses. By providing a detour, the canal has spared seamen more than a million trips through the "world's biggest sailors' graveyard," the dreaded Cape Horn around the southern tip of South America. It is estimated that more than eight hundred ships met their doom in those treacherous waters. Plus, the Panama Canal saves two weeks of sailing between the Atlantic and Pacific Oceans.

Panama is known not only for the canal. For quite some time it has served as a favorite location for tax evaders and money launderers. You can get a mailbox and an apartment lickitey split in this super tax haven. Information concerning financial holders and the money remains anonymous. Panama's government and citizens know about this and are, of course, officially against it. But behind closed doors the whole system is welcome, and it will most likely not be changed.

These circumstances clearly led to Panama City's rapid development and impressive skyline. The service sector, including the canal, provide the foundation for Panama's economy, and banks and the trade industry are a close second. Luxurious houses, the warm climate, and an affordable cost of living make the tax haven complete.

March 2015

An e-mail from the Australian family arrived a few days before the trip was scheduled to begin. It said something like,

> Some friends of ours accepted our invitation a couple
> of days ago. We would like to take them with us.
> Unfortunately there is no room left for you. We wish you
> well. Good luck!

I read the e-mail twice. *What!?* Like a dark cloud, an oppressive heaviness surrounded me. It was devastating. My smile vanished into fatigue and a headache. I literally had to hold my head up with both hands so as not to let it hang down.

What was I supposed to do now?

I forced myself to take a few deep breaths. It wasn't the cancellation itself that disturbed me so deeply but the timing. The best time to find a boat had almost passed. It was now the end of March. I had spent the optimal time for finding a ride waiting for the Australian boat. Plus, I had cut my time in Ecuador and Colombia short so as not to waste these very weeks. My chances of finding a place were slim indeed. I ruffled my hair in desperation.

The words the Australian had said just after shaking my hand echoed in my head: "I took your advertisement off the message board. You don't need it anymore." I asked, just to be sure, if I should keep any other irons in the fire. He had said, "No, that won't be necessary."

All of that and not a single, solitary word about perhaps inviting friends instead of me. That lying—

I paused. Even though everything inside cried out to curse him,

I did not want to break my new resolution. I had firmly decided to never wish ill on anyone. No exceptions. But the frustration had to come out somehow. I changed tack. I would not curse them but bury them in blessings: *Have a good trip! Good luck! Sunshine! Health! Safety! Coconuts! Peace!*

It was almost laughable. I had to be careful not to become cynical. But my new approach did help. There really is something to the proverb: you reap what you sow—not only in regard to outer circumstances but on the inside as well. I noticed that my words, as difficult as they were to claim, changed my inner attitude. The concept was so simple. *And yet the way down is so much easier than the way up.*

"I'm back to looking for a boat," I told my Panamanian hostess, to explain why I was back in Shelter Bay.

"I'm sorry to hear that."

"It's okay. I'm sure something better will come along."

I did not give her that answer because I was feeling optimistic. On the contrary, it was obvious that my chances were pretty slim, and I did not *feel* certain. *Don't doubt what you can't see—even if you don't feel like it.* Now that is true faith! Reading the Bible was starting to change me.

To beat the traffic I got up before daybreak and rode the bus to the north side of Panama. That morning I took up where I had left off exactly one month ago. My fears were confirmed. A month ago five boats left the canal every day, whereas now the number had dwindled to one or two. And many of these were headed toward places such as Mexico or Chile. That's not where I was going.

However, there was also something good in store for me. I met some old acquaintances, including a Swedish guy about my age whom I had met on Gran Canaria. He was on a trip similar to mine. There he was, sitting on a lawn chair in the shade of a little house, looking at the docks. He started his trip by riding a bike from Scandinavia to Portugal, and then hitched a ride to Gran Canaria.

I remembered hearing him say, "I would like to go up the Amazon River in a kayak. Fitness studios aren't for me. I need a real goal!"

He'll never pull it off! I had thought quite honestly. *It's already almost a miracle that he made it to Gran Canaria.*

He had changed from a pudgy, immature kid into a strapping, wiry young man. His blond, shoulder-length hair, tan skin, and curly beard reminded me of a Viking. He looked really good, even robust, and with no trace of his former childishness. He hadn't paddled up the entire Amazon, but he had, nevertheless, made it from Ecuador to Brazil in a kayak he built himself. *Respect!* And his Atlantic Ocean crossing was pretty daring too.

When the young Swede couldn't find a boat to sail from Gran Canaria, he and four other hitchhikers bribed the police with one thousand euros to let them steal a broken-down, rusty, fifty-foot sailboat that had been confiscated by the coast guard years ago. With no motor, no radio, no lights, and practically no sailing experience, they somehow managed to sail over the Atlantic. Even I thought that was a suicide mission. They used a pocket GPS and rough maps for navigation.

About halfway through the trip, a.k.a. the middle of the ocean, they had some bad luck: the mast broke. They dragged onward even slower than before. It was questionable if they would make it to the other side. To hold a steady course, they improvised a new mast out of a spinnaker pole and continued bobbing along. In spite of strict rationing, they ran out of provisions about four hundred miles from the coast of French Guiana. Since they didn't have a radio, they couldn't signal for help.

When their hunger became overwhelming, and still with no land in sight, they took drastic measures. Using liquor bottles and anything else that would halfway work, they started a signal fire on the boat. This is the one and only time I have ever met someone who intentionally set their boat on fire!

In an unbelievable stroke of good luck, a Venezuelan fishing boat discovered them. The cutter's captain brought them to Trinidad and Tobago, but there they ran into trouble with the immigration authorities. As on all self-governed islands, you have to either be registered on a boat or have a plane ticket home to gain admittance. They each had to buy a ticket to Martinique to get in. Martinique is a fully integrated part of the French state, and, as such, it is part of the European Union. For Europeans, it is the closest landmass with jurisdiction.

When they finally reached South America, they not only had barely escaped with their lives but also had spent way more money than a simple round-trip ticket from Gran Canaria to South America would have cost.

I couldn't help but shake my head in disbelief. "How long have you been looking for a boat?" I asked.

"A couple of weeks."

"And?"

"Nothing," he replied.

"You sure know how to encourage a guy," I laughed. It may not have fit the circumstances, but I was somehow feeling upbeat.

"Checkmate!" my opponent smiled at me. We were now tied with one win each.

The next match would seal my fate. Our fingers flitted over the board, returning the pieces to their starting places.

"How long are you going to stay here?" I asked my chess partner, who was from the Flemish part of Belgium. Although he was only in his midthirties, his short-cropped brown hair had already started to recede. To compensate, he had a well-trimmed anchor beard. He didn't seem to put much effort into his appearance, but he was, nevertheless, very attractive. He was on a trip around the world with a South African captain. The yachts floated gently on the Shelter Bay water next to us as the neighboring table ordered lunch. Later that evening it would be impossible to find a seat on the terrace at the marina restaurant.

"Not much longer." We turned the board around, and the Belgian opened the match with his knight. "I'm not traveling just for fun anymore. I'm mixing business with pleasure. I'm filming myself for a TV documentary: *In 80 Dates Around the World*—that's what it will be called. My mother is of the opinion that I should be looking for a life partner. That's how I got the idea for a trip around the world looking for suitable candidates and documenting it for posterity."

I laughed so hard that I almost knocked over a chess piece by gasping. *Could his mother have imagined such a thing?* "Do you really think you will find your future wife this way?"

With a big grin he said, "No, but it's a good reason to travel, and it covers the expenses. In the end, no one knows what the future brings." He looked at me. "And you, how are you paying for your travels?"

I had to stop and think—not about his question but because, if I wasn't careful, he would take my rook. "With any job or opportunity I can get my hands on. In Venezuela I remodeled a bathroom for the military police, in Guiana I dug for gold, in Rio de Janeiro I sold fruit salad on the beach, in Peru I pumped fuel at a filling station, and here I help take boats through the Panama Canal. Getting by is not really about how much you earn. It's about how much you spend. You can be a millionaire, but if your expenses are more than your income, you'll still go broke."

"True." He nodded in agreement and took my rook. "But surely your room and board must cost more than you make with all those odd jobs."

How stupid of me! I regretted the loss of my rook. "As far as housing, I usually sleep in my tent or my hammock, and sometimes in someone's house if I am invited. I usually hitchhike for transportation, so that doesn't cost anything, plus I get to make friends with new and interesting people. Then it is a win-win. I never eat in restaurants, and I don't go to bars."

Now he had to laugh as he kicked my queen off the board. "I get your secret. Lay off the beer, and you have plenty of money."

"That's about right." I winked at him. I surveyed the board and laid my king down. *Defeated. I talk too much!*

Satisfied, the Belgian leaned back and said, "Come by our boat for a bite to eat later this evening. What do you say?"

***

The captain of the sailing yacht was a white businessman from South Africa. He had met the Belgian almost twelve years ago in Venezuela. Way back then, the businessman had asked the Belgian if he would sail around the world with him if he were to buy a boat.

"Um, yeah! Of course!" was his spontaneous answer. They kept in loose contact, and ten years later the Belgian's phone rang. "Hi, I bought a boat. Do you still want to sail around the world with me?"

"Um, yeah! Of course!" was his spur-of-the-moment answer yet again. They had started their voyage around the world one year ago in the Mediterranean and would end the journey in Africa, after a full two years of sailing.

The crew was complete with a young Afrikaner who had left Cape Town a few days earlier to join them. Whereas Africans are dark-skinned, Afrikaners (or Boers) are white—the descendants of farmers and seamen from Holland who had settled in the Cape of Good Hope more than three hundred years ago.

Crossing with this yacht would be a blast! Too bad they already have enough men on board, I thought. All three of them were great guys. Although there was no boat in sight for me, the time had not been wasted. I drank ginger beer for the first time that night. *What will they come up with next?* Most importantly, I made some new friends.

The Belgian and I played chess again the next day; then the captain and I went swimming and had deep conversations about South Africa. At sunset we had a *braai*—the Afrikaner's term for a barbeque. We laid big logs around a campfire to serve as benches and roasted chicken and potatoes over the crackling embers. Now and then the wind blew into the flames, spraying sparks into the night sky. Out on the sea, the container ships glittered like city lights.

"Christopher," the captain and the Belgian had stepped aside to talk and were now waving me over.

I got up. *What could they want?*

"We understand if you have other plans, but would you like to sail across the Pacific with us?"

Other plans? Not on your life! "Of course!" I said, excited and smiling from ear to ear. I gave a little hoot for joy. The next day would mark seven days since the Australian canceled on me. Despite all my fears, something better *did* come along!

Third Leg

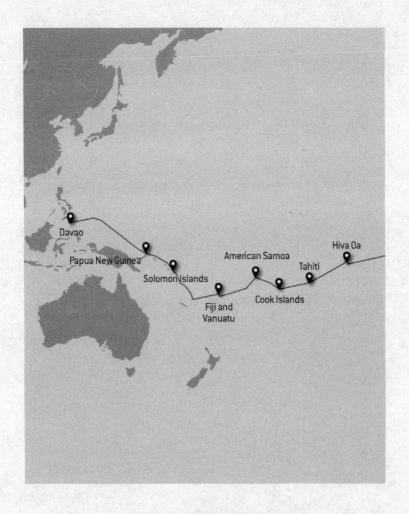

Davao

Papua New Guinea

Solomon Islands

Fiji and
Vanuatu

American Samoa

Cook Islands

Tahiti

Hiva Oa

THE PACIFIC

8

ENDLESS DISTANCES

April 2015

OUR FEET TOUCHED SOLID GROUND for the last time on the Monday after Easter. That day at noon we raised the sails and steered into the great blue—out into the Pacific, which is the biggest, deepest ocean on the planet. When asked, most people have the impression that the Pacific covers about a quarter of the earth's circumference. In reality, it stretches closer to halfway around the globe!

My heart pounded in my chest. If there were islands anywhere in the world where people lived in isolation from modern society, then it would be in the Pacific!

We started our three-hour shifts right away. First, the captain and I were responsible for the sails and the rudder. Then the Belgian and the Afrikaner relieved us for three hours. This meant you got only three hours of sleep at a time at most, but there was always someone with you to help navigate the boat and adjust for new weather conditions. And if someone fell overboard, the other person could sound the alarm.

Of course the chances of survival in such cases are not so great. According to the US Coast Guard, two out of every three cases of "man overboard" end in an unplanned burial at sea. One captain I sailed under put it like this: "On my boat there is only one rule: no one falls overboard!" Very few people die during storms while sailing because then they are hyperaware of safety. No, most people drown in calm weather on sunny days. Just when you don't expect it. It doesn't matter what you do way out there on the ocean—help will never reach you in time. Even rescue helicopters have limited gas tanks and can fly only so far before they have to turn back. If you are not near the coast, you are completely on your own.

A sudden tropical illness or appendicitis out on the ocean can easily end in breathing your last. That's why so many sailors take the precautionary measure of having their appendix removed. I kept mine. It may prove to be deadly someday, but not having one is deadly too. After all, life ends in death. Every time.

During the voyage across the Pacific, we spent our free time in the shade of the sails playing chess, reading, or having deep discussions. Once, during such a discussion, the Belgian and I got into a fight. It was a simple difference of opinion, nothing serious. Nevertheless, it led to one of the most important lessons I learned on my journey. When the Belgian went to his cabin to get some shut-eye, our captain set me straight: "If something that silly comes up again, let it be. Think about it! It is totally irrelevant how good your arguments are. If you don't win a person's heart first, you'll never convince them of anything. If you want to get somewhere, you can't have conversations that are based only on knowledge and understanding. You have to talk heart-to-heart."

My captain noticed that this plunged me deep in thought, and he added, "Most of our decisions are based on our feelings and not on reason even though lots of people try to convince themselves otherwise. That's why companies don't advertise with long pros-and-cons lists but with happy faces. If it doesn't reach your heart, it is just useless theory."

He looked me in the eye. "We didn't bring you along because we were in desperate need of another man, you know. Three people would have been enough. I wanted to bring you with us because there is something new in you. Something I find interesting."

"What do you mean?"

"In Panama you lived outside and ate rolls and bananas three times a day. Most of your clothes are worn out, bought from second-hand stores. You haven't seen your family for almost two years, and you are still far from reaching your goal."

I smirked. *Sounds like he wants to say: your life is pitiful.*

"In spite of all of that, you are always in a good mood and seem to be at peace with yourself. You give the impression that you have no real worries. You know who you are, where you are from, and where you want to go." He paused. "I don't have that kind of assurance."

"I think you are overestimating me a bit," I answered. "But what is true is that my problems and worries look smaller when I think about the fact that there is something beyond this life. And when I become consciously aware of how good things are actually going for me, then I get the feeling that the problem is already half-solved."

Two days later, barely having reached 85° west, we crossed the latitude point at exactly 0° north and 0° south. The equator. The earth's belt.

It was early morning, the breeze was fresh, and the skies were clear. Our boat cut a smooth line through the waves. *An absolute dream!*

This was the first time the young Afrikaner and I had sailed over that latitude. According to seamen's tradition, we were due for an equator baptism: a bit of torture symbolizing acceptance into the circle of experienced sailors. For a long time, the captain and the Belgian had been cracking jokes about the terrible things that might happen to us. Would we get a new, unflattering haircut? A piercing in an uncomfortable place? Would we be forced to drink toilet water? Yes, musing about these things was obviously a lot of fun!

As soon as our GPS showed that we had crossed the equator, the captain and the Belgian fist bumped each other, smiling. They got ready inside the boat and, a couple of minutes later, climbed back up on deck. The Belgian was wearing goggles and had thrown a long, sturdy rope over his shirtless torso. He was carrying a bucket full of torture devices. The captain followed him, wearing a white sheet like a toga. His dark, piercing eyes were framed by a black scuba mask with the snorkel swinging beside it.

"To the foredeck with the wretches!" he bellowed.

The Belgian pushed us roughly toward the bow. His ability to remain so serious was astounding! He then let the cord slide from his shoulder and bound us tightly to the forestay.

"Who are the intruders?!" The captain continued his bellowing. He sat on an imaginary throne on the dinghy across from us.

The Belgian introduced us. "New contenders, oh most excellent Neptune."

"I do not need anyone else! We have enough!"

"Your excellency's judgment is just, and yet it is written: from a foreign land they come to serve you, oh powerful Neptune. Here we have one from South Africa."

"Africa? The land with the zebras? I always wanted to have a zebra! But where are their stripes?"

"Their stripes? Oh yes, my lord . . . the stripes! Right away, oh all-merciful, Neptune!" The Belgian reached in the bucket and pulled out a spray can. He shook it and then sprayed thick white stripes on our bare skin, starting at the bottom and moving up. We were wearing only shorts because it was so hot.

"What ugly zebras!" Neptune brooded. "Far too puny. They are lacking fire!"

"Aye aye! Fire, oh mighty one!" The Belgian's hand disappeared in the bucket again and pulled out two carrots and a bottle of extra-hot chili sauce. He poured at least ten servings of hot sauce on the carrots and shoved them deep into our mouths.

Can you spit fire from eating spicy foods? If so, we surely would have done so right then and there! Our heads turned bright red and our eyes and noses ran a marathon.

"*Hahaha*! Very sweet, these two!"

"Sweet? Yes sir, oh lord of the fish . . . and zebras!" Then the Belgian unscrewed a bottle of maple syrup and poured it over us.

"Delicious! Is there more?"

"Right away, oh lord of all lords!" He squeezed a tube of tomato paste over each of us.

"What a celebration! Open our best vintage!"

"Of course, oh eternal Neptune!" The Belgian pulled out a water gun filled with red wine and sprayed us in the face.

"And crush the sign of my power over them!"

"With pleasure, oh most powerful of all powerful!" With that he smacked a raw egg on each of our heads.

"There is only one thing missing! The smell of the sea!"

"Very good, most aromatic of all aromas!" The Belgian opened a can of sardines and placed an oily fish on each of our shoulders and on our heads.

"Behold! True zebra-fish! Now they are a part of my kingdom! Permit them to enter!"

They untied us. In other words, we were allowed to go wash up. We smelled awful! It took more than a half hour of hard scrubbing to be even partially presentable again. But the memory of our equator crossing was worth it!

The afternoon was partially cloudy but still hot. We passed the Galapagos Islands and, as expected near the equator outside of hurricane season, there was little wind. The boat rocked slowly back and forth as the waves splashed a never-ending rhythm against the bow.

The islands that inspired Charles Darwin's theory of evolution were nowhere in sight. We kept an eye out for almost a week, and we finally spotted another boat that first appeared as a little gray spot on the horizon.

A Spanish-speaking voice suddenly came from the radio in front of the Belgian: "*Tenemos pescado para regalar!*"

"English, please!" He tried to communicate that he did not understand. But I had already sprung up and, to my crewmate's relief, took the microphone.

"Can you please repeat that?" I said in his language.

It turned out to be a fishing cutter from Ecuador that had caught an unusually large amount and wanted to share with us. He listed off kinds of fish as if it was a pizza delivery service—or a fish delivery service. Out of all the types of fish he listed off in Spanish, tuna was the only one I recognized.

"Sounds great!" I confirmed that we would like some, and they instructed us to meet them at our stern. I quickly hung up the microphone and ran to the others on deck.

Oh my goodness, they're already here! Behind us, just a stone's throw away, the bow of a massive fishing boat rose and sank with loud splashing noises in the water. It was at least twice as wide as our boat and towered four times higher into the sky. The cutter's steel was freshly painted white. Dark smoke swirled behind it when the helmsman increased the speed to close the distance between us.

"Watch out for the gap," the captain warned. "Their steel and our fiberglass would not get along."

To maneuver, we took down the sails and changed over to machine power. The barge came closer.

"If they wanted to, they could just steal our boat and throw us overboard," I mused.

There are, in fact, organized pirates in the northern regions of South America nowadays. However, most reports of captured ships are just poor fishermen seizing an opportunity. We sized up the eight or nine Latinos pushing to the front of the cutter. Most of them were wearing simple undershirts and shorts.

"I considered that too," said the Belgian. "But it's too late now."

"Catch!" one of the fishers bellowed over the noise of the diesel motor. He swung a line to us from fifty feet away. The Afrikaner and I secured it. *At least there are no grappling hooks on it!*

The sailors then attached a black trash bag to the line and yelled, "Pull it in!" Together we pulled the sack over the water toward us. The rope swung wildly to and fro. I imagined the plastic ripping and spilling the contents into the sea.

But it held. As soon as the sack reached our railing, we hauled it into the cockpit and then released the line.

"Let's see if they are unloading their kitchen scraps on us," the captain joked.

But when we cut open the plastic bag with a knife, we found superb specimens of fresh-caught tuna, and they threw in a two-foot-long back end of a gilled and gutted shortfin mako. I was still amazed that the sack could carry all that weight.

So much for pirates! In Europe this gift would have sold for hundreds of euros. Our enthusiasm was just as great.

"You'll be eating sushi until it comes out your ears!" our captain said and made a ferocious face. We all laughed.

The crew on the Ecuadorian cutter tooted their horn twice and waved as we shouted our profuse thanks to them. Then they brought their ship about. I chatted with our benefactors, thanking them again over the radio while the others emptied our cooler of anything we didn't need, making room for the fresh delicacies. *What a generous thing to do!* The fishermen had gone far out of their way and put out a lot of effort just to give us a treat.

I remembered a quote said to be from the author of one of the most famous books in world literature: "You have not lived today until you have done something for someone who can never repay you." John Bunyan had penned those words more than four hundred years ago, along with his book *The Pilgrim's Progress.*

You do not need to be well read or rich to live by this simple truth. The fishermen had proved as much. You just have to do it.

The southeasterly winds finally picked up as we passed the Galapagos Islands, blowing us farther into the open sea day by day. Two weeks later we cut up and ate the last of our fresh fruits and vegetables. From then on we had only dried goods, like rice or noodles, with canned foods.

To save drinking water, we always cooked with almost one-third seawater, so we didn't have to use the saltshaker at all. We used saltwater for washing up too. One morning I put the kettle on to make hot chocolate. I enjoyed the deceptively pleasant-smelling cocoa and slurped it into my mouth. My eyebrows shot up and then back down. With the nasty liquid in my mouth, I made a horrible face as I scrambled to spit it out. *So freaking gross!* I found out later that the kettle had fallen in the salty dishwater, and someone had put it back on the stove and forgotten about it—until I found it!

As funny as such things are in retrospect, you have to be on your guard not to become resentful. Due to very close quarters and sleep deprivation, almost everyone catches themselves thinking at sometime or another, *He did that on purpose!*

In fact, these paranoid delusions come from many forms of cabin fever. It is a natural part of being at sea, and if you expect it to happen to you, it is a lot easier to recognize and keep in check. I usually found it freeing to "err on the side of the accused." If you don't know for sure, then just assume the best. Of course you could be disappointed or even hurt by another person, but I still think it is better to assume that someone is better than they are many times over than to falsely judge even once. It's good not only for the other person but also for you. If you assume the best about others, they will assume the best about you.

Positive expectations can even call out the good in another person. Negative expectations can do the opposite.

9

PIGS AS CURRENCY

AFTER THIRTY-ONE DAYS AT SEA, the mountains of Hiva Oa peeked out of the darkness into dawn. Hiva Oa belongs to French Polynesia and is one of the Marquesas Islands that is inhabited by tribal warriors.

What could we expect so far away from civilization as we know it? Wild people with bows and arrows? Colorfully painted chiefs? Natives with wooden pegs for piercings, loin cloths, and tattoos?

Such things can be found on the Pacific Islands, but not in French Polynesia. Other than tattoos. In spite of my joy upon reaching solid ground, I detected vague disappointment upon entering the bay. Hiva Oa has not been an untouched, ancient civilization for quite some time, despite what my research had led me to imagine.

Long ago the mountains were lined with primitive huts inhabited by cannibals. In fact, only the bite-marked shoes remained of the first missionaries to Hiva Oa. Early sources describe how the Polynesians impaled their enemies on stakes and roasted them or wrapped them in the leaves of banana and breadfruit trees and then baked them in fire pits. They did this either as a sign of victory, or maybe just because the missionaries were tasty.

Nowadays modern SUVs and pickups roll along asphalt streets lining the mountains. You won't find huts made of stakes and leaves. And instead of prepared skulls and warriors' weapons, the modern houses are equipped with electricity, running water, and satellite TV.

Reports from the earliest discoverers told of human sacrifice, fertility rituals, and tribal warfare. Upon our arrival we discovered a bank, a hospital, a police station, and other amenities one would expect to find in a modern society. Instead of plundering the neighboring islands with canoes, the young people hop on an airplane to go study in Tahiti, the largest of the 118 French Polynesian islands. Some even go to Paris.

Yes, Paris. Since the French Polynesian islands are officially part of France, the Belgian and I didn't even have to get our passports stamped. Even though Europe is on the other side of the world.

France's financial support enabled French Polynesia to reach a Western standard of living. The Polynesians earn their income through agriculture, tourism, and pearl trading, which would not be sufficient on its own.

Their culture is in no way backward, in spite of the former prevalence of cannibalism. More than seven hundred years ago, long before Columbus found his way to America out of sheer luck, the Polynesian people managed a trade network around the Pacific, crossing distances of close to 1,500 miles. They went for weeks at sea through currents and changing winds with neither compasses nor sextants—and certainly no GPS—without missing the tiny islands they were aiming for. Had they miscalculated by only

2 degrees, they would have sailed past their goal, out into the open sea, and to their deaths.

That's crazy when you think about it! It is like traveling from Quebec, Canada, to Miami, Florida, with no streets, no maps, no signs, no navigational device, and no one to ask for directions along the way. Not even mountains or forests or any other landmark were available for orientation. I don't know about you, but I can get lost in IKEA, even with all the signs!

The only things the Polynesian sailors had for guidance were currents, waves, stars, the air, and birds in flight. Instead of nautical maps they used songs and stories to guide their way. Several Pacific cultures rely on songs for orientation.

Another famous example of this art form is found in the dreaming track, or songline, used by aborigines in Australia to travel hundreds of miles through the barren steppe. Dreaming tracks are not visible paths, but lines of songs that stretch over and across the wild lands. The fascinating part is that the text only plays a minor role in the songline. The decisive factors are the rhythm and pitch. If you pay attention to the sounds in your surroundings and observe the landscape while walking, you'll recognize and join in the song. The songline helps you to find not just your destination but water, shelter, and everything you need for your journey.

Along with their extraordinary navigational abilities, the Polynesians are known for their tattoos. For the natives of the Marquesas Islands, this artwork often covers a person's entire body. Contrary to popular belief, they are not the inventors of this art form. Even the five-thousand-year-old Ötzi mummy from the Ötzal Alps had tattoos.

The occupants of the Marquesas Islands are, however, masters of this art form. In days gone by they had no written documents, so the fine patterns on their bodies bore witness to their heritage, successes, and family, as well as personal status. The decorations were also said to have the power to release spiritual strengths. The tattoo artist used comb-like utensils made from animal teeth. It looked, and indeed was, excruciating, and the wounds often became disgustingly infected because the instruments were not sterile. It often took an entire year for the wounds to heal—and some people kicked the bucket in the meantime. That's the risk the men had to take on those islands, and to a smaller degree, the women too.

Polynesian priests were responsible for tattooing the people. They prepared for this task by undergoing years of training, precise rituals, and strictly observed taboos. The word *taboo* comes from the Polynesian language family and means both "forbidden" and "holy."

After a week on the Marquesas Islands, we sailed toward the atolls of the Tuamotu Archipelago. Atolls are doughnut-shaped islands with a lagoon in the middle. They are made out of coral reefs and, therefore, rise only a few feet above sea level, and they are mere hundreds of feet wide.

Seeing such tiny and apparently fragile landmasses out in the middle of the vast ocean left a deep impression on me. The dazzling white beaches are picturesquely decorated with coconut trees, and the turquoise-blue water is so clear you can easily see fifty feet down to the ground underneath.

Aside from the surreal beauty of the atolls, I was fascinated by the pearl farms run by the locals. I learned that, nowadays, real pearls are not as valuable as one might imagine. An average pearl doesn't cost a fortune, more like one US dollar. A very valuable pearl may cost ten dollars. That means a real pearl necklace doesn't have to be expensive.

It is the combination of colors, sizes, and the gold and silver work that makes pearl jewelry valuable.

After gaining this knowledge, we felt ready to invest in a few souvenirs. The opportunity presented itself as soon as we landed on Takaroa, where we met a local woman who invited us to take a look at her handmade pearl necklaces. She led us through the palm trees to her home, which was located in the only village on the entire island. Like most Polynesians, she was stocky and had dark-brown, curly hair with small eyes and a round face. She wore a simple T-shirt and shorts. Many Polynesian women seemed somewhat masculine to me, and according to their menfolk, they know how to pack a punch. Rumor has it that disagreements between the sexes are often settled with their fists.

The woman's sandy yard was bordered by a dark-green, chain-link fence and ringed with lush green bushes, some of which were in bloom. The little house was painted light pink. Like all houses there, it was built on blocks a good arm's length above the ground to protect it from flooding.

"Wait here," she said and disappeared into her house. There was a sack full of oysters in front of the entrance. *We're in the right place!*

When she came out, she apologized: "I just realized that I sold all of my jewelry on the last flight to Tahiti! This is the only necklace I have left."

She handed the treasure to the captain for him to inspect. There were three pearls in a row with a golden sheen, next to three pearls with red overtones, and the next three were green. The necklace repeated this pattern thrice for a total of twenty-seven pearls. They were all the same size and perfectly formed.

"How much?" our captain inquired.

"We are actually not allowed to sell pearls to tourists on this island, so don't tell anyone. I usually sell a necklace like this for one hundred twenty US dollars."

As far as I could tell, it was a good price. The pearls alone were probably worth more than that. *And in that setting!*

Our captain bit his lip a little, as if making a difficult decision. "I'd like to bring my girlfriend in South Africa something, and this necklace is beautiful! But I set myself a limit of one hundred dollars."

The Polynesian woman nodded sympathetically. "Well, that's fine. It would do my heart good to give you a fond memory of our island. I'll take a hundred."

Satisfied, our captain pulled out his wallet, paid, and we took our leave.

"Too bad you took the necklace; otherwise, I would have!" said the Afrikaner in envy as we climbed in the dinghy to row back to our boat, anchored in the lagoon. "You can sell that for several hundred dollars, easy!" We all agreed.

The next day we set sail again and reached the Ahe atoll the following night. A pearl dealer met us there too. He came right to the boat. Or should I say "she"? It was a rae-rae. Remember I first came in contact with rae-raes on the San Blas Islands, east of Panama, with the Guna Indians. Rae-raes are typically the strongest boys in their family and are raised as girls to help the mother run the household. Considering how strong most Polynesian women are, it is curious that they would want help from anyone!

Meeting him made me realize how pointless it is: all the pressure we put on ourselves in Europe over our appearance. The concept of beauty is so different in other parts of the world. In America tanned skin is considered beautiful, whereas most Asians prefer a "posh pale." In Africa being fat is the ideal of beauty; in Europe the ideal is skinny. In Europe pants are stylish for men, but in Fiji it's skirts. Beauty is definitely in the eye of the beholder.

"It all looks good," said the captain after the rae-rae had spread out his wares on our little table in the cockpit. His goods were priced at several hundred dollars each. "But we already bought pearls in Takaroa."

"Really?" The rae-rae furrowed his brow. He was taller and broader than all of us but still wore mascara and a long ponytail. His stylish sunglasses were pushed up on his head. He didn't wear women's clothes, but he carried a black patent-leather purse for transporting his jewelry.

"Yes, but you can still do me a favor." The captain disappeared below deck to get his new purchase. "What would you say these are worth?"

"If I may." The rae-rae took the necklace and rubbed two pearls together. Then he held it close to his eyes to get a better look. "How much did you pay for it?"

"One hundred dollars." The captain was visibly proud of the great deal he had gotten.

The rae-rae laughed and gave the necklace back. "It's *made in China*!"

Horror spread across our faces. "Are you sure?" I protested. *Whaaat? But the oysters in front of the pink house. . . . It all seemed so legit!*

The rae-rae pointed to where he had rubbed the pearls together. Something white was peeking through. "That's plastic. You can rub the color off."

Our captain rubbed a couple of pearls together and then picked at the coating with his fingernail.

"That witch!" he hissed through his teeth bitterly. "If it weren't against the wind, I would go straight back there!"

We all learned something from that event. First off, it's best not to invest in something you know nothing about. Plus, the woman had said, "We're actually not allowed to sell pearls to tourists on this island." If you take part in shady dealings, then you should expect to get the wool pulled over your own eyes!

From the Tuamotu Archipelago we sailed to Tahiti, where we removed my name from the crewmates' register. They planned to continue on to Australia, and from there back to their home in Africa.

The captain made a generous offer: "Come to Africa with us. You can work your way north from there!" Many people dream of traveling through Africa. Staying with that boat was appealing because it was sure to offer a quicker route back home. But that wasn't my dream. I wanted to go to Asia, Korea, and Japan. Since almost all the trans-Pacific sailboats had to make a stop in Tahiti, this was the best place to look for my next boat.

"You are right. We all have to stay true to ourselves." My captain not only understood my decision but supported me in it.

Since I was expecting to be boatless for up to a month in Tahiti, I bought a French-German dictionary. It would be a good opportunity to learn French. But Tahiti turned out to be a much better location for boat hunting than I had assumed. Instead of taking a month, it took only two hours to find a boat!

My new captain was a Norwegian businessman in his mid-sixties. He was headed to Asia, where he planned to have the wooden deck of his boat repaired. That was also to be the end of his worldwide voyage.

He was hoping his grandson would join him for the last leg of his journey, but the grandson had to cancel. Since the trip would be more comfortable and manageable with two on board, he was happy to take me along as the next-best thing. It was perfect! We hit it off right away, and the boat was awesome—a Swedish Hallberg-Rassy 49, which is one of the finest boats in its size category.

There was just one problem: the hatch in my cabin could only be opened a crack before it fell shut again. Thank goodness I had my French dictionary! It fit perfectly in the hatch! So it served a purpose after all.

Our goal was the Cook Islands. They are officially a part of New Zealand and are inhabited by the Maori people. After the Cook Islands, stormy weather blew us to American Samoa instead of Niue, as we had planned. It's hard to win an argument with the forces of nature.

After we had repaired the minor damage that the storms had caused, we finally left American Samoa and sailed into the Polynesian Triangle, which stretches from New Zealand to Hawaii to the Easter Islands and is inhabited by stocky giants decorated with tattoos and floral wreaths—the Polynesians who perform *hakkas* (war dances).

The term *Polynesian* comes from the Greek words *poly* ("many") and *nêsos* ("islands"). Hence, the Polynesians are the people from "many islands." They are one of three prevalent ethnic groups and cultures on the Pacific atolls. The Micronesians, who live in the northwest Pacific Ocean, are much smaller in stature than the Polynesians. The third group is the Melanesians, whose name comes from *mela*, meaning "black" or "dark."

Our arrival at Fiji and Vanuatu marked our entrance into the area inhabited by the Melanesians. The Melanesians' pigmentation is among the darkest found anywhere outside of Africa. Another phenomena presents itself as well: one out of every fifteen Melanesian children, whose appearance is otherwise similar to Africans, has white-blond hair! Surprisingly the Melanesians have the highest percentage of blonds outside of people of European descent. But there is no genetic connection. That means this characteristic—as opposed to blue eyes, for example—cannot be traced back to Western ancestry.

Physical appearance was not the only difference in this region; it was much less developed. In Vanuatu I finally felt that I had reached a place with minimal Western influence. I could smell the adventure!

Upon our arrival on the island of Tanna, I immediately noticed that the houses were quite primitive, built out of wood with palm fronds covering them. The few exceptions were brick houses owned by local merchants, to which supply boats made regular trips. The streets were made of sand. There were few vehicles. People just walked from village to village barefoot or in flip-flops. The men wore simple T-shirts and shorts, and the women wore brightly colored dresses or skirts with T-shirts.

I was struck by the impression that most people simply didn't do anything. The people of Vanuatu seemed able to sit next to each other in silence for hours without getting bored. The island certainly provides a pleasant setting. The weather is gorgeous, you never have to freeze, and the fertile earth produces enough food for everyone in just a few weeks.

In the tropics, getting by on only three months of subsistence farming a year is not unusual. During sowing and harvesting seasons, people are pretty busy, but in between they are free most of the time, surrounded by glorious, untouched nature with mountains, jungles, meadows, and beaches. All that beauty with no sign of dangerous or poisonous animals. There are hot springs to provide roomy bathtubs out in the open. And since the temperature of the hot springs sometimes reaches the boiling point, you don't even need to light a fire to cook. To me, it really did seem like paradise!

One of the residents said to me, "If I don't feel like it, I just don't work for a couple of weeks. Sometimes longer."

Taking off whenever you feel like it? No matter how long? Where can I sign up?

I've heard that most doctor's appointments in industrialized Western nations can be traced to one problem: stress. In spite of all the modernization and automation, I get the feeling we have somehow gone wrong. Perhaps we should help ourselves to a bit of the Vanuatu attitude toward life and realize that one harvest is enough for the season.

Tanna Island is full of wonders. Among the sightseeing opportunities is the volcano, Yasur, which has been active for about eight hundred years. It currently erupts every three minutes, but in such small quantities that, with a healthy dose of respect, you can approach the crater even during an eruption. Our plan was to do just that!

We set anchor in Port Resolution Bay. The famous sailor James Cook named it after his ship the HMS *Resolution*, which he had sailed to that location more than two hundred years ago.

With our boat were two others manned by young men and women about my age. They were alternative travelers. More to the point, they were neo-hippies who had founded a sailing commune with their own old yachts. They financed their travels with circus performances, donations, and profits from selling crafts. A pretty unique project considering how expensive boats are. But so far it had worked out just fine.

I had already made friends with some of them in Fiji during a two-month repair job on the yacht. Since there were so many of us adventurous youths from various backgrounds all in one place, it made sense that we would want to explore the volcano together.

Fifteen of us started out one morning from the beach in Port Resolution, carrying our backpacks. Someone had shown us a narrow trodden path that led over the mountain range to the next bay. Most of us walked barefoot like the natives, who had beaten down the earthen path so that it felt like the ground was bouncing a little beneath our feet. Wild bushes, ferns, trees, and vines rose up beside the path, creating a green thicket. Crickets chirped, insects hummed, and the plants exuded the hearty, fresh smell of pure nature.

The curtain of leaves became thinner as we approached the peak, offering a clear view of the sparkling sea. Upon arriving on the back side of the mountain, we met many natives. They worked their high-altitude fields by hand. The steep incline protected their crops from hungry swine and other animals that were kept in the valley below.

We shook hands with the locals and exchanged a friendly smile. Conversation was not possible since Vanuatu has almost 120 different languages and dialects. Inherited from colonial times, English, Bislama—a simplified, broken form of English—and French are the official languages. The degree to which the natives have mastered these languages varies widely depending on the region.

I struck out with the three fastest members of our group, and we got quite a ways ahead. (I was also carrying someone else's supplies, but thanks to hauling my backpack around for so long, I hardly noticed.) Therefore, we were the first to skip over the rocks and roots down to Sulphur Bay.

Like a threatening watchdog, Yasur the volcano was crouching at the far end of the bay. Dark clouds of smoke rose out of its crater and floated over the scorched landscape, then wafted up into the blue sky. The path led us past mighty trees that did not have normal trunks but seemed to be made of intertwining roots that emerged from the ground and seamlessly turned into branches. The trees' diameters must have measured fifteen to twenty feet, maybe even more. In the crowns of these giants, massive bats made their homes. The natives call them "flying foxes," which gives you a feel for how big these creatures can be.

"They are my favorite animal," one of the natives confided to me. By that he didn't mean "my favorite animal to pet" but rather his favorite ingredient in a national dish.

Behind the giant trees stood a native village. Women swept the dirt floors daily with kikau brooms made from palm leaves, which gave the floors a unique, well-kept appearance. The village was decorated with scraggly fruit trees, among which pigs, chickens, and dogs ran around. Otherwise, the village seemed deserted and unexpectedly quiet. It was not until we reached the middle of the settlement that the path opened up into a wide, sparse, sandy square. Several older men were squatting in the dust next to a spacious shelter in the middle of the square.

The village council, I supposed. They hadn't noticed us yet, but a couple of them got up. From that I deduced that the meeting had probably just come to a close.

"Hello." I made myself known from a distance with a friendly wave as we approached the square. The men froze and stared at us. They did not appear displeased, but surprise and curiosity were written all over their suntanned faces. A man with a white, bushy beard, tangled gray hair, and a dirty plaid shirt made a gesture for us to sit down with him.

We sat, legs crisscrossed, at a respectful distance and repeated our greeting. The older man sent someone away, and we waited until he came back with another man wearing a black T-shirt and brown shorts. He was about forty years old and had a close-cut, black beard.

"This is Chief Isaac Wan," the younger man introduced the man with the white beard in English. "I am Fidel, the Speaker."

In Fiji, as well as in other villages of Vanuatu, it is considered impolite to directly address the chief. Therefore they have speakers to facilitate communication with the leader. This is also practical due to the many languages spoken in that region.

We introduced ourselves with our names and country of origin. I explained that we had come with boats to Port Resolution and came further on foot to see the volcano. Fidel translated for the older man.

"Who is your chief?" they asked. A normal question to ask. Not in Europe, of course, but when you are on a Melanesian Island in the Pacific Ocean, it is a normal question. The country folk, almost without exception, belong to tribal structures.

"He is the captain of a ship. A Norwegian," I explained, and they seemed satisfied. The status of a captain fulfilled their expectations.

After we had gotten past the important matters, my four companions asked for permission to continue hiking. They were in a hurry because they wanted to climb up the volcano that afternoon. I stayed behind to wait for the rest of the group.

There I sat, crisscross applesauce, in the open square with about twenty curious natives, answering their questions as Fidel translated. He had been stationed there by the government as a teacher, so his English was perfect. "Is Germany next to North America?"

"No," I laughed. "But we have a lot in common."

I told them about my homeland and how many Germans dream of living in a place like this. To illustrate, I drew in the sand with a stick.

"Are there very many pigs in Germany?" they asked eagerly, as if that were a way to gauge the strength of my homeland.

"Don't you know about the noble German pig, the Edelschwein?" I feigned surprise and could barely suppress my amusement. We call pedigree pigs *Edelschwein*, or "royal pigs."

Luckily they did not understand my joke. In most countries people asked me about German cars: BMW, Audi, Mercedes, Volkswagen—but on the Vanuatu Islands they asked about our pigs. And why not? There, these animals serve as capital and status symbols. If you have enough pigs, you don't have to worry about becoming poor or not having a wife. Not long ago, pigs were still generally accepted as currency. They also need them for rituals. To ascend in the tribal hierarchy, you have to kill a pig. It may sound strange, but it is comparable to our practice of winning votes by sponsoring town banquets when running for mayor. Extremely influential chiefs have achieved their status by killing many hundreds of animals. *A schnitzel restaurant would be an absolute hit here!*

"Why do you fly an American flag?" I pointed curiously at the tattered stars and stripes blowing around on top of a bamboo pole. A Vanuatu flag hung on a second flagpole. Behind the two poles stood the only concrete house in the village. *Looks important.*

"It's to honor the USA. You see, John Frum freed us and led us back into our custom lifestyle."

I wasn't sure if I had heard the liberator's name correctly, so I started with what I had caught: "Custom?"

"That is our traditional lifestyle. The kava and all of our rituals belong to the custom. And we live without money. We give and take what we need."

There were so many questions I was dying to ask. But I wasn't allowed to look in the concrete house until the Norwegian captain had made his way to the village. It was apparently their "holy of holies."

"Everything is documented here," Fidel informed us as he unlocked the door. The Norwegian captain and I went inside. There was a large painting of the volcano on bare concrete to the left. A hallway in front of us led to various rooms.

"*Yasur* means 'god' in our language," Fidel explained. "The volcano is where John Frum and his men live."

"So this John Frum is your god?"

Fidel chuckled. "John is a spirit and an American. He is very powerful. He said if we pray to him, he will return out of the volcano someday and bring us gifts."

"What kind of gifts?"

Fidel's eyes glazed over. "Everything! TVs, refrigerators, pickups, houses, factories, boats, clocks, medicine, Coca-Cola . . ."

Then it dawned on me: *These people are followers of a cargo-cult!*

During World War II, hundreds of thousands of US soldiers were dispatched to the Pacific to establish support posts for the war against Japan. The completely natural, untouched island inhabitants could not explain where the white men had gotten all of their goods in such a short amount of time. They had never seen anything like it. Things like canned goods, soft drinks, radios, candy, Jeeps, and so on. Some of the stuff had been thrown out of cargo planes, and therefore had literally fallen from the heavens. The conclusion was obvious: the Americans were magicians who could make all these things appear out of thin air! How else could it have happened?

This misinterpretation reached its pinnacle after World War II, when the allies withdrew and many of these wonderful objects were pushed off of cliffs with bulldozers or, on rare occasions, bequeathed to natives.

They were left wondering, "Why did the Americans leave us?"

The elders had a ready answer: "They were dissatisfied with us!" As a result, cargo-cults developed in Melanesia in an attempt to prove themselves worthy for the Americans to return and bring gifts once again. The members of the cults built docks, cleared land in the jungle, and even built bamboo towers to provide safe landing for airplanes. But their expectations turned into disappointment, and most cargo-cults disappeared soon after. The followers of John Frum belonged to one of the last valiant representations of this persuasion. It seems plausible that the cargo-cult's name came from a soldier who introduced himself as "John from America."

"Has anyone ever seen this John Frum?"

"Yes, Chief Isaac," Fidel nodded and pointed to a white chest with a painting of the volcano, marked with the word *door*. "He climbed through a secret entrance into the volcano and spent a night with John Frum there. Isaac is a great magician. None of us can go in the volcano without dying."

The Speaker brought us into the next room, where the villagers stored all of their relics from World War II: the jacket of a Thompson Caliber 45 machine gun, an old walkie-talkie, and tan uniforms.

"We wear the uniforms every year when we raise the flag on John Frum Day, February 15." *One day after Valentine's Day.* "John Frum will return on that day to lead us into a new era."

"How many people in Tanna are waiting for John Frum to return?"

"Many. But we are the center. Next to the volcano. In contact with John Frum. In the south a misguided village called Yaohnenen thinks that Prince Philip is John Frum's brother."

"You mean the British queen's husband?"

"Yes. The prophets there say that he is god, and that he will come bearing gifts. A few years ago five of their men traveled to England to be heard at Buckingham Palace."[1]

This island with only thirty thousand inhabitants is full of surprises! Unbelievable!

⁂

The rest of our group trickled in over the next few hours. The villagers invited us into the shelter in the middle of the square. This was their church, where they sang songs about John Frum's return every Friday, all night long.[2]

Poor things. Hopefully he'll come back soon!

---

1   There is a documentary about this notable encounter in the TV series *Meet the Natives*, National Geographic, https://www.nationalgeographic.com.au /tv/meet-the-natives/. For more information, see https://en.wikipedia.org/wiki /Prince_Philip_Movement.

2   "John Frum Cargo Cult Song," 0:54, YouTube video, published on December 31, 2014, https://www.youtube.com/watch?v=2SQBuweNByk.

There were carpets made of woven palm twigs lying between the narrow benches around the perimeter of the hut. When we were all present, three of the hippie-sailors used the opportunity to delight us with some songs. There was a music major from Quebec, who played her 160-year-old violin accompanied by a French guitarist and a drummer from Canada. It is difficult to describe the enthusiasm and fascination written on the faces of the natives. Within a couple of minutes they had lured the whole village into the square that earlier had seemed so deserted. The "coconut Wi-Fi," as we call their inexplicably quick communication, had carried the curiosity lightning-fast to all the nooks and crannies of the area. Men, women, children, and even dogs and pigs pressed into the shelter as if it were Black Friday at a department store.

This is probably the first time they have ever seen a violin. As Fidel and I observed the impromptu concert from the outside, I inquired about the volcano.

"You should probably approach Yasur from the other side. That's where the official entrance is and where the ranger collects the entrance fee."

"And the fee is . . . ?"

"Thirty-five hundred vatu per person."

That was about thirty-five dollars. I was pretty sure the hippies wouldn't dream of paying that much, even considering the tight time schedule we were on. I described our situation to Fidel, and he spoke with the chief.

After a while he informed me of their decision with a nod: "Tell your people that they are the guests of Chief Isaac. You can stay with us tonight. Later, when it is dark, we'll show you a hidden path to get to the volcano. We have never gotten any of the money from the ranger, and we also don't agree with turning the holy place of John Frum into a business."

Thank John Frum!

When the musicians had finished, Fidel showed us a hut that they had quickly cleared out for us. *They sure are good hosts!* After that, we played a little soccer with the young people and bathed in the hot springs.

10

THE VOLCANO

"CALL YOUR MEN TOGETHER," Fidel ordered when we returned at dinnertime.

It had become clear to me that the villagers thought I was a Speaker for my captain. Probably because I was the first to arrive. So they turned all the important matters over to me.

"We are going to Nakamal. A holy place. To drink kava. Then we will eat."

There are a lot of holy places here. "Just the men?" I asked.

Fidel made it crystal clear: "Women are forbidden at Nakamal. Someone will bring food to them in their hut. You all come with me."

So we split up. Five of us followed the Speaker, who led us a mere two hundred yards out of the village to an embankment just past a little clearing. About a dozen natives joined us.

"This is Nakamal. That means 'Place of Peace,'" Fidel explained and indicated that we should sit on the tree stumps, which were placed in a square around a little hill.

The hill was only about six feet tall. Fidel hacked the peel off a thick root that another man had brought. The hill must have been made from the peels of these roots over many years.

"The kava in Vanuatu is the strongest there is," Fidel proclaimed, smiling proudly over the root.

I knew the plant from Fiji, where it is used for a greeting ceremony: *sevusevu*. If you go to a new village, you must bring dried kava root to the chief as a sign of respect. He then has it ground and made into a drink. Then you get intoxicated together. *That's how you make friends!*

Twilight descended upon us as the crickets and insects chirped, announcing the arrival of night. Someone started a fire next to us; the flames licked along the thin twigs and chased away the shadows that had stretched out from the tree branches like long fingers.

When Fidel had peeled the root, two boys, about ten years of age, were brought to him. They were dressed in costumes made of long grasses, and they each laid a two-foot-long banana leaf in front of them. Then they each shoved a cube of kava in their mouths and started chewing.

"These two are in training. Only circumcised boys who have not yet laid with a woman are allowed to prepare the kava," Fidel explained.

The boys spit greenish-brown slobber in the banana leaf, each popped another cube in their mouths, and kept going until they had chewed up all the kava. To put it nicely, two piles of incredibly unappetizing-looking pulp had been collected in the banana leaves.

Why do I have the feeling I know where this is going? I thought and grimaced unintentionally. One of the natives brought a wooden bowl with some water in it. He then smacked the mass from the first banana leaf into a big bundle of palm fibers that functioned as a natural cheesecloth. He swished the clump around in the bowl. The more he rolled it around, the murkier and greener the water became until it had the color and consistency of lentil soup. (I could make other comparisons, but out of tact and respect for the reader, I'll refrain.)

The man poured more liquid in the bowl and repeated the procedure with the second glob.

"The chief and you first," said Fidel, and he filled two coconut shells to the brim with the mixture and handed them to us.

"Thank you, but I just couldn't . . ." I tried to show honor and respect as I eyed the swampy broth in my hands. I didn't sound all that convincing. The Norwegian seemed unsure as well.

Fidel noticed our hesitation, but luckily he misunderstood and thought that we were pondering the proper way to complete the next step. "You go away from the group, look at the bushes, then drink all the kava at the same time. Spit vigorously on the ground, say a prayer to your god, and come back."

Well then. I can't wait.

We got up and went to the edge of the clearing. With our backs to the others, we glanced at each other reluctantly.

"It won't kill us," I whispered.

"No, probably not," answered the Norwegian, but he didn't sound so sure. We hesitated, but that didn't help matters.

"On three?"

"One, two . . ."

We lifted the containers and gulped it down all at once, so fast that it dribbled over our chins. *It tastes just as bad as it looks. Disgusting!*

When I lowered the bowl, my mouth became numb. According to the directions, we spit noisily on the ground and stared in silence out into the darkness. *Thank you for this experience*, I prayed, as instructed, to my God. I had grown much closer to Him during my travels. *Please protect us from stomach problems!*

That drink was a harsh, crude version of the other kavas I had tried. Commercial kava is milder. It seemed to me that kava is more common in the West Pacific than alcohol. In heavily populated areas you can find kava bars. It is a beloved intoxicant that does not inhibit your cognitive abilities. It just relaxes you and makes you happy and sleepy. And you don't feel a hangover the next day. A little like marijuana. It is traditionally used in Melanesia, Micronesia, and Polynesia for religious rituals, medicine, and, of course, recreation.

We went back to the others. The next two took a turn and so on until everyone had drunk.

"Another?" Fidel offered.

"Oh, thank you, but we want to leave enough for all of you," I pretended to be generous.

One bowl was enough. Gratefully, the natives were happy with this answer. After they had finished it off, they brought us taro roots, sweet potatoes, and manioc. Just little bites, nothing filling, so as not to wash away the feeling of intoxication.

"Now listen to what the kava says," Fidel suggested.

Then no one talked. We sat silently on the stumps, listening into the night. Even the animals got quiet, as if the command to be silent pertained to them too. The fire crackled and threw its warm glow on our skin. I thought I could hear the sea in the distance. Moonbeams peeked through the leaf ceiling, creating a glittering mosaic. The volcano jutted out over the treetops, glowing mysteriously up toward the stars. The earth rumbled, and fiery balls shot into the night sky before Yasur swallowed again, letting out a deep grumbling noise.

"Do you feel anything?" murmured one of the sailors.

We shook our heads. But I didn't need a kava high. I already felt like I was in a dream, completely overwhelmed by the surroundings. I was honestly glad that I hadn't gotten toasted. We had a long night ahead of us.

After about an hour the silence ended, and we went back to the women. Holding our flashlights in our mouths, we took anything unimportant out of our backpacks and met in front of the hut.

"Ready?" a villager asked before leading us to a path. "Just follow this trail to the volcano and climb up."

"Aren't you coming with us?" I was surprised. Fidel said the man would lead us.

"No, I'm tired. You'll find it, easy. Good night." He said his farewells and left us alone.

I was a little disappointed at first, but he was right: orienting here was not hard. There weren't many directions you could go, and every few minutes the volcano announced its presence with long, low grumblings.

As soon as we reached the scorched earth at the foot of the volcano, we turned off our flashlights. We didn't want to risk being noticed since we weren't allowed to be there. The whole idea was crazy! But, luckily, you are usually not alone when you make stupid decisions.

We trudged through the gray sand in the moonlight, nearing the silhouette of the grim giant. The mountain kept spitting threads of glowing lava over its rim. The earth shook as if trying to warn us not to come any nearer to the volcanic pipe. Swaths of dark smoke wafted over the orange glow. We had to be very careful with each step to not fall into one of the fissures or gullies lurking all around. They coursed through the entire area like a network of arteries.

"Someone is there!" a Spanish guy in our group whispered. There were two yellow globes of light shining at the volcano's summit. We couldn't make out anything else in the darkness, but the globes were moving quickly in our direction.

"Is it the rangers?" a girl from New Zealand wondered.

"They couldn't have seen us. It's too dark." I tried to calm them down, but I doubted my own words. I frantically looked for a place where we could hide. "Here!" I pushed the others into one of the ditches eroded by the weather. We followed the chasm deeper into the hillside. No one spoke. We were all afraid of getting caught. The walls rose up to the left and right. *Like a labyrinth*, I realized.

Suddenly strange voices mixed in with the sound of the night wind. *It's the watchmen!*

"Hide! They're coming this way," whispered the Spaniard.

How did they know we were here?

The earth shook. The mountain exploded once again into the night sky. It felt a little like war. We turned off into one of the side arms of the gulley and pressed into the shadows of a small overhang. One of the strangers shone a flashlight on the path that we had just left. We held our breath. No one dared to move. A silhouette passed the entrance to our hiding place.

And stopped.

Come on! Keep moving! Even my thoughts seemed loud to me. The beam of light swung in our direction but then back the other way. Sweat ran down my forehead. The outlines of two more figures came into view. The strangers exchanged a few unintelligible words and then started moving again.

They didn't see us. Their dull footsteps faded into the distance. We exhaled. "Onward!"

We quietly left our hiding place and went uphill. It was hard work, which we hadn't expected. We sank ankle-deep in the mixture of sand and ashes covering the hillside. With every three steps up we slid two steps backward. Finally we crawled on all fours just to gain some ground.

Every couple of seconds the volcano shook and scattered glowing lava rock at us, forming little avalanches that rolled over the surface.

"This is freakin' crazy! Climbing on an active volcano!" laughed the music major from Quebec.

"Indeed," the Norwegian captain wheezed in agreement and rolled onto his back. "I can't go on. I'm three times your age." We climbed on for about half an hour.

"Come on! We're almost there!" We tried to keep him going even though the darkness prevented us from seeing how far we still had to go.

With a little help the Norwegian rallied, and we made good progress for a while. But he sat down more and more frequently to catch his breath. Finally we reached a ledge that was partially protected from falling stones.

"Enough! At my age a person has to know their limits, and I'm way past them." He groaned and fell down on the rock. "I'll wait for you here. My legs won't go any further."

I protested. "But you can't possibly miss this!"

He lit a cigarette. "You just watch me, young man." He took a long drag and defiantly crossed his arms on his chest as he exhaled.

It was actually amazing he had made it that far. "But it could be hours before we come back." I expressed my concern.

"Nope. You go on. I'll wait." He was determined.

Well, there's nothing I can do. So we left the captain on the ledge and scrambled up, trailing behind the music student, who couldn't wait to get up there. In less than ten minutes the incline leveled off and we reached a plateau. Jagged basalt boulders covered the ground like giant chocolate sprinkles on a birthday cake: the residue of the volcano's rocket projectiles. *Not like I've ever been there, but this looks like Mars!*

A mere hundred yards in front of us, poisonous sulfur swaths wafted out of a giant hole, lit up by demonic-looking fire from deep within the earth. Through enormous cracks, the mountain threw new fireballs into the starry firmament again and again. I had never seen anything so breathtaking! *What would it be like at the crater's edge?*

But that had to wait. I didn't want to enjoy this moment while someone else was missing it. "See you in a few! I'm going to get the captain!" I said and hopped down the incline. *If he only knew how close he is! He would kick himself.*

I hurried as fast as I could in case he had decided to head back alone. I had to be careful not to cut my legs on the porous, jagged rocks in my haste. Then there was another problem. I couldn't find the trail. Everything looked the same up here. Ashen, barren, and rugged.

"Captain!" I called over and over as I wandered downhill. The thought shot through my head: *If there are rangers on this side, I'm making a big mistake!* But I did it again, anyway: "Captain!"

No response—from the captain or from a ranger. The wind and bizarre rock formations swallowed my cries. I worked my way sideways. *Wait a second. Was that a glimmer of light?* I strained to make something out in the darkness. *What do you know?* A flicker of light flared up. *A cigarette! That's him!*

"Hey," I said, coming nearer. The captain looked up. "It's just a few yards. If you don't come, you'll regret it!"

"That's what you said before," he countered.

"But now it's true! The crater is just a couple of minutes away!" I raved about what awaited him, and he took the bait.

"Okay. But if it's not as close as you say, you're paying for my helicopter ride back." He struggled up, and we made our way to the summit together.

Right when we reached the plateau, an enormous blast seized

us. The earth shook under our feet, and mighty thunder sounded
out. Molten lava burst out of the volcano's center and flew over our
heads. An indescribably powerful boom sounded, and the volcano
catapulted a second surge into the air. It was as if hundreds of burning lamps were raining down around us.

My heart raced. We tried to predict if we would have to jump
to the side in a split second to avoid imminent death. Amazingly
the aggressive onslaught avoided the spot where we were standing.
Pure adrenaline!

Laughing, I punched my captain's back. "The mountain is
happy to see you!" I gestured to the boiling pit in front of us.

We stopped to listen. A violin mingled with the mountain's
grumblings. The sound led us to the others. There, a mere hand's
width away from the edge of the bubbling crater, the girl from
Quebec sat, lost in the music of her violin. The mournful melody
had a magical effect, pulling us into the overwhelming power of
creation. And she—or so it seemed—was preparing for its pompous
demise. *Surreal!* It was a moment I will never forget.

"Where are the Spaniard and the girl from New Zealand?" I
asked the group, worried.

They calmed my concerns: "Up there. They are taking pictures." They pointed up at a ledge a little ways off. I approached the
raging, gaping mouth of the volcano and looked in. The magma
bubbled up like the wrath of a subterranean beast. The sea of fire
frothed and raged until it sunk its greedy fangs anew into the
crater's edge and exploded in fury. Bizarre shadows flickered like
grimacing faces on the crater's walls.

Did people used to sacrifice humans here? The shadows looked
like caricatures of tortured souls trapped in the throes of death. The
flames boiled beneath them like the gaping mouth of hell, throwing
up burning embers into their eye sockets and mouths, giving them
the illusion of life. Every hair on my body stood straight up.

Who are you, mortal man? The overwhelming drama in front of me took over. *What are you compared to this volcano? What is this volcano compared to our sun? What is our sun compared to the three hundred billion other suns in our galaxy? And our galaxy compared to the thousands of millions of others in our universe? In half a millennium everyone will have forgotten us. No one will know your name. In seven billion years the dust of our planet will be spread throughout the universe. You mean nothing.*

Unless you mean something to someone.

A distant whistle awoke me from my musings. The lava boiled up, and with a screeching crash threw a burst of flames out of the crater. The destructive force crashed out onto the rim. And onto the ledge where the two from Spain and New Zealand were taking pictures.

We had put our lives in danger; that much was clear. But none of us had seriously considered the possibility of someone dying. My heart pounded in my chest.

"Hey! Are you okay?" I screamed into the wind and hoped for signs of life. But there was no answer.

A few seconds later, which felt like an eternity, peals of laughter rang out. "Thank God!" I sighed. *They're okay.*

When we found each other, I was surprised to see that the Spaniard had his arms around the New Zealander's shoulders. He was limping but still smiling. His pants were ripped, and his knee was bleeding.

"He was so scared he just fell down," the woman told us, laughing.

"A lava ball *this* big almost hit me." The Spaniard threw out his arms dramatically. "It was wild!"

"You guys are crazy." The captain shook his head. "You could have died."

What is life worth when it is over? The weighty questions took hold of me once again. I watched the fumes dancing over the crater, how they turned into thin strands and then disappeared. Just like the torrid sparks that lit up only to be extinguished seconds later. *Worth*, I thought, *is what someone gives you. And what you can give to others. Life is what you make of it before it leaves you. How can one have value that doesn't disappear? Life that endures?*

As unbelievable as it may sound, we got used to the threatening discharges after a few hours. And we got cold. The summit was too high and the wind too persistent for even the flickering oven underneath to warm us. Long after midnight we made our way back to the village and slept in the modest hut on palm mats that the followers of John Frum had provided.

Before setting sail the next day, the captain and I gave 3,500 vatu to the rangers as back payment to show respect for the official rules. We sailed on, hopping from island to island. The inhabitants invited us to village festivals and gave us floral wreaths to honor us. Many gave us fruit and invited us into their homes. In return we repaired their electrical appliances and solar panels.

"White skin knows everything," was the frequent compliment received in such situations.

On the island of Malakula, a native took me with him to a neighboring village to pay his last respects to his grandmother, who had passed away that same day. The path led by a bay, where colorful reefs sparkled beneath the crystal-clear water. The luscious leaves on the bushes surrounding the beaches looked healthy and well cared for. Brilliantly colored blossoms decorated the green so artfully that it looked like a skillful gardener had thoughtfully planned and planted it all. Sweet potatoes, squash, manioc, bananas, cabbage, corn, kava, limes, tomatoes, melons, papayas, cocoa plants, and coconut trees interwove unobtrusively among the lush vegetation. The cozy houses were built out of natural materials.

"How old was your grandmother?" I asked the man as we sauntered in the shade of the palm trees. He wasn't in a hurry. *Why should he be? We have nothing else planned.* I took a deep breath of fresh air and enjoyed the idyllic surroundings.

"I don't exactly know," he answered.

"What was her name?"

He considered the question. "I don't exactly know that either." *Excuse me?!*

Along the way we met many people who were also on their way to pay their last respects to their grandmother. *The good lady couldn't have had this many grandchildren! Maybe they just call her that because she was old.*

As we neared our destination, a heartrending howling and mournful cries cut through the thicket. At the head of the path leading directly to the deceased's home, a native pastor greeted us and shook everyone's hand as they passed by. Suddenly, the men around me lowered their heads and broke out in deep sobs and groans. I lowered my gaze as well. *This woman must have been very loved.*

We reached a sandy courtyard with a few huts in it. A throng of about one hundred people filled the space. They had come from all over the island and kept on coming. Their faces were etched with pain, and they wailed and cried so much that it felt like the end of the world. Suddenly I stopped. *Something is missing! Where are their tears?* I sized up the mourners a little closer. Then I saw through the drama: their sorrow was just an act!

Well, if that's how it works . . . I laid my arm over my eyes and broke out in shrill mourning cries along with them. For about three minutes we exchanged the torment of our souls. A middle-aged woman in a flower-print dress, probably the daughter of the deceased, fell on each person's neck, one by one. She seemed to be the only one crying real tears.

After a while my escort signaled for me to come with him. We sat down under a mango tree out of eyeshot of the crying chorus. Everyone was in a good mood again. On the one hand, this way of expressing respect for the dead and solidarity with the relatives was disconcerting to me. But on the other hand, it created an atmosphere in which no one had to be ashamed of their emotions. It was even desirable to share grief with each other. *These people recover more quickly from a shock than we do*, I speculated. It also impressed me that it was in no way considered sissy behavior for men to cry at such an occasion. It reminded me of Jack Handey, who said, "It takes a big man to cry, but it takes a bigger man to laugh at him."[1] *Otherwise the big man will punch his lights out!*

August 2015

On the neighboring island of Pentecost, we encountered a fascinating custom. Every year they hold a festival that celebrates the forerunners of bungee jumpers. The participants build towers out of limbs and bark straps that are fifty to one hundred feet tall. Then, secured by just two vines tied to their ankles—which are exactly long enough for the jumper to barely touch the ground—they jump off the towers. A tradition that has paved the way for many a broken skull.

I backpacked for two days on Espiritu Santo Island, hoping to meet the followers of the Jimmy Stevens cult. In the eighties this man had declared the island to be the independent "State of Vemerana" and made himself the first prime minister. When Vanuatu was granted independence, the real prime minister struck down the revolt and Stevens went to prison. After being released in

---

1   From *Deep Thoughts* (London: Warner Books, 1996).

1991, he took a couple dozen wives and sired about four dozen children before dying of stomach cancer. The Nagriamel Movement that he founded is somewhat cultish in nature, and according to reports, the followers wear only loincloths to this day. *Where else can you see something like that?*

My captain accompanied me to a small city, where we planned to get a replacement part for the boat shower. After fixing the shower, I hiked alone farther inland. The locals had indicated which direction I should go and explained that I would reach the village where the people wore loincloths in about five or six hours. The sun was high in the sky, and the paved streets soon turned into red dust under my feet. The buildings gave way to thick jungles and barren pastures. The trunks of the enormous palm trees looked like antique columns. I imagined them once serving as supports for mighty arches. Now they were the dwelling places for birds.

A motor rattled up behind me. I glanced over my shoulder. *A white pickup.* I moved off to the shoulder. *Should I try to hitchhike here?* That was certainly a foreign concept on this island. The truck passed by as I thought about what to do, and my outlandish appearance made the decision for me: it stopped.

The driver leaned out the window. "Where are you going?"

"To the village of Jimmy Stevens," I said, and he gestured for me to climb on back. Some farmers who had just hocked their produce at the coast moved closer together, and I squeezed in with my backpack. Then the pickup traveled on, happily oblivious to the countless potholes and their effects on the human cargo in back. Thick dust blew on the truck bed and we pulled our T-shirts over our noses.

"Have you heard of Formula 1?" I asked them over the racket.

I made out a smirk on one of the faces. My question was met with counterquestions. After I had shared a little about myself, a man with a long face; a black, curly beard; and thick lips introduced

himself. "I am a neighbor of Jimmy Stevens. You will spend the
night at my place tonight." It sounded more like a statement than
an invitation, but I was glad. "How long would you like to stay?
Two or three nights?"

"Only one night unfortunately. We set sail the day after tomorrow," I explained apologetically. He nodded in satisfaction.

The truck bed emptied out bit by bit as farmers jumped off at
their destinations. We did not climb off until the very end, at the
outskirts of a village.

"Jimmy Stevens had twenty-three wives," my host told me as
we walked through a thick forest along a muddy path. At the path's
entrance was a broken-down hut with a half-naked man in the
doorway grimly whetting his machete. I smiled at him. He looked
up from his work and stared even more grimly at me. *I'd better not
take any pictures here*, I decided and walked a little faster.

"He was a great chief," the man with the thick lips continued,
obviously impressed with his description of Jimmy Stevens. "He
killed more than one thousand pigs!"

"My goodness!" *That's about fifty pigs per wife*, I estimated. *I
wonder if I should breed pigs here. Just for fun, of course.*

At the end of the trail, we came to his property where his
family lived. The only house for miles with a corrugated-iron roof
belonged to him. The funding for this was evident: kava root was
drying in the sun in front of his house. There were six more buildings nearby, all made of wood and palm twigs. Roosters strutted
around the courtyard, and someone had hung colorful laundry on
a line between two houses.

"My relatives live in these houses." The man pointed to the
simple frames.

"And that shelter there?" I asked. The structure looked like the
gathering place of John Frum's followers. Inside, someone had hung
up twirled tobacco to dry.

"That's the Jimmy Stevens ceremonial hall. Every settlement here is required to have one," the man answered.

He then introduced me to his family and showed me around. I was disappointed that most of the people were normally dressed. Those who were running around half-naked did so out of religious conviction, not because they were primitive. *Too bad! For me. Good for them, of course.* The rough paths, simple huts, and open fires did have a primitive feel, but there was also a health clinic with pictorial directions using bananas to show the proper use of condoms.

My host took me to a kava bar that evening. It consisted of a roof supported by posts, a big pot full of the mixed beverage, and a couple of little stools to sit on. *Not at all like the ambiance we enjoyed in Tanna.*

"Fathers come here to drink away their children's school money!" the man said, pulling his lips into a grin. When he saw my worried expression, he assured me that he did not do that—of course not.

We emptied three bowls of the slushy intoxicant and sat down in a dark corner. Then again, every corner was dark. There were no lights other than the red, solar-powered LED in the entrance. A few villagers joined me to talk about German soccer. But the more they drank, the sleepier they became, and no one wanted to talk anymore. The mood was kind of oppressive. I was happy when my host had drunk enough and wanted to go to sleep.

"Do you know what jackfruit is?" the man with the long face asked me the next morning. We were sitting by the fire, and I was helping him peel kava roots with a rusty knife.

"I don't think so," I said, shrugging my shoulders.

"Then I'll make lunch while you go with my son." He called his five-year-old son and gave him directions in his dialect. The little guy was swallowed up in a big striped T-shirt, and he chewed his fingernails timidly. When I got up, however, he jumped up and hopped along happily in front of me, leading me over the border of a pineapple field in the jungle. As we followed the foot trail, the boy pointed several times at barbed wire glittering underneath the leaves on the ground. *What the heck is that doing here?* As usual, we were barefoot.

Suddenly the boy stopped. "There!" He pointed at a somewhat short, deciduous tree off to the side of the path. Fat, yellow-green fruit, about as long as your arm, grew on the smooth bark of the thin trunk. The skin was covered with little knobs. I carefully climbed through the vegetation and picked a jackfruit, twisting it to free it from its stem. Tucking it under my arm, I teetered back. About halfway to the trail something cut deep into my right heel. It was impossible to see what it was through the thick plants, but it felt like the blade of a machete.

I picked up my foot to get a good look. It was shooting a thin stream of blood like a water gun, spraying the bushes around me. *Nothing tragic.* I calmed myself down and hobbled behind the boy on the way back, leaving red tracks behind me.

Back at his property, my host and his wife washed my foot. They got two vines from the edge of the property, rubbed them in their hands, and pressed them into my wound to stop the bleeding. The first plant didn't seem to do the trick. When they removed the plant, the blood was still spraying out of the nicked artery, painting thin lines on the lawn.

Just like in Monty Python!

"What about the health clinic?" I inquired.

"They're closed today," said the long-faced man. I had to laugh as I imaged the fine print disclaimer: "Open Monday through Friday from 10:00 a.m. to 6:00 p.m. Whoever bleeds to death out-side of business hours is liable for their own death." As funny as I thought it was, I also realized how vulnerable the people were in case of a real emergency. If I had suffered something more serious than a small laceration, things could have been very bleak! *And things like that happen so fast.*

For the third bush-medicine treatment, my hosts heated the stem of a waist-high plant with shiny, pitcher-shaped leaves in the fire and pressed the gel-like juice into my open wound. It felt surprisingly good. Soothing. And the bleeding stopped too. Using the rest of the stem and a cloth, the man tied a bandage on my foot. "You'd better stay another day," he ordered.

"I can't. We sail tomorrow."

"Then I'll go with you. I need to sell a bag of kava anyway."

We set off after lunch. "The pickup doesn't come today," he informed me after we had crossed through the muddy trail. He threw his bag of kava over a fence into a cow pasture and climbed over. "We'll take a shortcut through this field to the next place where cars drive by."

"How far is it?" I wanted to know. The bandage didn't fit in my shoe, so I was hobbling along barefoot again.

"Just a few miles."

A few miles?! If I had known that we had to walk so far . . . I still would have had no other choice. Breaking my word to the captain and delaying his departure was out of the question. He probably would have worried about me too. I had no way to get in contact with him.

"Off we go!" I said to encourage myself and climbed over the fence, limping behind him. The wound opened up again after a mile or two, and blood seeped through the cloth. I tried to ignore it. The longer we marched along, the looser the bandage got, until finally I removed the last shreds. We were about halfway there. My calves and hips hurt from my abnormal gait, and I got farther and farther behind this neighbor of Jimmy Stevens. Cow manure and dirt caked in my wound and formed a crust. *At least it's not bleeding as much.* The hot air shimmered over the ground. It seemed an eternity before we finally reached the farm road.

"Here is good." The long-faced man positioned himself at a curve in the road. I plopped myself down on a rock and cleaned my heel with water from my bottle.

We waited. After two hours in the blazing sun, a cloud of dust appeared on the horizon, signaling an approaching vehicle. We waved our arms to stop the truck, but he drove on by.

"Sorry, already full," my companion said and clicked his tongue in pity.

"How many cars pass by here each day?" I asked.

"No one knows exactly," he answered.

Another hour crept by. I pictured myself hobbling the whole way back that evening. Then another pickup drove by, and this time we got lucky. There was just enough room.

✦

"Well, did you see the naked men?" my captain greeted me as he rowed up in his dinghy.

"Not only that. I got into it with a machete too!" I showed him my wound.

"I hope you learned something."

"Yep. I found out what jackfruit is." I grinned.

In the words of the poet Ewald Christian von Kleist: "Pain makes it possible to feel joy, just as evil makes us able to recognize good." That's why I am happy to this day to have two healthy feet. We often learn to appreciate something only when it is gone!

I introduced Jimmy Stevens's neighbor, and we showed him the boat. He was probably the first from his village to see a yacht from the inside. No wonder he was overcome with amazement.

We held a steady course to the north, maneuvering through the Solomon Islands. Although the people here are also Melanesians, there is less kava consumption. Instead, they have a tradition that would make any dentist break out in a sweat: the corridor leading from the Solomon Islands over to Southeast Asia, even as far as Pakistan and Africa, is inhabited by people who chew betel nuts. Although hardly anyone in the West has heard of these nuts, they are the most-used psychoactive substance in the world next to coffee, tobacco, and alcohol. This intoxicant is similar to nicotine or a mild dose of cocaine. The stupid part is that it attacks your gums and turns your teeth into unsightly reddish-orange stumps.

These nuts, which are actually palm tree seeds, are chewed with mustard stick (the leaves or buds of a pepper plant) and lime powder. Cooking coral to produce lime powder has become a favorite on the islands. In some countries people pep up their betel nuts with tobacco or spices.

"I could never have children in a place like this," my captain commented. "The rotting mouths the women have from that stuff would be an immediate turnoff!"

Obviously tastes vary widely, and the population of the Solomon Islands is growing—with or without teeth.

※

We landed in Papua New Guinea next. The culture there is anchored not only in betel nuts but also in witchcraft, polygamy, and, to a certain extent, cannibalism and ritualized abuse. All this in the twenty-first century. Therefore, be warned: the following section is both shocking and disturbing.

Fortunately the traditions I learned about in that region have decreased significantly in recent years. Yet tribes in Papua New

Guinea—such as the Sambia or the Etoro—still separate their sons, ages seven to fourteen, from their families and force the boys to have intercourse with older men for many years. These tribes believe that true manhood is transmitted through the sperm. They consider it the counterpart to the mother's milk. They even believe that the older men are doing the children a favor. They "generously give" the strength of their manhood to raise the younger ones to become fierce warriors.

The German government classifies this as child abuse. But according to anthropologists, 10 to 20 percent of the Melanesian tribes have practiced and cherished such traditions. At a minimum, it was tolerated by the other tribes. They hold the spiritual conviction that sperm is a male elixir, making child abuse desirable in the Sambia and Etoro tribes.

If spiritual beliefs result in these kinds of morals, would we be better off believing in nothing at all?

Theists *believe* in a god from whom all life comes, a god who gives everything meaning, worth, morals, consciousness, rights, freedom, and the like. Then there are agnostics. They *believe* that you can never know if what you believe is true. Therefore, they are determined not to be determined about anything. And what about people who say they *don't believe*? Explicit atheists, for example? In their own way they are believers. Instead of believing in God, they *believe* in nothing. When confronted with the universe, they believe in a nothing that exists without the universe. In a certain sense this belief considers nonexistence to be so powerful that literally, from out of nothing, everything—matter, energy, laws of nature, characteristics, space, and time—spontaneously came into existence.

It's hard to wrap your mind around all of this!

"Out of nothing comes nothing," seems to be a reasonable assumption. However, an explicit atheist who fully accepts the big bang theory completely contradicts the nature of nothing, actually *believing* that everything came into existence out of nothing, through nothing, and for nothing. Atheists don't want to believe in anything that has not yet been scientifically proven, which means a person is made up of a pile of lifeless atoms. Morals, meaning, worth, rights, consciousness, and reason are only an illusion because none of these have substance that can be proved in a laboratory. Thoughts and feelings are merely deceptions and chemical processes.

To believe in only what can be proven scientifically is to say, "I believe only what I see." That, according to science itself, is shortsighted. After all, it's been only in the last century that we discovered what we see constitutes less than 5 percent of the universe. The rest is dark matter and dark energy, and we don't even know what those are. So far we can neither see nor feel them. It is possible that dark matter, like a ghost, is passing through us at this very moment without us knowing it. Who knows how much more there could be that we have not yet discovered?

Everyone believes in something. Even those who don't want to believe. The great French author Victor Hugo concluded, "To believe is difficult; not to believe is impossible."[2]

However, isn't it also important to seriously think things through and not believe just anything? If nothing else, the Sambia and Etoro prove that blind faith can have serious, long-term consequences. We base the answers to all of life's important questions on our beliefs: *What is right and wrong? What will I do with my time, my money, and my strength? How do I treat others? Who am I, what can I do, and what can't I do?*

Our beliefs determine our deepest motives. I believe that life is a marvelous gift, and I want to treasure it and use it well. After my experience in Papua New Guinea, it became clear to me that I had

---

2   Victor Hugo, *The Man Who Laughs*, in *The Works of Victor Hugo*, vol. 5 (New York: T. Y. Crowell, 1888), 150.

gotten things backward. I had based my whole life on becoming happy myself, believing that happiness would enable me to help others. Now I believe that God put me in this world to be strengthened through Him and thereby able to help others—that's where I will find happiness. At first glance it doesn't seem all that different, but it changed how I thought about everything.

Every day, more and more.

The German bus stop, closest to my house. I walked one kilometer to get there. (July 1, 2013)

That first day of my travels, I took the train to the highway, where I would begin hitchhiking around the world. (July 1, 2013)

Seven days in Paris on a budget of five euros a day. I ate a lot of couscous and baguettes that week! (July 31, 2013)

Always hitchhike with a smile or two—just in case you lose one! (France, August 19, 2013)

Sailing to the Cape Verde Islands. My favorite spot on the yacht, breathing in freedom! (Atlantic Ocean, December 23, 2013)

My first Christmas without family! I once heard it said that home is where your loved ones are. All the wonderful people I met certainly made me feel at home. (Mindelo, Cape Verde, December 25, 2013)

Levera Beach (a.k.a. Paradise), Grenada (January 17, 2014)

Aranka gold mines in Guyana (May 30, 2014)

One step away from a several hundred meter free fall on Mount Roraima (Venezuela, July 10, 2014)

© Felipe Monteiro Vazami

Hiking back from Roraima with Felipe (July 12, 2014)

© Felipe Monteiro Vazami

Favela in Rio de Janeiro, Brazil (October 2, 2014)

Eye candy for the soul: Ipanema Beach, Rio de Janeiro. I sold fruit salad on this beach to earn a few bucks. (October 3, 2014)

Salkantay trail—fifteen thousand feet high—on the way to Machu Picchu (Peru, November 3, 2014)

© Wilfried Texier

Salar de Uyuni: the world's largest salt flats. I worked here as a tour guide. (Bolivia, December 15, 2014)

This is where I was trying to sleep while in Atocha when my life was saved by a donkey. (Bolivia, December 22, 2014)

In Cartagena, I had a suite with an ocean view ;-). (Columbia, February 15, 2015)

With the bald Canadian—full of surprises! (Cartagena, February 17, 2015)

Boat hunting at Shelter Bay Marina (Panama, March 25, 2015)

The sailors' "Equator Baptism" (Pacific Ocean, April 11, 2015)

A captain with wisdom to offer (Pacific Ocean, May 4, 2015)

Cargo-cult painting depicting the Yasur volcano (Island of Tanna, Vanuatu, September 20, 2015)

Public meeting space for villagers (Island of Tanna, September 20, 2015)

Village concert (September 20, 2015)

A nighttime eruption, Mount Yasur (September 21, 2015)

Traditional living on the island (September 21, 2015)

The fiery abyss at dawn (September 21, 2015)

With my friend from Baywatch ;-), Cuatro Islas (Philippines, February 9, 2016)

On fire for underwater exploration on Cuatro Islas (February 29, 2016)

Early morning, the last breakfast before the storm (East China Sea, April 27, 2016)

Shortly after our arrival in Busan (Korea, April 29, 2016)

Hitchhiking around Korea with my sign: Anywhere (September 12, 2016)

On top of Wolchulsan Mountain, 360 degrees of awesomeness! (Korea, September 20, 2016)

Experiencing Korean Buddhism,
Daeheungsa Temple (September 21, 2016)

Saying THANK YOU!! (Seoul, October 11,
2016)

Osaka, Japan (October 30, 2016)

The Great Wall of China at Badaling
(December 22, 2016)

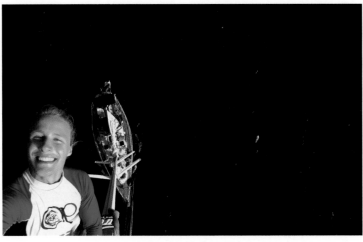

Doing some repairs on top of the mast (Indian Ocean, March 18, 2017)

After an evening church service where I was invited to preach, close to Lahore, eating on the bed of an elder (Pakistan, July 3, 2017)

Happy ending with the woman of my dreams, inside the Colosseum (Rome, Italy, August 6, 2017)

The happiest family reunion! (Rømø, a Danish island in the Wadden Sea, August 21, 2017)

With my partner in crime, one week before I proposed (Erzhausen, Germany, December 13, 2017)

Fourth Leg

ASIA AND THE
MIDDLE EAST

11

STORM AT SEA

I EXPERIENCED THE FULL EXTENT of a standstill when we reached an area near the equator that sailors call the doldrums—and for good reason! Windless waters dominate this region, which meant that our voyage from Papua New Guinea was less of a daring adventure and more like a two-week visit to the sauna. But as we Germans say, *Everything has an end. Except a sausage—which has two!*

In the southern Philippines brightly colored canoes went rattling by us as we arrived in the Bay of Davao in Mindanao. I was amazed to see that the fishermen had attached two bamboo supports on either side of their boats to stabilize them. At full throttle, they lifted the supports out of the water to reduce resistance. These outrigger canoes were fast as well as stable. *Clever! Of course the people here would optimize their vehicles. After all, the Philippines are an island country, and boats are a vital means of transportation.* To this day more Filipinos are active in global shipping than any other nationality.

"Hopefully none of them will get the bright idea to climb on board," my captain mused as one of them overtook us with its loud, stinky motor. "Four people were kidnapped a couple of weeks ago in the marina where we are going to dock," he exclaimed. "And one of them was Norwegian!"

"Well then, maybe they already have enough Norwegians." I winked at him. I, too, had done some research because I wanted to debark in the Philippines and find a way to travel to Korea and Japan. Islamic terror organizations active in the region were responsible for brutal attacks. And this even though the Philippines is the Asian nation with the highest percentage of Christians. About 90 percent of Filipinos identify as Christian, a holdover from about three hundred years of Spanish rule during colonial times.

"I'm glad you're so relaxed about it. Could you picture yourself staying for a while to help me remodel my boat?" he offered.

"It depends on the price." I needed a little cash for the next leg of my journey.

I started work a few days after our arrival. The captain had left to spend Christmas and New Year's in Europe, so I was on my own. Just a few yards from the wharf where the hostages had been kidnapped, I spent two months, eight hours a day, toiling in 90 degree weather under the blazing sun. To avoid getting sunburned, I wrapped myself up like a nomadic Arab. While roasting in the heat, I thought about my festively decorated homeland, and a deep sense of solidarity rose up in my heart for baked apples, which are treated so inhumanely, just like me. Cored and stuffed with raisins, spices, and sugar, they are baked until they practically melt into a puddle.

When I get back home, I will start a protest: save the baked apples!

I tried to motivate myself with such thoughts, making my tribulation a little easier to bear.

I was making just over two dollars an hour. I began to seriously doubt if the job was worth it, especially while sanding the fiberglass deck, when countless itchy splinters found their way to my skin and lungs. In northern Europe this would be considered exploitation. But I didn't have much of a choice since there were few opportunities to earn money in the Philippines. I had already worked for weeks in other countries for less than one dollar an hour. Compared to that, I was making bank! *Plus, I'm learning life lessons.*

I spent Christmas and New Year's Eve with a welcoming Filipino family I had met in church. Along with Filipino, English is one of the national languages, so they could understand me quite well. But I was also interested in learning some of their dialect. I was astounded that their language not only has many Spanish words but also shares commonalities with distant Pacific islands. For example, in Filipino, *mata* means "eye," the same as in Fiji, Maori, Indonesia, and Malaysia. If you just read this, pat yourself on the back. You just learned how to say *eye* in more than seventy languages. Congratulations!

This begs the question: Why are these languages so similar? How did people get to these islands, and where did they come from? Madagascar, off the coast of Africa, and the Easter Islands near South America are on almost exactly opposite sides of the globe, but they have something in common: the inhabitants have the same origins! Somewhere between 3,000 and 4,000 BC, brave fishermen left the coast of China for Taiwan. There they developed their knowledge of canoe building and set sail with the first outrigger canoes for a population migration known as the Austronesian expansion. They went to the Philippines and then onward to the west side of Indonesia in the Indian Ocean. By AD 500 they occupied the Easter Islands as well as Madagascar. A thousand years before Columbus, they had already traveled similar stretches of ocean! Although the Easter Islands and Madagascar are separated by half the globe, the word for the number two is *roa* in Madagascar and *rua* on the Easter Islands.

I am overcome with fascination when simple interactions with natives lead me to pick up the trail of such amazing connections. If I had not yet figured it out, I definitely knew by then: *it's a small world after all.*

As soon as I presented my work on the wood deck to my captain's satisfaction, I said goodbye to the older Norwegian with whom I had spent almost nine months. I would have to be patient for at least two more months for the sailing season to Korea and Japan to begin. The window of time is small, and only a handful of boats set sail in that direction. I would need a ridiculous amount of luck to find someone willing to take me with them.

In the meantime, *Focus*, a German magazine, published an article about me. Later I got a message on Facebook from Michal, a girl from Germany. She said, "I think what you are doing is good!"

I answered her, she wrote back, and soon any time Internet connections allowed, we began writing longer and longer messages to each other from opposite ends of the world.

Since the time and opportunity presented themselves, I was able to volunteer for a month on the Island of Leyte, which had recently been destroyed by a powerful typhoon. On our day off a Filipino I had befriended took me swimming on a beach. Had I ever wondered what it felt like to be a movie star? A funny mistake was about to give me a pretty good idea.

"There's a space over there!" I pointed to an empty parking place. Dozens of cars lined the wet, sandy path. It had rained that morning, but the sun was out and droplets sparkled on the tropical plants lining the pathway. My Filipino friend pulled his white Ford Ranger into the spot and turned off the engine. In the privacy of the tinted windows, we put on our swim trunks, then got out on the soggy path and shut the car doors. The sea, accompanied by the rhythmic beat of electronic music, roared in the background through the fresh air. The wet rocks crackled under our flip-flops.

"There's a surfing festival on the beach," my friend told me as we sauntered toward the water. He was short, even for a Filipino, but very muscular. His hair was undercut and he wore the top part in a ponytail like a samurai warrior. "Do you want to check it out?"

Several hundred locals were thronging in front of a stage where three women with backward baseball caps were dancing to a big vibrating beatbox.

I shook my head. "Maybe later. Let's go swimming first."

I started jogging at a loose, relaxed pace. The Filipino passed me, and soon we were sprinting, racing until we plunged into the foamy waves. The ocean spume sprayed on our faces, moistening our lips with the salty water. A strong wind blew over the surface, but underneath the current felt like a bathtub filled up with warm water! And the best part: we were the only ones in the ocean! We had that entire section of the beach to ourselves while the others were watching the show. We reveled in the inebriating sensation of the breakers swirling us around in a steady rhythm.

A larger breaker came down on me, and as I surfaced—rubbing the saltwater out of my stinging eyes—a surfer floated past. I raised my hand in greeting, and he gave me a friendly nod.

"Chris," my friend said from behind me. "Maybe we'd better get out of the water."

"Why?" I asked, turning around. "Are you cold?"

He gestured to the beach. The show had ended, and the mass of people had started lining up on the beach. "So they won't think we're with the pro surfers," he laughed mischievously.

"Oh, you're right," I agreed. While trudging through the white water toward the beach, I felt for my hair band but couldn't find it. My long blond hair fell around my shoulders, and my turquoise-blue shirt clung to my skin, accentuating every muscle. Behind us, the surfer I had greeted caught his first wave. I was a little jealous—surfing was high on the list of things I wanted to do!

I surveyed the crowd on the beach, staring at the ocean. *What the heck?* I awkwardly noticed they were not staring at the surfers behind us. They were staring at *me*! Maybe they thought that I was the only foreigner for miles around who had come to participate in the competition. *And I had never in my life even stood on a surfboard!*

"They're all looking at you," my friend whispered.

"I know! What should I do?" I whispered back.

"Better stay in the water," he advised.

"But you just said . . ." I wanted to protest, but he cut me off.

"Yeah, but look!"

A cameraman and a reporter with a microphone had positioned themselves to intercept us as we came out of the water. *Oh no!* We scurried through the water like poor imitations of *Baywatch* characters, just a stone's throw away from the crowd watching us. Some people whistled. Others filmed us with their cell phones.

How embarrassing! Get me out of here! When we had lost the reporter, we ran along the beach toward our SUV. When we reached the crowd, a girl next to me clapped her hand to her mouth and screamed hysterically. *Oh, please no.* Some of the others pressed up next to me for a quick selfie. It was like that one domino that knocks all the others down. The tumult around me convinced every last skeptic that I really was a famous surfing star. *Ridiculous!*

"What should I do?" I cried, wringing my hands as the multitude streamed toward me.

"Just make your way through," my friend laughed. "I'll wait for you at the car."

"What? You can't leave me alone!" I frantically raised my arm and pushed by a couple of people to rejoin him.

A group of pretty girls jumped in my way. "Just one picture, sir!"

I sighed and squatted to be at their height for the picture. *Mistake!* Now the others screamed, and more selfie-photographers closed in around me, the contagious insanity spreading through the crowd. *Help! Where are my bodyguards?* From all sides the natives pushed toward me. If I wasn't a head taller than everyone else, I probably would have suffocated. I desperately chiseled my way forward, pulling what felt like a big bunch of grapes made of human beings along with me. I forced a tight smile so as not to look too pitiful in the countless photos being taken.

"A selfie, please!" The Filipino girls kept pushing their phones up to their faces.

"Where are you from?" one girl asked.

"Germany," I admitted, and the crowd swooned and cheered.

"Sir, the last Miss World was from the Philippines, and her father was German!" a girl exclaimed, eyes beaming.

Oh, you're not trying to suggest . . . I put my hand in front of my eyes and pushed on. The more I insisted that I had nothing to do with the surfers, and the more people who got their pictures taken, the more the situation calmed down. I finally broke through the crowd and hurried along behind my friend. We took refuge in the white truck.

"What? You want to go already?" the Filipino laughed. *Wise guy!* Chuckling, he started up the car. "They've never seen anyone like you except in Hollywood tearjerkers."

We drove down the sandy path. At the end of the parked cars, two tractors approached pulling long trailers filled with teenagers. My friend hit the button to roll down the tinted window on my side.

"What—no, I . . ."

"Come on," he insisted, grinning. He slowed down to a walking pace next to the first tractor. "Now!"

I stuck my smiling face out the window and waved. "Helloooo," I called out, accompanied by my friend honking the horn.

A few Filipino girls looked at me, screamed shrilly, and strained to touch my hand. Then the rest of them caught the fire and hooted and whistled at me.

My friend at the wheel almost died laughing. "Again!" He choked on his tears from laughing so hard and hit the brakes as we passed the next tractor.

This trailer had been alerted by the tumult of the other one, so all I needed to do was lean out the window. The crowd went wild! They jumped up and down and screeched so jubilantly that I was afraid someone would fall off the trailer. I was also concerned about my friend who, doubled over with cramps, was hitting the steering wheel and couldn't stop laughing.

"Man!" He gasped for air. "Why didn't we film that?"

I used to think Asians were rather shy, but that's not true. You just have to catch them doing what they are passionate about. Take karaoke, for example. Anyone who has sung karaoke with Asians knows what I am talking about. Even the most delicate, shy Asian hiding behind a pair of glasses turns into a rock star in a karaoke bar! A rock star with rock-star glasses! I'm not exaggerating when I say that Dr. Bruce Banner's transformation into the Incredible Hulk is small potatoes in comparison.

But along with karaoke and surfing legends—*cough cough*—the Filipinos have another great love: basketball.

Basketball is to Filipinos as soccer is to Germans. An improvised basketball hoop can be found on almost every street corner for children to start practicing from a young age. If there are no streets or balls, the locals tie a wire ring to a palm tree and throw coconuts through it. *Where there's a will, there's a basketball!*

And yet it pains me to say that this is a tragic, unrequited love affair. As they say on the islands, "The Filipinos love basketball, but basketball does not love Filipinos." Of course, this is not surprising in a region where the average adult male is just under five feet four inches tall. Therefore, Filipinos only play a *small* role in international basketball. But I find it admirable that they still remain true to their love.

◯ February 2016

Next, I traveled to Manila, the capital of the Philippines. The parents and siblings of the Filipino who had brought me to the beach took me in for a week. His mother is a dentist. "Before you go, I am going to check your teeth, *anak*," she said. *Anak* means "son," and they truly had become like family to me. Not only did she take care of a little cavity that had snuck in, but she removed my wisdom teeth as well—all for free! If she had not removed them, they could have given me lots of problems, forcing me to cut my travels short.

But as luck, or something more than luck, would have it, I found myself in the right place at the right time. It was like winning the lottery over and over again. Could it happen one more time? It would have to if I was to find a boat for the next leg of the journey.

"Come in!"

I turned the door handle and entered the Subic Bay Yacht Club's port office in the northernmost marina in the Philippines. The yachts that were sailing to Korea and Japan would probably come by here.

"How can I help you?" said the man behind the desk to my right. To my left was a plate-glass window. Since the office was located on the fourth floor, we had an excellent view of the docks in the marina. Boats gently bobbed up and down in the water, and you could barely hear the metallic clinking of the lines striking against the masts.

I introduced myself: "I work on sailing yachts. Which boats are sailing northeast?"

The man behind the desk laughed. "Sailing?" He stood up and went to the window. "You see all those boats?" he continued.

"Yes." *I'm not blind.*

"And do you see all the people?" he asked.

"What people?" I replied, confused. Other than a couple of Filipino cleaning crews, there was almost no one to be seen.

"Exactly!" And with that, he returned to his desk. "Most of the boats are kept here, and the owners come every couple of months to spend a weekend."

"So no one takes off from here in the direction I want to go?" I was grasping at straws.

The man at the desk nodded. "But you can hang up your flyer, just in case someone comes in."

One last question: "How many yachts make the trip from the Philippines to Korea or Japan each year?"

"From all of the Philippine Islands? Between three and five. But it could be less."

Oh my goodness! Between three and five?

I was prepared to be disappointed, having encountered lots of naysayers along the way. Be it people or circumstances, something is always trying to convince you of how impossible something is. "That won't work," they often say. "No one has ever tried that before!" Or "People have tried that, and it didn't work!" I was no longer impressed by such statements. But if the man was right, my chances were not nearly as rosy as I had predicted.

Still, I won't give up yet. "When is the season for the yachts to stop here that want to go northeast?" I kept digging.

"It starts now. My best tip is the Rolex yacht regatta from Hong Kong. It meets at the end of the month. Maybe there will be a yacht from Japan there."

That's better than nothing! I thanked him, left the office, and went down to the docks. As the saying goes: *If opportunity doesn't knock, build a door.* I planned to do just that. Once again I found myself knocking on every boat, making personal contacts.

I spent most days in the yacht club until the Rolex regatta met, so I could meet as many people as possible. At night I slept in a park by the ocean. It wasn't exactly the safest place, and an older married couple who had cared for the park for years thought that my plans were a bit harebrained. They lived in the caretaker's hut on the perimeter of the park.

"Hang your hammock next to our hut in the light, then you should be okay," they said. As usual, I stowed my backpack in a trash bag and put it directly under my hammock.

"Yes, there is a boat from Japan here," the British skipper of a super yacht informed me. He had arrived on one of the many yachts in the regatta from China, and, like most of them, he wanted to take part in another local race. I had slipped into the welcoming festivities for the participants to make contacts with sailors. "You'd better be quick, though." The Brit leaned over the white tablecloth. "The Japanese want to take off tomorrow morning."

"Oh, they must have enough crew members, then." I sunk back in my chair, disappointed, and stared at the ceiling. *Doesn't look good.* Not the decorations, of course. They were fabulous! The pavilion was covered in classy white trimmings. Lanterns glowed overhead and, behind the artistically trimmed bushes, the moon reflected off the dark water.

The man grinned as if he knew the solution to my problem. "At least the rum is free."

That was not exactly what I was hoping for. But I laughed anyway, "Thanks. Got any other ideas?"

"How about going to Hong Kong and then to Taiwan? Maybe you'd have more luck there."

I had already thought of that. I shook my head. "There's probably no one going to Hong Kong who needs help on board."

Now the Brit got serious. "Come on! Don't give up so quickly. Everyone has a bad day now and then. Setbacks rarely cause failure. It's usually a lack of faith in yourself and what is possible."

While I let this idea sink in, my conversation partner gestured to the crystal decanters at the buffet. Then he said, "I think I can toss back two of them by myself. What do you think?"

Oh, these sailors . . .

Against all odds, I got up early the next morning to try my luck with the Japanese boat. As I had guessed, they had a full crew and left without me. I stood downcast on the pier watching as the yacht sailed away.

Another door closes. What I really needed was a little miracle. Even if other boats were sailing in that direction, would they need help? "Setbacks rarely cause failure." I contemplated the Brit's words. *He's right. If for some reason it doesn't work out, it won't be for lack of trying.*

As I had often done in hopeless situations like this, I contacted a few friends and asked them to pray for me. Maybe you believe in prayer, maybe not, but I have had some pretty astounding experiences with it.

I also went back to the regatta to make more contacts. Not sitting still and doing everything in my power gave me hope. And what do you know? Just a few days later there was a miracle waiting for me.

"I want to introduce you to someone," a Russian captain whom I had met in the lobby said to me. "He just came in from Thailand."

We went through the revolving door and into the luxurious interior of the club that also served as a hotel. The floor was made of sand-colored marble, and in the middle of the room, a broad staircase with green carpet led to the second floor. There were comfortable armchairs made of mahogany and light, velvet upholstery near two of the four columns. In one of these chairs a tall man with straight, black hair and an angular face sat talking on the phone. We waited until he finished. Then he stood up, shook our hands, and we all sat down.

"The kid here wants to work on a boat that's headed to South Korea." The Russian captain got straight to the point.

The man with the straight, black hair looked at me without smiling. "Good for you," he said, but his facial expression remained cold. He had a heavy Russian accent. "Can you sail?"

"Yes," I replied. "I've already sailed around two-thirds of the world. I'll work for free."

The black-haired Russian smirked. The first facial reaction that I could detect. "My boss will be pleased."

Doesn't sound like it! I furrowed my brow at the lack of enthusiasm in his tone.

The two men conversed in their mother tongue for a while. Then the man with the black hair turned back to me. "The yacht must be brought to Korea for a regatta. The skipper will arrive from Vladivostok in couple of days. Then all of you can go."

"'All of you'?" I asked, surprised. "Aren't you going with us?"

The man smirked again before pointing to his cell phone. "I just quit. That . . . [not for tender ears] won't pay me!" *That explains his bad mood.* "Bad for me. Good for you," he went on, narrowing his eyes. "I'll let you know when you can go aboard."

April 2016

As soon as the skipper from Vladivostok arrived, things went fast. The winds seemed to be favorable, and we didn't want to lose any time. Although typhoons are unusual during those weeks, there was still a risk of being surprised by one of those pesky buggers. The more favorable weather we could use, the better.

With that, we fastened the sails, filled up the gas tanks, and stored about one hundred liters of rum, hiding it in the stern of the boat—all on the first day.

"What do we need that for?" I naïvely inquired about the alcohol.

"For my friend," said the Russian skipper with a wink. He did not need to mention that he would not be paying customs.

The captain was in his early fifties, with frizzy white hair and a short beard. He had a charming smile and, in spite of his little pot belly, looked quite athletic. The kind of man who is up for anything. Like smuggling rum. Another Russian in his late forties made our crew complete. He was a wiry man with a dry sense of humor, a good head on his shoulders, and his heart in the right place. Too bad he wasted all his money on alcohol, cigarettes, and prostitutes. *Smart is not always wise.*

Our yacht was equipped for racing, and as soon as we left the bay, the boat clipped along at an easy seven knots northward. We spent our time in shorts until we reached the latitude of Taiwan; then the temperature became crisp. The ever-increasing layers of clothing were proof of our fast progress.

After only five days we passed the Japanese island of Okinawa. The trip could hardly have gone any better!

But then, on the sixth day, the skipper had bad news. "There's a storm front rolling in," he said grimly, relaying the weather report he had received via satellite. "We'll take a course to the Korean island of Jeju-Do, where we will seek shelter for two days."

"But it's another three hundred miles to Jeju-Do!" I interjected.

"We're cutting it close," the skipper admitted, "but we're going at almost eight knots. It's possible to make it there in forty hours."

In the meantime we had started wearing heavy-duty clothing for the cold weather. Wind and waves came over the bow. The yacht was sailing at a constant angle, and foam continuously sprayed into the cockpit. Not exactly comfortable. But it was fun!

Since no one wanted to prepare a complicated meal in those weather conditions, we just warmed up some bags of buckwheat with the camping cooker. The Russians call it *grechka*, and we ate the little kernels with milk and sugar.

That evening the wind died down so drastically that we had to use the motor. This had the skipper worried. The time we had to reach Jeju-Do was slipping away. We couldn't afford for anything to go wrong.

The wiry Russian woke me up at 1:00 a.m.: "The engine stopped!"

No, not now! I got up, sleepy and stunned, to go help. We thoroughly inspected the engine for over an hour but couldn't find the problem. It wasn't until I shone a flashlight on the murky water on the bow that I saw it—and was horrified. Something that looked like a human ponytail was hanging in the propeller. *A corpse in the water?* There are pirates in the waters off of the south side of China. Why not to the east?

Upon closer inspection I realized what it really was and yelled to the others: "It's algae! The propeller must be blocked."

With a shake of the boat, we reached the seaweed and pulled it out of the blades. But our joy was short-lived.

"Not again!" The skipper was perturbed as the propeller got blocked once again. And this time the plants were out of reach. We finally had to glide along with the weak wind pushing us at three knots per hour.

Well then, that's it!

Since both Russians had hardly slept that night, I navigated the yacht alone the next day. Thick fog surrounded us like a gray bell and the water and air were icy cold. Countless drops of condensation cloaked the deck in a shimmering veil.

The East China Sea really is special, I thought. Although we were a hundred miles from land, the ocean bottom lay no more than one hundred yards below us. *Unusually shallow.* The sea had a greenish color, and giant fields of reddish-brown algae floated around like pools of blood. There were also piles of trash and buoys from the fishermen. Now and then a Chinese cutter peeled out of the hazy wall that floated over the water. *How does that thing stay afloat?* I wondered. *It's totally rusted through!* It was also amazing that they could find fish in such shallow water. Little triangles on our screen showed that there were dozens of these tub boats near to us.

The eerie weather changed during the night and left us in complete calm. We were stagnant in the moist cloud of haze. It rained off and on. Otherwise it was dead still. *The calm before the storm*, I thought. It was a bizarre sensation, being trapped in this shallow soup. I pictured the Chinese on board their fishing boats. *Are the fishers slurping rice noodles with soy sauce in the glow of a greasy lamp?* These men spent most of their existence on the water. I wish I could have asked them what to expect.

Before dawn had chased the night away, the little triangles had fled from our chart plotter. *Yes, they know!* Only we remained. Unable to flee to safety.

Our breakfast eggs were not very appetizing that morning. Maybe there wasn't enough salt. Or maybe it was the tense anticipation of what lay ahead that spoiled our appetites. The smooth water splashed gently on the hull of our yacht, and we stared silently into the thick fog that had swallowed the sun for days.

Suddenly something moved. "There!" The wiry Russian raised a hand. A little ways off, the water shook. Like a shudder, the vibration overtook the surface until it grabbed our boat. It passed through our hair like cold fingers. *Wind!* The draft gained strength and awoke the waves sleeping in the sea, whipping them to life.

"Reef the big one and raise the storm jib!" the captain quickly commanded and sent us onto the foredeck while the sea came to life around us.

We had barely carried out his orders when the sails filled, and in no time they brought our bow through the frothing floods. Foam sprayed the glowing orange storm jib on the point of the boat, creating a warning contrast to the dull gray. Thankfully, the current had cleared the propeller so that we could use the motor to control the boat in spite of the troubling weather. I watched the display of nature in utter fascination—I had never experienced such a swift, stark change. Eventually exhaustion overtook me, and I went below deck to get some sleep.

BAM!

What the heck was that? I sat up in a daze, only to be shaken by another sudden jolt. A drawer scattered silverware all over the kitchen as it came loose from its hinges. *What the . . . ?* Another massive hit on board, as if the sea was trying to break our ship into pieces. The fiberglass walls creaked and groaned under the powerful blows. Half-asleep, I latched on a safety harness and climbed up, staggering into the room overtaken by chaos. Anything not tied down rumbled around like a large puddle on the floor. Bags of rice and cereal, plastic cups and bowls, and even the heavy kettle. My heart pumped all the common sense out of my head.

Where are the others? I scrambled over the stairs to the cockpit. The night was pitch-black. The wind howled against the rigging, and raging waters poured over the ship's rail.

"Hey! Is everyone okay!?" I called into the roaring din. I still couldn't see anyone. My eyes had yet to adjust to the darkness. Someone answered me out of the night with an impressive torrent of Russian curse words.

Thank God! Looks like nothing has changed. But how long could it last? The storm was driving us at a forty-five-degree tilt. Under the thundering claps of the mountainous waves, the tilt seemed to be increasing by the minute. I could make out the skipper above, holding on tightly to a security line with one hand and clutching the tiller with the other. So many curses came from his mouth that I asked myself how he could still concentrate on steering the boat. The other Russian was handling the winches in front of him.

"We have too much sail out!" I called to them. That was the only thing that could be responsible for the severe angle.

"YOU THINK?!" roared the wiry man in distress.

Good. They already know. I clasped my harness on and climbed up the steep side of the yacht toward the others to get a better look. A torrent of icy water washed over me, kicked up by the wind and by each and every raging wave. I bit my lip so as not to curse like the Russian.

To lessen the pressure on the sail, the men had lowered the main boom over the water so that it floated just inches above the surface. If it were to submerge, it could break the mast. That was obviously why we could not shorten the mainsail: at that severe of an angle, pulling it in would be suicide, especially with the main boom so far off the deck. Plus, the storm shook the sails with such power that no one could pull them down. *But still, too much surface area of the sails is terribly dangerous in a storm!* Under these circumstances, falling overboard would mean certain death. The poor visibility would make it impossible to be found. You would become hypothermic in no time and then drown.

"Did you try steering into the wind?" I called out to the skipper. That was the only chance of reaching the mainsail.

The white-haired man answered by gritting his teeth and pushing the helm away from himself to go into the wind. I got ready to scurry to the mast and pull in the sail. As usual when you bring the ship about, the wind felt even more brutal than before. The deafening noise increased to a shrill screech. At the same time our foreship crashed so violently through the crest that I was afraid our ship would explode. The water sprayed and rolled over the deck and crashed against our bodies, making us wet to the core. I trembled. The biting cold went straight to the bone.

"Forget it!" the skipper bellowed and turned the boat away. "We'll just destroy the bow!"

We clumsily pulled back around and assumed our former tilt. The attempt had failed.

"Thanks," the wiry Russian said, angry. With his free hand he wiped the ocean spray from his face and added, "For nothing!"

I understood his frustration. My rubber boots had turned into an aquarium and my fingers were frozen stiff. How bad must it be for the two Russians who had been out there for so much longer? But still, if the wind picked up, it would fling the rigging at us. Or tilt our yacht so far that it took on water and we would sink. Turning into the storm was terrifying, but in my opinion, it was still the only way.

Sometimes the biggest risk is not to take a risk and just wait. You have to be proactive to change things. If you are passive, things change you. It was up to us: the situation was what we made of it. Or as Aristotle said, "We cannot direct the wind. But we can adjust the sails."

This did not seem to be the appropriate moment for philosophizing. I tried my suggestion again: "If we turn a little slower, then . . ."

"Enough! Shut your cakehole!" the furious Russian on the winches yelled.

Well, that's not how I imagined it would go. I looked to the skipper for help. He was cursing under his breath while manning the rudder. He had dismissed my idea and was concentrating on other things. I anxiously sat down on the higher side of the boat to counterbalance the tilt a little bit with my weight. *Oh well, that's how things go. When you want to change something, it often gets overruled by the majority.*

A frosty swell of water washed over me. Then another. My teeth chattered. *No, it's not the majority that's the problem, but those who don't win the trust of the majority.*

It was pitch black all around. We couldn't even see the next wave before it hammered down on the boat. The moon and stars were nowhere to be seen—only the navigational lights, glowing red and green on the pulpit. We had turned on the white anchor light on top of the mast for better visibility.

The most unbearable part of being passive is the uncertainty, I pondered, staring into the darkness. None of us knew how bad the storm would get or how long we would have to hold out. And yet our lives hung in the balance. But, instead of changing our circumstances, we surrendered to them.

Now we can only hope that nature will have mercy on us. Although I didn't like it, I had to admit that our best chance was to stick together.

"Go get some rest. I'll relieve you," I said to the wiry man. He hesitated for a moment, as if unsure. Finally, he nodded and I went to his side. Secured with one extra hook, the Russian went to the deeper side of the stern to tie up the diesel canisters again. The waves had already knocked three of them overboard. Then he climbed inside the boat and handed a bucket of water to me to empty before lying down between two sailing bags to sleep.

The skipper and I stayed outside, fighting the storm until the bearded Russian couldn't go on. He traded off with the other man. Then I was relieved. We rotated like that all night long. One person held a steady course while the other readjusted the sails to make it as easy as possible for the one at the helm. The third person rested. Our angle decreased as dawn approached, the first sign that we had survived the worst of it.

"What do you think?" the skipper asked me as I took over steering the next morning. His red pants and jacket were soaked through and drops fell from his hair as well as his nose.

"I think you look like Santa Claus at the swimming pool," I answered, grinning, and then I added, "At least you've finally taken a bath!"

The skipper laughed. "You'd better not be expecting breakfast." He gave an exaggerated stretch and disappeared into the cabin. Through the opening I saw him pouring a bowl of cereal.

Dang it!

It wasn't until the following night that we were finally able to replace the storm jib with the normal mainsail. The day after that we sailed into the marina at Busan. Next to Seoul, the capital of South Korea, Busan is the country's second-largest city and an economic center. Eighty percent of South Korea's container cargo goes through these harbors. The skyline is correspondingly impressive with buildings up to 80 stories tall. In comparison, the highest skyscraper in Germany has only 65 floors, which is half as many as the tallest building in South Korea, which is 123 stories tall.

During my stay, I planned to learn the language. Learning Korean was surely the key to understanding the Asian mind-set better. It was certainly the key for Koreans to understand me at all!

It took me just three months to learn Spanish, Italian, and Portuguese. Three months should be enough to learn Korean. I put myself on the fast track without realizing how much I had overestimated. You can learn to read Korean in just two hours. But speaking it is an entirely different story! Instead of using thousands of characters like Chinese or Japanese, Korean has just ten vowels and fourteen consonants. That's twenty-four symbols, almost like our alphabet. Anyone with Internet access, two hours, and the desire to learn can participate with numerous sources of online help. Having said that, it may not be essential for most people to be able to read Korean, but exercising the little gray cells never hurt anyone.

Since I knew modern technology makes learning a language much easier, I purchased a cheap, used smartphone from a man from Bangladesh. Up until then I had traveled completely without electronics. That was the first smartphone I had in my life. I figured it out pretty quickly and right away discovered a program called "The 1000 Most Commonly Used Korean Words." *Bingo! That sounds perfect for me.* For starters, I decided to learn thirty new

words and one grammar concept a day. A lofty goal, but I wanted
to be a good student.

A couple of weeks later I had learned more than seven hundred
words. I finally realized that the "1000 Most Common Words"
had probably been taken from the newspapers. I could translate
"employee," "standardization," and "research and development" in
my sleep, but I still couldn't ask for "food and drink" or find out
where the "toilet" was. *Fail. Especially if I really had to go!* But, if out
of the blue I urgently needed to discuss the economy or politics, I
was well prepared.

12

GANGNAM STYLE/IN A BUDDHIST MONASTERY

I STAYED ON THE RUSSIAN BOAT until the yacht regatta. We took second place out of more than fifty boats! *What a nice memory of our time together.* Then I said goodbye to my new Russian comrades and hitchhiked inland into the mountainous region of Korea, all the way to the historical city of Gyeongju.

The sun had just set as I reached a lake near my goal. The temperature was still pleasant and mild. I toyed with the idea of going for a swim. *If the Koreans were to see a blond European rising up out of the dark water, they would probably get the shock of a lifetime!* I laughed, discarding the idea.

My muffled steps echoed on the bridge leading to the other shore. *The water looks truly magical.* I leaned on the wooden railing in silence, losing all sense of time. I was captivated by the scene! All around me, decorative lanterns changed from blue to red. Classical Asian music played from speakers nearby, and not far away a cherry tree stretched its limbs in the warm night air.

I'm really in Korea. Who could have guessed? It became clear to me in that moment just how different Korea is from the other countries I had visited. For the first time since Europe, I was in a first-world country. *Everything looks so harmonious and safe!*

There are, in fact, practically no murderers, terrorists, or thieves in Korea, and drug abuse is a rare exception. What is there to be afraid of? Okay, other than North Korean rockets, of course.

Since daily life is so safe, totally absurd fears have crept into the Korean population. It's a little bit like our immune system: if it doesn't have anything to do, it attacks totally harmless things, thereby developing allergies. That's how it is with most Koreans, who, for example, are deathly afraid of fans. Not the imposing metal rotary blades of industrial ventilators, but little fans that you set on the dresser on a hot summer evening. Most Koreans believe that if you leave a fan running overnight, it will suck the oxygen out of the room, and you will suffocate in your sleep. Another theory is that vacuums make you unable to breathe, and yet again, you suffocate. This has not been proven scientifically, and there has never been a single death of this nature, yet this fear is so deeply ingrained in the people that even the Korean government requires safety labeling on fans, warning that they should not be left on overnight. For this reason, many Korean fans are equipped with a timer to turn them off automatically.

First-world problems! I laughed to myself and then continued on my way to the other shore, where I set up camp for the night behind an abandoned outhouse.

The next morning I hitchhiked to the city center. The driver asked where he should drop me off, and I made a hand gesture for him to wait while I thought about it. *I should have looked up the words ahead of time!* I was actually looking for a supermarket to stock up on inexpensive food. I hadn't found any for the past three days and had been eating only instant noodles. Truth be told, my stomach was a little queasy.

In my head I formulated a sentence to the effect of: *"Please let me off on your way in an area located near a retail district including groceries."* In reality I said: "You. Way peripheral. Many people buy. In out."

For crying out loud, I don't know the word for "groceries," but "peripheral" springs to mind!

To my surprise, the driver nodded eagerly and said, "Oh, oh, oh!" as if he knew exactly what I meant. *Well then! Maybe my Korean is not that bad after all!* My chest swelled from the success of being understood—and then collapsed again when he dropped me off at the train station instead of a supermarket. *Next time will be better, for sure.*

Whereas the buildings at the lake were traditional and aesthetically pleasing, the city center was industrial: everything there was stark, colorless, and purely functional. The buildings were rigidly straight with right angles, just like the roads that ran through them. To save space, there were no sidewalks, only narrow gutters at the sides of the streets. Plaster crumbled on the walls between dirty signs, and gray smudges disfigured the façades. A sad sight.

Other than a lonely flowerpot placed by the side of a driveway, my eyes sought in vain for plants. I was surrounded by a concrete jungle that had banned nature to its outskirts. Although I was happy I didn't live there, another thought continued to plague me: *Still no grocery store! I need a break.* My stomach growled, and my calves ached under the weight of my backpack. The sweaty straps dug their artificial fibers uncomfortably into my shoulders.

Luckily I turned into a narrow side alley and noticed immediately that the architecture had changed. The farther I followed the curvy path, the more obvious it became that I was entering the rich part of town. I peeked curiously through a wrought-iron gate into a green garden. A U-shaped apartment complex enclosed the manicured premises. The sloping, elaborately decorated corners of the roof stretched over a terrace that wrapped around the building. A pair of pink slippers sat on a stepping-stone leading up to the terrace. *So cute!*

The path wandered into an open park with a 7-11 convenience store on its outskirts. Exhausted, I unfastened the clasp and let my backpack slide onto a pillar next to the entrance. Leaving it there, I went in the store. I was not worried about anyone stealing it. It was far too heavy to carry while running away, and anything valuable was packed deep inside. For 1,500 won—just over a dollar—I got two plastic containers of instant noodles at the counter and used the water dispenser to fill them with hot water.

The fourth day in a row of instant noodles. It's time for me to find some proper food.

I perched with my lunch on the step in front of the store. While slurping up the noodles, I admired the cherry trees and felt strength gradually flowing back into my limbs. These trees look more delicate than European cherry trees. Although they had bloomed weeks earlier, the fruit was still small and did not look ripe.

An older Asian man wearing a dark-blue sports jacket came up and put his hands on my backpack's shoulder straps. He had tanned skin and thin black hair with bits of white running through. He reminded me a little bit of my grandfather, partially due to the crooked teeth poking generously out of his mouth. The man took hold of my backpack and lifted it about an inch. Groaning, he put it back down and laughed. His kind, brown eyes scrutinized me. Then he pointed back and forth between me and the backpack.

You're not the first person who couldn't pick it up, I thought, amused. Countless people had that reaction when they went to see how heavy it was. They usually made a comment about it being full of gold or rocks. This man probably said something like that. Whatever it was, I couldn't understand him.

A younger man in a white sweater with a soccer logo came up behind him and translated into bad English: "He want know where you from."

"*Dogilesso wassoyo*," I tried to answer in Korean.

"Ahh, from Turkey?"

I really need to improve my pronunciation! Not Tokil, but Dogil!
"No, not Turkey, Germany," I replied, falling back on English. *Isn't it somewhat obvious from my blond hair and blue eyes?*

The men conferred with each other. Then they continued by asking the same questions that I got asked almost every single day in Korea: What was I doing there? How long had I been there? When did I plan to go back to Germany? Tell me about your family.

Ironically, many people also wanted to know which flavor of instant noodles was my favorite. I had learned the answer to that one: "Shin ramyun." The flavor of shin ramyun doesn't get boring because it's so spicy that it numbs your tongue, and then you can't taste anything anyway.

"My father ask if you want to come with us. You can sleep in our house tonight. Far from here," said the younger man. At least I think that's what he said. His English was very exotic. *But still better than my Korean.*

"Come with you? Now?" I asked, unsure.

The man in the sports jacket made a gesture as if to eat quickly. Clear enough. Surprised and happy, I said, "*Nae, nae!*" and gulped down the last few noodles. (*Nae* means "yes" in Korean.) When I was finished, I bowed, which is important to be polite in Korea, and added, *"Daedanhi gamsahamnida,"* which means something like "Thank you very much." I followed the man in the blue jacket to a group gathered under a cherry tree.

Clueless, I looked to the younger translator and gestured to the group. "Your family?" He nodded.

"Wow! Very big family!" I was amazed and followed the older man to an empty tour bus.

"Choe Yong Mun," the older man introduced himself as after I caught up to him.

"Christopher."

Since Koreans always say their family name first, his first name was actually Yong Mun, but I didn't know that at the time, so I called him Choe. But that wasn't so bad. He couldn't really remember my name, anyway.

Choe gesticulated to communicate that I should put my backpack on the back seat of the bus. *They rented a whole bus? Amazing!* We returned to the group together. I felt a little uneasy about leaving my things in a stranger's vehicle, but what could happen in Korea? The group was meandering among some red poppies.

Just as we joined them, a young girl, about twelve years old, hopped over to me. "You, me, picture?" she asked. The rest of the group had already surrounded me, taking pictures and bombarding me with bad English. "You welcome in Taiwan!" a man offered enthusiastically with his big camera swinging from his neck.

I suddenly noticed that most of them were wearing Buddha talismans. "Uhm—Taiwan? Are you from Taiwan?"

"Yes, yes, all from Taiwan," the man answered, gesturing around the circle.

"Didn't you say that this was your family?" I whispered to the young man in the white sweater.

"No, no. Not family. Many. Those there," the man pointed to a man, woman, and the twelve-year-old, "a family. These two.

Grandparents. And there, another family. This here, my wife." He pointed to a young Asian woman at his side.

I interrupted him, nodding at Choe. "Is that your father?"

"No. Not my father." He laughed as if I had asked a stupid question.

"So then, you are a tourist group?"

"Yes, yes. Family. For three days in Korea. Tomorrow back to Taiwan."

It finally made sense. I couldn't understand any Korean words because they were speaking Chinese! Choe was the local tour guide. That did not reveal if he would really help me. Maybe he just wanted to include me in the group and charge me later for the tour? I had run into things like that more than once in other countries. *Choe seems nice, but that could be deceptive.* I had a hard time figuring out Asians.

Perhaps I should thank them and go my own way? Instead I decided to stay and let myself be surprised by how things unfolded. In retrospect, I often had interesting experiences when I just listened to my gut and let myself get drawn in to what was happening around me.

"Mogda." Choe broke me out of my thoughts. *What did that mean, again?* "Mogda," Choe repeated and brought his hand to his mouth, just like before, like he was holding a spoon with soup in it. *Oh yeah, food!*

He led the whole group to a restaurant. The aroma of chicken broth wafted through the room. My stomach growled loudly. I wanted so badly to eat with them. But I just couldn't afford it. *It's high time I found a job!*

Choe noticed my hesitation. He pulled me by the shirtsleeve to a table behind the counter where two members of the tour group were sitting. He indicated that I should wait. Then a waitress pushed a cart up to our table and served up bowls of Korean food. We each got a bowl of rice and some seaweed soup. In the middle of the table, the server added bean sprouts, pickled garlic cloves, chopped onions, whisked eggs, fried lotus, and kimchi. Kimchi is fermented cabbage, and, along with rice, it is served at every meal in Korea—like sauerkraut used to be for the Germans. However, kimchi is loaded with chili paste, so you have to get used to how spicy it is.

When we began eating, Choe came up with three more bowls of rice and a bowl of spiced fish and put them around me. Then he picked up the metal chopsticks from his place setting and started eating. "Mogda!" he grinned. He picked up the tab for me. I was ashamed that I had been suspicious of him!

After dinner we went to a hotel. Choe must have told a joke over the bus microphone. At any rate, the Taiwanese broke out laughing. My neighbor leaned over to me and explained in English, "He just told us how you ate enough for a whole family. Heh, heh!" I had to laugh too. *When he's right, he's right!*

In the hotel Choe took me to a bedroom that he shared with the bus driver. The room was modernly equipped with a flat-screen TV on the wall, an electric kettle for making tea, and a bathroom. *Finally a shower!* But unlike most modern hotels, I noticed that there were no beds! I later learned that even the king of Korea ate and slept on the floor all the way up until the twentieth century. Although Western-style chairs and beds are increasingly popular among the younger generation, many Koreans hold true to their traditions. Which is why I had to remove my shoes before walking on the hotel's light-wood flooring—like everywhere else in Korea. That was embarrassing because my socks did not exactly smell good. *But who walks around on the table and the bed in their shoes?*

We took three thick, rolled-up mats with pillows and blankets out of a closet and spread them out on the laminate floor. Our sleeping accommodations. I think this arrangement is not half bad, at least if you do not mind sleeping on a hard surface. In a small apartment it would save a lot of space. And the best part is, you don't have to make your bed! Just roll it up and put it in the closet where it doesn't bother anyone. *Done!*

Choe suddenly pressed his phone up to my ear. "Hello?" I said, confused.

"Hey, I'm Choe Yong Mun's wife. My husband wants to ask if you want to go with him on the bus to Busan tomorrow."

Wow! Whereas Choe spoke no English, his wife's was decidedly good! "That sounds great! But I was actually planning to go to Daegu tomorrow." I declined the offer. I had just come from Busan. Plus, I didn't want to overtax Choe's hospitality.

Choe took the phone back to hear the answer. After a few exchanges he put the phone to my ear again.

"My husband really wants you to come along. Tomorrow night you'll both take the train to Seoul, and I'll cook for you."

What a generous offer! It was very appealing. But a train ticket would definitely be expensive, and I didn't want Choe to have to foot the bill. *Better hitchhike.*

The bus driver sat next to me in his undershirt and underwear, sipping his tea. I couldn't help but notice that he was shaking his head. *Is he trying to signal that I shouldn't turn him down again? That would probably be very impolite.*

"Okay, I'll go along to Busan," I said. Choe smiled, satisfied.

After breakfast in the hotel, we drove to Busan as planned. There, we checked out a Korean favela. At least, that's what they called that part of town. It has nothing to do with the poor districts in South

America; it was more like a hip cultural center. The only similarities were that the small houses were painted with bright colors and it was built on the side of a mountain. Our tour then led through Yongdusan Park, which is less of a park and more like a platform on a forested mountain that floats above the city of Busan. When I got out of the bus, I tasted the familiar ocean air of a port city. It felt like home. A hint of pine and deciduous trees mixed in with the gentle breeze. If I closed my eyes, I could almost imagine that I was back in Northern Germany.

Choe pinched my shoulder and tapped his watch. *"Han shigan"*—"one hour"—he indicated and shooed the remaining Taiwanese and me out of the parking lot. Unlike the others, who immediately went to canvass the souvenir shops, I wandered to the south end of the park. My gaze fell on a green and red pavilion with a giant bronze bell hanging inside. The bell was so big that it left barely enough room for one person. I wanted to jump over the barrier and hammer the bell with the wooden beam that served as a mallet. *That would be a mighty sound!* But besides the fact that it was probably not allowed, the wooden beam was chained up. *Looks like I'm not the first person to have that idea.*

When the hour was up, we met at the entrance to the highest level of the park. Mosaic tapestries depicting turtles, reindeer, and birds were affixed above the stairs. Enormous pillars protruded out of the massive overhang at the top, giving the entrance an imposing atmosphere. Choe positioned himself in front of one of the pillars, waved his little tour guide flag, and started his speech about the location. The Taiwanese pressed into a half circle around him, listening to his performance, which he conducted in Chinese for their benefit. I strained to see if I could recognize any words, but all that came to mind were scenes from kung-fu movies. *What a funny language!*

Then Choe suddenly came over to me and grabbed my sleeve, pulling me with him to his spot in front of the pillar. *Maybe I was*

*right and this really is about kung fu, and now he needs an opponent to
fight. Too bad no one here can understand my jokes. Maybe I'll write
a book about it someday.*

Without letting go of me, Choe continued speaking and poked
me in the chest with his finger every time he emphasized a word.
Everyone stared at us. I couldn't help but giggle. I was still thinking
about kung fu.

Then to my surprise, Choe whipped out his wallet and gave
me almost fifty dollars' worth of Korean won. I looked at him in a
complete daze. Now he was the one giggling. A Taiwanese man broke
out of the group, posed for a snapshot with me, and handed me some
money that was worth about ten dollars. Another came up to the
pillar, again with money in his hand. We took pictures for his family
and he gave me a donation. It went on and on, until everyone in the
group had taken a turn. All together, they gave me about 140 dollars!
Choe had blindsided me with a minibenefit! *What a tour guide!*

Part of me felt super awkward taking money from people and
not doing anything for it. But then again, the members of the tour
group seemed to go wild for the chance to take a picture with me, as
were quite a few Asians. I was overcome with emotion and beamed
with joy. Choe had shown me so much neighborly love, even though
we couldn't really even talk to each other. Love is shown by deeds,
not words, as they say. If that isn't proof, then what is?

That evening we took a high-speed train through the Korean landscape toward Seoul, the capital city. To Choe's delight, I bought a
ticket with the money from the photos. Choe and his wife planned
to have me stay in their home while I was in the grand metropolis. I
didn't want to overstay my welcome, but if I were to stay somewhere
else, I would need money.

I've gotta get a job! So using the Wi-Fi that worked perfectly, even though we were traveling at about two hundred miles per hour, I sent an e-mail to a friend I had met in Busan. She had told me about a friend in Seoul who was looking for a private English teacher. *That's at least a start.* In the e-mail I outlined my qualifications in short sentences and added a picture to identify myself.

I received a prompt response:

> Unfortunately, we no longer need an English teacher.
> Nevertheless, I'll forward your e-mail. Good luck!

I have to admit, I was a little disappointed. After all the manual labor I had done, it would have been a nice change of pace to use my head. *But whatever. It was worth a try.*

And indeed it was! To my surprise, another e-mail soon arrived:

> Hi, a friend showed me your e-mail. Next Monday we are filming a commercial for our company's product: smart shoes for golfers. I have some questions for you: Are you available on Monday? Can you swing a golf club? What is your shoe and clothing size?

Wait a second . . . golf?! I've never held a golf club in my entire life! Unless . . . does minigolf count?

After some discussion it turned out not to be a problem. I would play the part of the trainer. After all, the trainer doesn't have to be a good golfer; he just has to be a know-it-all. *Yep, I can do that!* [1]

---

1   "IOFIT Smart Shoes (Without Narration)," 0:48, YouTube video, published by Salted Golf (IOFIT) on June 30, 2016, https://www.youtube.com/watch?v=UKyx6gu1nLY.

After a few days with Choe and his wife, I said goodbye and moved into a kind of dormitory. I had earned the first month's rent with the ad for golf shoes, filmed on a private course owned by Samsung. At that golf course, a permit alone probably costs thousands of dollars. *I didn't notice anything about the grass that was worth that kind of money. But it was pretty!*

My new home was in Gangnam. Yes, the part of town that inspired the song "Gangnam Style." Although the hit tune had long since disappeared from popular culture, the first thing I did in my new place was to dance "Gangnam Style." *Stupid? Maybe. But still funny!*

Thanks to a good Internet connection, my communications with Michal, the girl from Germany, grew more intense. It was almost scary how well we understood each other. We became like a mutual "living diary" for each other, talking and writing about simply everything. The only thing we didn't talk about was the tingly feeling that became increasingly noticeable the more we spoke with each other—at least, that's how it was for me. But we avoided that topic.

"Did you strike it rich?" my aunt wrote to me when she found out I had gotten a room to myself. She, of course, couldn't see that it was about the size of a bathroom. In Germany, the law states that the minimum space for human occupancy is seventy-five square feet. *I'm a little shy of that at forty square feet!* My aunt had also seen the Internet pictures of me on a yacht and on the golf course. *And now she thinks I'm rich! Hilarious.*

"I'm not as rich as you think," I said. From a material standpoint, I had practically nothing. But I was more than satisfied with what I had. Or as Lao Tse put it more eloquently, "He who knows he has enough is rich."

In this sense, yes, I was rich.

In the following months I was able to finance my stay with other little acting jobs, including an advertisement for Samsung. I also took part in a medical study in Busan. They wanted to test growth hormones on men with European ancestry. That didn't sound so good at first, but since the drug is already a successful seller in the Asian market, I figured it was pretty harmless. Not to mention that Sylvester Stallone supposedly used the same substance to supplement his muscle-building routine. And what man wouldn't want to have a body like Sly Stallone's?

So I signed myself up, was judged to be an acceptable test subject, and they invited me to spend two weekends in a hospital in Busan. I've honestly never earned money in a more comfortable way. In total, I lay in the hospital with my laptop for four days, having my blood drawn every hour. The pay amounted to about two thousand dollars. That would not have been a lot of money if had grown a third arm or something, but my body did not change—not for the worse, nor did I look like Sylvester Stallone. *You can't have it all!* I was still grateful for this source of income.

Since I had plenty of time, I studied vocabulary and learned about the country's history. And what a history it is! After World War II, Korea was split into two zones: one occupied by the Soviets, and the other occupied by the Americans. This was at about the same time that Germany was split into East and West Germany. The immediate result was the Korean War in the early 1950s, which turned South Korea into one of the poorest countries on earth. Many cities were in ruins, fields were destroyed, and starving families wandered through the icy Korean hillsides in search of herbs and plants to eat. This dire situation did not change much until the 1960s. What happened then was unimaginable.

What if I told you that Afghanistan, Albania, or Somalia, for example, would transform into one of the world's leading commercial powers within the next four decades? You would probably laugh at me. It sounds absurd. That's why South Korea's advancements mark perhaps the greatest economic miracle in all of human history! Even though Korea had practically no natural resources or education system, they became the world's tenth-biggest economic nation by the early 2000s. Within only forty years South Korea went from being the second-poorest country in the world to speeding past countries such as Spain and Australia! Today this country, which has a smaller population than Germany, has on average the fastest Internet and the highest concentration of industrial robots worldwide.

How did the Koreans do it? Through hard work, for the most part. They have a "fast-fast" mentality or, in Korean, *balli-balli*, which means their work may not always be the most efficient, but that is outweighed by working a lot and working quickly. The Koreans work over forty hours a week per person all year long! *That's not so hard*, I thought at first. *I often work forty hours a week. Sometimes more!* But you can't forget that vacation time, sick leave, and holidays have to be counted too. Taking this into account, the average German works only thirty hours a week. During the economic boom, most Koreans worked forty-eight hours a week.

But hard work has disadvantages too. Competition is so stiff that employers expect their workers to put in overtime without pay, staying until their superiors go home for the day. If you don't, you will be fired and won't be able to find work elsewhere. If high school graduates don't make it into one of the top five universities, the families' disappointment is so crushing that many young people see no way out other than to jump off a bridge. According to the World Health Organization, Korea is number one in suicides worldwide.

So intense hard work has an ugly side. But it is still impressive how South Korea or Singapore—another example of dramatic economic improvement—have proved that, even starting at rock bottom, you can reach the top.

But hard work alone won't do the trick. There is another ingredient hiding in the Korean recipe for success. I can dig a hole and fill it all day long and still not accomplish anything. Plus, the average German currently has a higher economic output than the average Korean, even though he or she works only thirty hours a week compared to Koreans' more than forty a week.

The other important factor is focus on continual development and better education. If you want to improve something, you have to improve yourself first. A single generation of Koreans started by producing clothing, and then learned to make cars and ships, and finally electronics as well. The Korean company Samsung started with textiles and groceries, and now they own the world's largest share of smartphones on the market. That would not have been possible if the Koreans had not invested much of that hard work in education.

As the 2,500-year-old wisdom from neighboring China says, "Learning is like rowing against the current. If you stop, you go backward." I would say, *If you are done with learning you are done for.* The Koreans would say, 배움에는 왕도가 없다: "There is no short cut to learning."

* * *

After three months in student dorms in Gangnam, I decided to hitchhike farther through the country. Even though I had crammed some rock-solid Korean vocabulary, I still couldn't really talk. The best way to practice was to have no other choice.

So I stuffed everything into my backpack once again and headed south. I wrote "somewhere" in Korean on a piece of cardboard. This indication of my direction confused quite a few people, but at the same time it led to some unique experiences. For example, one Korean farmer spontaneously took me to the mountains one afternoon to show me a monastery called Daeheungsa.

Instead of being at the peak of the mountain, as one might expect, the facilities were built in a sinkhole so the forested cliffs protected the area from all sides. The atmosphere was peaceful and picturesque. Like a skillful artist, late summer had sprinkled the green with red, yellow, and orange dashes of color, and the monastery's heavy, wooden halls with its pointed, elaborately decorated roofs fit so nicely into the landscape that it seemed like it had been there for centuries.

The farmer brought me to a sandy square at the entrance and introduced me to a monk. Like most Buddhist priests, his head was shaved to symbolize the desire to be free of illusions and ignorance. He wore a long gray habit to remind him of ashes and the past. The farmer bowed to the monk in a special way, and I tried to imitate the respectful gesture.

"Where are you from?" asked the monk.

"*Dogilesso wassoyo*," I answered in Korean, confident that my pronunciation had improved quite a bit.

"So, from Turkey!" he said.

Nooooo! Why can't anyone understand me? "Germany," I corrected with a smile and tried out the vocabulary I had recently learned. "Europe. Reunification. Cars. Merkel. Germany."

The monk nodded and let it be. He turned away and started talking to the farmer. *I hope I wasn't rude.*

While the two of them conversed, my thoughts drifted to what I had learned about Buddhism. Buddha's fundamental assumption, on which the religion is based, is that life is full of suffering and pain, permeated with troubles, doubts, sickness, and the like. *I wouldn't be a very good Buddhist. I honestly think life is pretty wonderful.* The worst part, according to Buddha, is that suffering does not stop when you die because you are reborn again and again. The only way to break the cycle is to separate from everything that causes suffering.

That made me think of math exams. But Buddha said that the origin of suffering lies deeper, in what we *want*. Therefore, math tests are painful because we want to get a good grade—or at least pass. You have to separate from all wants and desires. That basically means separating from your identity, belongings, family—Buddha is said to have left his wife and son—from urges and even from thoughts, opinions, and feelings. If you are successful in detaching from all of these things, dependent on nothing, then you have reached nirvana. Nirvana doesn't mean a kind of paradise, as a lot of people think, but "extinction" or "disappearance"—a state of being released from feelings, wishes, and thoughts.

"Do you want to stay the night here?" the farmer addressed me. He had finished chatting with the monk. I looked at my feet, a little uncertain. My inner curiosity wanted to cry out, "Yes!" But I had decided that I always wanted to enrich others as well, and this monk didn't seem to be very interested in me. Maybe because of my awkward response to his question about where I'm from.

"Thanks, but I'm okay," I declined quietly, knowing that a direct no is considered impolite in this culture. But I was clear enough. I hoped.

The monk reached into his gray habit, took out a smartphone, and called someone. When he finished, he nodded in agreement: "No problem. The German can sleep here."

Sleep here?! But . . . Although it was embarrassing to communicate so poorly, my curious side was rejoicing. I was sure that I could learn a lot in the monastery.

After I said goodbye to the farmer, another monk came to get me and led me to my room. He was about my age and, unlike the other man, his robe was brown.

"Why is yours brown?" I tried to start a conversation.

"I'm a novice. I've only been here for three months," he said in very good English.

Woohoo! Someone understands me! Thick, black-rimmed glasses rested on his wide nose. "How is it that you speak such good

English? And how long does it take to get from being a novice to a proper monk?" I dug deeper.

"You ask a lot of questions."

If you only knew. I grinned. "I'm just getting started."

We reached a square in the temple area with two traditional timber buildings to the left and right. There were five dark wooden doors covered with bleached paper in each building.

"This is your bedroom." The novice opened one of the doors. Other than a desk and a fan, there was no furnishing inside. Two folded blankets and a rice pillow were sitting on the desk.

"One blanket is your bed, and the other is to cover up," he explained. "That passage leads to the bath. Unfortunately there is only cold water. Please don't leave the fan running overnight. You know, it's dangerous."

I nodded obediently.

After the sun had gone down, I was writing in my journal when I heard a soft knock at the door. I opened it and saw the novice. "What . . . ," I started to ask, but the young monk quickly put a finger to his lips. Then he gestured for me to follow him.

I slipped into my shower sandals and closed the door quietly behind me, feeling my way behind the Korean man. He led me on a path uphill in the dark night. I tripped a few times on slippery rocks because it was so dark, painfully stubbing my toes. The novice still wouldn't let me use any light. *If I had known we were going mountain climbing, I would have put on better shoes!*

Finally we reached a distant building. "That's the tea house," he whispered and pushed open a sliding door. "Take off your shoes," he murmured.

I slid off my sandals, and we crept through along the entrance hall in our sock feet. Then he pushed another door open, led me into an inner room, and finally turned on a light. The walls were made of light-colored wood and paper, through which the lighting cast a warm, pleasant glow. In the back of the room stood a long floor table set with many tea cups and pots.

"We will perform a tea meditation. Monks in my rank are actually not allowed to do it yet, but I have very nimble fingers." The novice winked at me through his glasses. Then he went behind the short table and proceeded to pour water from a ceramic vessel into an electric kettle. "Have a seat."

Using wooden tongs, the young monk made a little tower out of tea cups. When the first press was ready, he poured the tea in the top cup so that it went cascading over the sides into the other cups like a fountain. Then he poured out the cups using the tongs and poured a second press. This one was for us to drink.

"What now?" I asked in anticipation.

"Now we talk. That is the heart of meditation." The novice chuckled.

"Aren't you afraid of getting in trouble if someone finds us?" I asked.

"The others are all watching TV or sleeping right now. Just like every night. They won't find us."

I was baffled. "Monks watch TV?"

"Don't you?" he threw the question back at me.

"Not very often," I admitted. "It makes me kind of lethargic. That's why I never got a TV." I sniffed the tea's delicious aroma and took another sip. "Why did you come to the monastery?"

My conversation partner leaned forward a bit. "Searching for peace. My studies were very stressful."

There was a tone in his voice I couldn't quite figure out. "Then you've surely come to the right place," I confirmed. The surrounding nature alone could hardly have been more peaceful and idyllic.

"I don't know."

"What? You don't know?!" *Again with this tone. It sounds almost like . . . is he disappointed?* I reached for the teapot, but the novice picked it up first and poured more tea for me.

Then he continued thoughtfully. "Buddha said we are all alike. But here I often feel like a slave."

What?! That came as a surprise. "Whose slave? The other monks'?"

The novice did not grow agitated, but he did not deny it. I took his silence as confirmation. "Maybe it's just supposed to be like that at the beginning of your training? To teach you something?" I suggested.

The young Korean pulled up a corner of his mouth. "Many of the monks look a lot more gentle on the outside than they really are, but it's actually very hierarchical here. Like in the army."

With all of that, it wasn't hard to understand why he would be moody, especially considering other things I had found out. For example, they beat the drum for the wake-up call at 3:00 a.m., and the strict daily schedule makes it impossible to get more than six hours of sleep a night. *I'd get pretty sick of that after a couple of weeks.* Apparently sleep deprivation got to some of the monks, and they became short-tempered with the poor novice.

"What do you think? Was it a mistake for you to come here?" I inquired.

"I think everything has a price. We don't get peace without giving something for it. Buddha said, 'No one saves us but ourselves.'" The novice poured more tea. He did not seem willing to disclose any more.

"You are a Christian, I assume? What does your faith say?" he said, turning the tables.

I furrowed my brow. "Do you really want to know?"

"You people from the West are so strong and powerful when it comes to business," said the young monk. "Why are you so hesitant and shy when it comes to your religion?"

Interesting observation. "If you will permit me," I began, "I'll start with Buddha's saying: 'No one saves us but ourselves.' I don't believe we are in any way able to save ourselves. Trying to do so just puts more pressure on us to perform. Demands and expectation that we can never fulfill. I believe that God alone can save us." I knew that was challenging to his faith, but he had asked for my honest opinion.

The novice shook his head. "Each person has to do something to make progress. It's that way in Christianity too. Do good, keep the commandments, things like that."

"A lot of people think that is true," I agreed, "but Christianity is really very different. Being a Christian is not about good deeds or following rules but about a relationship with God. And because He loves us, a desire grows inside of us and also the strength to do good. I am convinced that nothing can change us like love. And nothing grants us as much peace as knowing that we are loved."

A deep stillness ensued. My words echoed in my own head. I truly believe that a deep longing for love is the motivation for most of what we do in life. And we spend a lot of time trying to earn love and recognition with accomplishments and good performance. It's funny. If we know that money can't buy love, then why do we think accomplishments can?

The novice collected our cups and washed them in a bowl with old tea water. He looked me straight in the eye. "That was the tea meditation. We should go to sleep now."

I stayed in the monastery four days—enough time to see what the novice meant by a hierarchy "like in the army." I helped him for a few hours each day gardening and cleaning, and I observed how people treated him. In my opinion it was not promoting his inner peace as much as he had hoped. Quite the opposite. I wished him well. *I hope he finds what he is looking for.*

After leaving the monastery, my hitchhiking took me further through Korea until I finally returned to Seoul. I had spent almost six months in that country, and although at first it was hard to imagine, I could now communicate with the people using normal, daily speech. I finally had the opportunity to do what I had wanted to do earlier: I could thank all of the wonderful people who had helped me during my stay.

I invited Choe and his wife to a Korean barbeque restaurant. It was nothing compared to what they had done for me, but I was so excited to be able to speak with Choe man-to-man! It was a little like talking to my own personal hero for the first time.

As in almost every country, I would have liked to stay longer. But it had been three years since I had left home, and I hadn't seen my family in all that time. Something was telling me that it was time to move on.

I traveled one last time to Busan and took the ferry to Japan. The ferry was equipped with this incredible hydrofoil technology that lifted the passenger ship almost completely out of the water, dramatically decreasing the resistance. We put the 125-mile stretch at sea behind us in less than three hours. Our ferry, although it weighed several tons, looked like it was floating over the water. *Crazy! Twice as fast as a normal container ship, easy!*

13

THE WORLD'S BEST SOUP

UPON MY LANDING in the port city of Fukuoka, the immigration officer seemed worried. It looked as if I would not be allowed to enter Japan. And in that case I would have to either pay my own way back to Korea or maybe even go to Germany. I was horrified. *I didn't picture the end of my journey coming as such a surprise!* The problem was that I didn't have a plane or ferry ticket to leave Japan. The Japanese wanted to make sure that if I entered the country, I would also exit it in a predictable amount of time. *Bureaucracy . . .*

I was completely at the mercy of the immigration officer, so I tried to be friendly while describing my plan to go to Tokyo to get a visa for China and then travel to Shanghai. I also gave the addresses of contacts that I had in Japan, thanks to my many travels. The addresses, thank the Lord, seemed to convince her. She stamped my passport and I was allowed to enter.

I visited a tourist office in the port terminal to find out how I could continue traveling. Fukuoka did not have a lot to offer, other than that ramen noodles were invented there. *How special could a noodle soup be?*

While trying to exit through the glass doors into the sunny parking lot, a middle-aged woman started talking to me. It was the lady from Immigration. I recognized her by the prominent birthmark on her right cheek, as well as her thin lips and round eyes.

Uh oh, what's going on? I wondered. *Did they make a mistake? Are they going to send me away after all?* But then I noticed that she was not dressed in her work clothes.

"I just got off work and have some free time. If you like, I can tell you a little about Fukuoka," she offered.

I breathed a sigh of relief. Apparently everything was okay. "Thank you, but I'm leaving right away for Hiroshima," I said.

"Then you have to go to the train station? My husband and son are about to pick me up. We can drive you there if you like."

Wow! Sounds great. The train station would probably be a good place to start hitchhiking to Hiroshima. I gratefully accepted the offer. While we waited together, she suggested I join her family for lunch. *I've definitely never had such a warm welcome from an immigration officer!*

Her husband and son picked us up in a white, compact Japanese car. That was an experience in itself. Whereas Europeans like streamlined, aerodynamic cars, the cars in Japan look like pastel-colored boxes on four wheels. The front part of the car is as squished up as possible, the passenger area is a square with right angles, barely tall enough to get in, and there is practically no backside. This questionable, lightweight design is called a Kei car and comes with tax benefits. To be honest, the functionality made it look like a big Playmobil car. Fun but somehow not realistic. However, if you think this market would be prime for fancy German cars, you'd be wrong. The Japanese are very loyal to their homeland's industry and avoid overseas products as passionately as a lazy student avoids homework. (Let it be noted here that studies show that homework is of minimal use anyway, unless the goal is to torture children. For that it is certainly effective!)

Thanks to the Playmobil cars, the street traffic looks like a playground. The white taxis straight out of anime and the children's school uniforms increase the sensation of being in a comic book. This society is, however, in no way childish. It functions like a Swiss clock. The Japanese *always* obey the traffic laws. Although this is impressive, I had to wonder if there is not a kind of island fever that alters people's brains. Just like in England, Australia, and Fiji, the Japanese drive on the wrong side of the road (the left, that is). For this illness I would like to send my get-well wishes to all island inhabitants!

Unlike the immigration officer, who had learned English as a child in the United States, her husband and son spoke no English. I found it interesting that the son, who was about my age, was wearing an FC Bayern-München jacket of a German soccer team. "A souvenir from a trip to Germany," his mother explained. *Whether you like this team or not, Germany seems to have made a good impression on him.*

We parked a few blocks away from the restaurant and walked the last bit. We had to walk in the street because, other than on main thoroughfares, there were no sidewalks. Something else was missing too. *Where is the color?* The entire area was various shades of gray and brown. There were no plants, and the tiled buildings looked like industrial buildings from the seventies. *I thought everything in Japan was modern!* I later found out that those buildings were very modern—but in Japanese culture, they try to attract as little attention as possible. But when the Japanese do decide that they want to attract attention, then they go all the way!

We came to an entrance in a building where two ventilators were having a blowing contest. It looked more like a back entrance rather than the front. The sliding door reminded me of something that should lead to a bedroom. Not at all like an entrance to a restaurant. A light-blue tin bucket bobbling in front of the door was the only thing that gave the nondescript building a hint of character.

"If the blue bucket is hanging here, then the restaurant is open. If not, it's closed," the lady from Immigration explained. I had just started to wonder why they don't use a simple door sign when she added, "The owner is kind of special."

Right when we were about to go in, a young employee shot out of the door, almost as if she expected us. She wore light blue, contrasting sharply with her black ponytails and apron. "You have to wait," she said quickly and disappeared back inside.

So we waited. And waited. And waited. Little by little people left the restaurant. *There must be plenty of room now!* But the employee still wouldn't let us enter. "The owner is kind of special," the lady had said. *I guess she's right.*

After an eternity, they finally let us in. Inside it looked like a normal street restaurant. Simple brown carpet with no decoration. Four brown tables just big enough for two to the left. About ten steps straight ahead you could see the half-open kitchen. I stifled a laugh: more than half of the tables were not occupied. *Why did they make us wait so long?*

"*ARIGATO GOSAIMAS!*" someone belted at us from the kitchen before we sat down. He was the oldest person in the room, apparently the owner, and it sounded like he had just ordered his archenemy to be executed. *Arigato gosaimas,* as I already knew, meant "Thank you very much" in Japanese.

A split second later both of the employees yelled in perfect unison, *"Arigato gosaimas!"*

Aha! It must also serve as a way to greet someone politely. We sat down and all ordered the same thing: pork ramen.

"ARIGATO GOSAIMAS!" thundered through the room. I unintentionally shrank back until I identified the source of this verbal attack: someone who had stood up to leave. Like gunshots from a pistol, the employees immediately replied, *"Arigato gosaimas!"*

I grinned at the immigration officer. "Very militaristic here!"

"It's like that in a lot of ramen restaurants. And this restaurant is even more . . . special."

A good amount of time passed before our food was served. I stood up to take a picture.

"STOP!" the owner bellowed in a tone that froze the blood in my veins.

"It is forbidden to take pictures here," explained the lady. "As I said, the owner is kind of . . ."

"Yes, I know, special!" I laughed.

In the meantime the restaurant had emptied out even more. Nevertheless, other guests who had arrived were forced to wait outside the door. Anytime anyone left or entered, they were addressed with an aggressive-sounding *"Arigato gosaimas!"* There was enough force behind those words to blow-dry your hair. *I wouldn't be surprised if the cook were slicing onions with a katana sword, screaming like a samurai warrior at the same time.*

"Itidakimas." We wished each other bon appetite, and I grabbed my chopsticks.

"Uhm," the lady whispered. "The owner has a rule that you try the soup before you eat the noodles. He is kind of—"

"I understand!" Smiling, I picked up the curved Japanese spoon, dipped it in the soup, and tasted it.

Whoosh!

I think I lost my mind for a moment. It was a taste explosion, catapulting me from the restaurant into culinary heaven. Without meaning to, I groaned uncontrollably. *Oh my goodness!* Eating that spoonful was like sinking my teeth into the juiciest, most intense, best-seasoned piece of pork roast ever to grace the face of the earth.

"*Oishi?*" ("Tasty?") The lady from Immigration was visibly enjoying the moment.

"Yes, unbelievably good!" And then I was swept away once again! "I've never—"

"SILENCE!" the owner interrupted in a murderous tone, and the employee explained quickly that talking is forbidden.

His demeanor is pretty weird, but for this delight I would gladly crawl on my hands and knees if I had to!

Now that we were silent, only the loud slurping of the guests could be heard. Slurping loudly when you eat noodles in Japan is considered good manners. It shows that the food tastes good. *If my mother only knew that my slurping was a constant compliment to her cooking, she surely would have reacted differently when I was a child.*

After lunch we thanked the great flavor-master and were catapulted out the door with one last explosive *Arigato gosaimas!*

Indeed, kind of . . . special.

October 2016

From Fukuoka I caught a ride with a Japanese couple headed toward Hiroshima. Once again, thanks to my offline translator app, we could understand each other surprisingly well. *So unbelievable what technology makes possible.* About halfway there, I found out my drivers hadn't actually planned to leave Fukuoka that day, but when they saw me with my sign, they thought they could do me a favor by driving me 150 miles to Hiroshima and back. When I figured that out, after an hour of driving, I insisted that they drop me off at the next rest stop so that I could hitch a ride with someone who was planning to go there anyway. We had already had lots of fun together and they had taken tons of pictures. If I had let them, they really would have driven more than three hundred miles, just to take me to Hiroshima!

When you mention Hiroshima, most people think about the atomic bombs dropped there by the US at the end of World War II. I had to ask myself why more than two million people live there nowadays. *Isn't the region still contaminated with radiation?*

I found out that there is a big difference between an atom bomb exploding in the air and on the ground. If it detonates on the ground, the radiation stays in the earth and surrounding area, causing long-term contamination. However, if it explodes in the air, as in the cases of Hiroshima and Nagasaki, the initial damage is more severe, but the radioactive material disseminates more quickly over a much larger area, and the long-term contamination is greatly reduced. The most dangerous materials are released within the first few weeks, and the rest spreads out so thinly that it is practically harmless. All over the globe, naturally occurring concentrations of radiation can be found that are higher than what remains from the atomic bombs detonated in Japan. These facts are what make nuclear power plants so questionable. If they blow up, there is only one place it can happen: on the ground.

I finally made it to the city that had actually been the first target for the bombs: Kyoto. This city had been Japan's capital for centuries, and later it remained the location of the imperial court, making it a highly treasured historical site. It is a miracle that it survived the war practically unscathed. For quite some time it was in first place on the list of cities to bomb, above Hiroshima and Nagasaki.

Luckily for Japan and all of us tourists, a single man stood against this decision: Secretary of War Henry Stimson. He had visited Kyoto twenty years earlier and had developed an emotional attachment to the city. Rumor has it he spent his honeymoon there. Motivated by these memories, he set about trying to get Kyoto removed from the list. Due to his direct line to the president, he was successful.

In retrospect, it is incredible that the fate of the more than two million people living in Kyoto at the time hung on one man, more specifically, one man's vacation memories. This is powerful proof for how much traveling can affect our behavior. Life experiences carry much more weight than dried-up theories. These experiences leave a permanent impression on us. I am more sure than ever that everyone can benefit from being abroad for an extended amount of time and discovering something new. Goethe said, "The best education for a clever person is found in travel." If Goethe said it, it must be true!

They have a saying in Japanese that every young person who wants to travel should know: "可愛い子には旅をさせよ." This means, "If you love your child, let them travel." Isn't that incredible? Since almost all parents love their children, they'll have to let them go! Worst-case scenario: they'll say, "I'm not interested in Japanese sayings. You're staying here." It's still worth a try.

In any case, I still think a trip is always worth the trip!

By the way, Japan is worth the trip too! Unfortunately Japan's worth also shows in its high prices. Therefore I made every effort to get to Tokyo as quickly as possible so I could snatch up a visa for China.

As most people know, Tokyo is Japan's capital city. But most people don't know what *Tokyo* means. In Japanese, *to* means "east," and *kyo* is a shortened form of *Kyoto*. So Tokyo is the Kyoto of the east, the capital city in the east. Just imagine if we did that too. Instead of Berlin, we would say "Capital City in the East."

Hamburg, where I am from, would be "The Middle of the World." We Germans do have some cities indicating location; they are just not poetic, such as Darmstadt, which means "Bowels City." *Fail.*

The basic attitude toward life is completely different in Japan. For example, whereas most Germans choose their profession to make money, it's about something else for most people in Japan: they use their work to justify their lives—to prove that they are worthy of living and that they can contribute something useful to society in their position. It's no wonder they would die for their work. Occasionally they actually do so. A word for working yourself literally to death has developed in Japanese: *karoshi.* For some, offering your life in service to your company is an honorable death. To me, it is tragic.

Great variation can be found within Japanese culture as well. The inhabitants of Osaka have earned a reputation throughout Japan for being crazier and more open than the rest of the country. The best way to illustrate this is with a simple street experiment. If you find yourself in Osaka and are feeling courageous enough, point your finger at a complete stranger and pretend to shoot him.

I tried it, and it worked! Just a point and the word "Bang!" is enough to make most people in Osaka spontaneously deliver a dramatic death scene. It doesn't matter if they are teenagers, retirees, or businessmen and businesswomen—they play along, and it ends in hearty laughter on both sides. Some of them pull their own imaginary weapons and pantomime shooting back at their attacker.

That is something that you'll only experience in Osaka!

December 2016

From Osaka, I took the ferry to Shanghai. Even though Germany was still so far away, I had the feeling that the greatest challenges were behind me. After all, from here I could go all the way home on solid ground. Further travel wasn't dependent on finding a place on a boat.

At least, that's what I thought.

Although hitchhiking is practically unheard of in China, it worked fabulously. The reason for this is that Chinese people are very curious and have no sense of restraint. Most of them don't seem to be bothered by anything. (Not the noise, nor the smells, nor the tight, crowded spaces. No one minds if you let your child poop in a plastic bag out in public. Yep, things like that happen all the time.)

For example, they apparently thought it was totally normal for dozens of people to surround me while I painted my hitchhiking signs. On such occasions many assumed I spoke fluent Chinese because the characters on my sign were so neat and detailed. I had just copied them carefully from my cell phone, of course.

Other than a couple of basic phrases, I communicated by means of an app on my phone. Once, a Chinese businessman and his wife, whom I had met hitchhiking, invited me to dinner in a restaurant. Since they had never met a white man before, this was a special occasion for them. He called a few of his friends too. When we arrived at the restaurant, the waitress led us to a private room. Such dining rooms are common in East Asia, making it possible to converse with each other undisturbed. The room was built with decorated tiles, dark wooden walls, and shiny trim. The businessman took my phone and drew some characters in the translator app. Then he gave it back to me to read: "Do you like Chinese food?"

I typed back, saying I would eat anything they ate. And more. The man nodded in satisfaction and ordered some food without looking at a menu. Then we sat down. At first, it was just the three of us, but the businessman's friends began to trickle in until there were seven of us. While they were arriving, the waitstaff kept putting more and more bowls on the large glass lazy Susan in the middle of the table until the wooden legs began to groan under the weight. There was soup with fish and beef, tofu, eggplant, chicken, fruit, peanuts (candied, salted, and roasted), mushrooms, and much more that I couldn't identify. We turned the lazy Susan around slowly so that each person could take some of everything.

The meal had barely begun when the shot glasses were filled. My host made a toast: "To Kis!" We clinked glasses and tossed back the booze. He meant "Chris," of course. That would be me. To be respectful, I made a toast back to my host. No one understood what I said, but the gesture toward the businessman made my meaning clear.

I had barely swallowed the fiery liquid before my neighbor tried to fill it again. "No, thank you. No liquor. Only beer. I am German!" I explained and held my hand over my glass. *If they go on like this, it won't end well!*

Luckily they understood and ordered a beer for me. It was a true feast. Every time a plate was emptied, a fresh dish was added. Cigarette smoke mixed in with the aroma of food. To my surprise, they threw their chicken bones behind them and dropped their cigarette butts on the floor. Sometimes they just spit them out. *That explains why there is only tile here and no carpet.*

Everyone at the table, other than the wife and me, smoked and drank like my parents' car. When we had filled our stomachs to the point of bursting, the four friends decided to try to get me drunk. One after another, they poured me a drink, clinked my glass, and chugged theirs down. I had to do the same to avoid insulting them.

It seemed a little unfair: four to one. Plus, I was out of practice since I had abstained from alcohol since being in Guiana. But in this situation I did have one crucial advantage: they didn't seem to notice that they were drinking hard alcohol while I was drinking beer—from the same size glasses.

It took a good hour before the four friends were lying on the table, and we had to call it a night. *And it's only a little after nine. Heh, heh.*

While traveling, I had heard lots of stories from Chinese people about their countrymen, and this evening fit their descriptions perfectly. It had very little in common with going to a Chinese restaurant in Germany. The excess of smoking and drinking, the toasts, the unusual table manners—not to mention that about two-thirds of the food did not get eaten.

That last part made me sad. But the New Year festival was not far away, and the Chinese always leave a lot of food uneaten during this time. It is supposed to bring abundance in the coming year.

Although Japan, China, and Korea are relatively close geographically, I was yet again reminded of how diverse these countries are. The food alone is completely different in China and Japan. Japanese and Korean people feel deeply offended if someone thinks they are Chinese because they think of the Chinese as some Europeans think of Americans: they are loud and have poor manners.[1] How could anyone confuse them? In the end, it all comes down to perspective. What is polite in one country is not in another. It is just as important to learn a country's body language as well as their spoken language.

I concluded that although it is wonderful to see diverse, sometimes breathtaking landscapes, that wasn't the best part of traveling. In fact, it comes in third place. The culinary experiences were definitely more fabulous and fascinating!

However, by far the best thing about traveling is meeting people along the way. A beautiful landscape can be enjoyed for a moment and then maybe later with pictures, although the reality can never be adequately relayed in pictures. But we carry the stories and people we befriend with us forever. They shape who we are.

---

1   Let it be known that the American translator said that Americans are loud and have poor manners, not me! Sincerely, Chris.

Upon arriving in Peking (Beijing), I quickly understood why you shouldn't visit China in winter: the city was engulfed in a thick, brownish-gray, smoggy cloud-soup. The pollution came mainly from factories outside of the city, but it was captured in the city limits due to weather patterns. Since the conditions were categorized as hazardous in the news, I bought a breathing mask in a drug store. I looked like I had just fled from a hard-core, techno rave as I went sightseeing in the city.

I was not alone; countless others also chose to protect themselves from the polluted air with a sweaty, sticky mask. It was worth braving the pollution, though, as I got to indulge in culinary delights such as original Peking duck and a few fried scorpions.

Although the smog seemed to be constantly present, the poisonous layer lifted the day I visited the Great Wall of China. Finally I could enjoy blue sky, sunshine, and oxygen! The part of the wall I visited had been restored so perfectly that I couldn't tell which parts were ancient and which were new. The orderly brickwork and pointed fortifications were simply gorgeous everywhere I looked.

However, the vast majority of the Great Wall is in disrepair. It was not built with stone but with clay and earth. Therefore, you can't take a romantic bike ride for days along the wall, as some people imagine.

Another widespread myth is that you can see the Wall of China from the moon. Unfortunately that is not possible, since it is nowhere near wide enough. But it's a great marketing gimmick! At the largest point it is about fifty feet wide. In comparison to the 238,900 miles that the moon is away from the earth, that would be like seeing a hair from a mile away with the naked eye. If you can do that, then you can probably see your house from the moon—as long as your house is at least fifty feet wide. Good luck!

Despite this little disappointment, the wall was very impressive. In terms of mass and volume, it is still the largest structure in the world. And it winds along large, steep cliffs. *It's mind boggling to consider how much time, energy, labor, and money it must have required to build!*

Considering its original purpose, the wall was perhaps the worst political investment made in centuries. This construction project, which cost hundreds of thousands of lives, was supposed to protect the Chinese from their northern enemies. It didn't work. Instead of storming the fortresses, the enemies just bribed the guards and ended up gaining free access. Tragically humorous. The devil's in the details. If you're not careful about the small matters, then the important things will come to ruin.

I spent Christmas in Xi'an, where the truly impressive two-thousand-year-old archeological site of the Terracotta Army is located. Then, I traveled south to Guilin to see the cormorant fishers at work. Instead of fishing with a rod and hook, they catch fish using lamps and a tame cormorant bird. They go out on the river at night and light their lamps. The light draws the deepest fish up to the surface, and then the cormorant bird jumps in the water and catches a fish. A string around the bird's neck prevents it from swallowing the fresh catch so that the owner can just snatch the fish out of its mouth. The pictures of this ancient craft were so phenomenal that I just had to see it with my own eyes.

Near Xi'an I slept in my tent in 25-degree weather. Just one day later and six hundred miles south in Guilin, I was able to walk around in a T-shirt. What a difference in temperature!

I struck out on foot to explore the area. While I was trekking along the unpaved paths, it was not my massive backpack that took my breath away but the landscape! The rich green rice and vegetable fields were polka-dotted with the yellow straw hats of Chinese workers digging in the earth and tying bundles of plants together. Spread out around the fields were simple houses with little bamboo forests and gigantic water buffalo. *I sure would like to ride one of those sturdy animals like the children here do!*

My gaze was captured most irresistibly by the enormous, peaked mountains jutting up out of the ground. They looked like sugar loafs—like something from a dream, simultaneously sur-real and familiar. A babbling brook flowed at the foot of the stone giants. *If I ever retire, this would be the perfect place*, popped into my head. *Provided the nature remains like it is.*

I followed a stony footpath to the village. It had gotten late, and the evening sun threw its warm glow on the white houses. A couple of dogs wandered around, and many of the doors were standing open so that you could peek right into the houses. I caught a glimpse of a por-trait of Mao Zedong hanging over an old-fashioned sofa. A Chinese family made up of a mother, grandmother, and four children sat in the front yard. *Dude! Real, authentic Chinese life in the country. That's just what I wanted to see.* I silently enjoyed the scene. I greeted them with "*Ni hao!*" when I walked past, and they smiled at me.

My feet led me to a stone pier with raft-like boats bobbing up and down next to it. They were made of six thick poles tied together. Upon closer inspection I was disappointed to see that the poles were made of plastic, not bamboo. *If there are any cormorant fishers in this region, this would be the spot.*

I let my backpack slide to the ground and squatted on the shore, quietly watching until sundown. The current made little eddies on the surface, and the silhouettes of bamboo reflected off the peaceful water in the darkness. People had begun cooking din-ner in their houses. The soft music of drums, bells, and something like a bagpipe floated over from the other shore. They must have been celebrating something because I also heard the delayed crack of fireworks from time to time.

As I was sitting on the shore, my thoughts drifted from the fishermen and celebrations to where I would sleep that night. That brought a Chinese saying to mind: "If you want to be happy for an hour, take a nap. If you want to be happy for a day, go fishing. If you want to be happy for a month, get married. If you want to be happy for a year, inherit a fortune. If you want to be happy for your whole life, help other people."

Valuable and challenging! I wasn't quite sure about the time estimates though. *Watching cormorant fishing would definitely make me happy for more than one day.*

The first person I met in the descending darkness was a middle-aged man going to wash his pants in a tin bucket. "Excuse me," I said to make my presence known immediately.

The man seemed irritated. But when I handed him my cell phone, he took it willingly. I had prepared the phrase: "Where can I find cormorant fishermen? I want to fish with them."

The man mumbled each word out loud. When he finished, he shook his head smiling. I quickly showed him how to respond on my phone.

Then I read the translation: "Cormorant no. Only for tourists. Fishing is forbidden everywhere."

What? He can't be serious! I asked what the boats at the pier were for. "Transportation. The government forbids fishing."

What a bummer! Well, I should have expected the enormous economic growth to have changed things, even in remote areas like this. Despite the fact that it fits so many stereotypes.

I thanked the gentleman and left him to his task of scrubbing his pants. *The magical atmosphere of this place was still worth the trip. Our earth is, beyond a shadow of a doubt, an unsurpassable work of art. This diversity, these details, this beauty!*

14

FORK IN THE ROAD

I SPENT NEW YEAR'S EVE on the phone with Michal. We both had the feeling that we knew each other well even though we had never met face-to-face—if you don't count video messaging. Getting to know someone this way was somehow strange but exciting too. It's so different from meeting someone in daily life. Concentrated. More intense. I, for one, felt the excitement between us growing more and more. I still didn't know if Michal felt that way or if she just thought of me as a good friend.

From Guilin I hitchhiked to Vietnam. Communist banners at the border reminded travelers right away who had won the Vietnam War. Hint: it wasn't the United States.

Even though you read a lot about restrictions and surveillance, what I experienced in Vietnam was quite the opposite: total freedom. In daily life, it seemed like almost everything was allowed—or at least not punished. So much happens through friendships and not on paper. At least not on bureaucratic paper. Maybe it has to do with the dense populations of such countries. It forces you to be very personal and intimate when dealing with people. Much more friendly than in the regulated, big cities in the West. In hindsight, this approach is much more humane—it made me feel welcomed; a warm, fuzzy feeling.

To my delight, Vietnam turned out to be a country full of good-hearted people, glorious landscapes, and delicious, exotic foods. It was also one of the most affordable countries in South Asia. But, you have to be careful what you order. Even though people talk about the Chinese eating dogs, our four-legged friends end up on the table much more often in Vietnam. At least that's what it seemed like to me. Cats, too, by the way. However, dogs are eaten in many countries where you wouldn't expect it, including Korea, French Polynesia, Northeast India, Hawaii, and sometimes even in Switzerland!

January 2017

When my visa ran out, I decided to travel to Laos and apply for another visa so that I could return to Vietnam right away. Vietnam had so many advantages to offer, and I had made lots of friends there. It was the ideal place to rent a room near the beach and write about my travels. Although I had kept a journal nonstop, I wanted to organize my experiences on paper before returning to Germany. After all, who could predict when or if I would have the chance once I was back in the middle of the quick-paced daily life of Germany?

Upon arriving in Vientiane, the capital of Laos, I went straight to the Vietnamese embassy. The sooner I had a visa in my hot little hand, the better. On the way, I met some gas smugglers who were planning to drive back to Vietnam in a week, and they were willing to take me with them. If I had my new visa by then, I could make it back to Vietnam to spend Chinese New Year with my friends.

On the corner in front of the embassy, I changed out of my dirty undershirt into a clean polo. Some official agencies have dress codes. *I don't want to risk it.* Then I went in. The office consisted of one bright, tiled room with a shiny, polished counter at one end. To the right, plastic chairs were attached to a metal bar, kind of like in airports.

The clerk gave me two forms that had become routine to me after so much traveling. I quickly filled them out. When I gave the documents back, she offered to process them right away for a surcharge. It seemed like a great offer, but since she asked for twice the normal fee, I declined. That turned out to be a lucky choice.

I was just about to go when a young, European-looking couple came in. Their dark tans and sun-bleached hair made it obvious that they weren't just out for a little hike, but had been on the road for quite some time.

"Where are you from?" I asked curiously.

"Poland," the man curtly replied.

"Been on the road for a long time?" I guessed.

"Yes. Many months. We came here without flying."

I laughed. "Really? Me too! What route did you take?"

Now they seemed more interested. "We came across Russia, Mongolia, and then China. And you?"

"I came the other way around. Over the Atlantic and Pacific. Soon I'll go through India and on to Europe."

"Oh!" The woman looked surprised. "Then you are planning to fly?"

Confused, I shook my head. "No, that's not an option for me. Why?"

"Then how will you get to India?"

"Through Myanmar," I suggested. After all, it's the closest way by land. I read up on it six months ago. At that time the borders were open.

"Sorry, bro," the man took over. "The border between India and Myanmar is shut airtight. We just checked. Otherwise we would have come that way too."

Gulp! If he's right, that will spoil my plans. And I just have to go to India!

I quickly said goodbye and beelined it for the nearest café with Wi-Fi. I left my passport at the Vietnamese embassy. Since I hadn't paid the surcharge, thank God, I still had until late that afternoon to let them know if I wanted a visa or not. It was already about noon.

My research showed that the Polish couple was right: Myanmar had closed the border to India five months ago. I had to scrap my plan. But I was absolutely not going to take an airplane. I didn't want to spoil the nice feeling of traveling that I had preserved so carefully. After all, when you fly, you get in at one place and get out in a completely different place without having experienced what is in between. I had already made it across the Atlantic and the Pacific without an airplane. I was determined to see it through to the end.

I had two options: I could go back to China and then travel through former Soviet-bloc countries on to Europe. That meant cold weather, more expensive visas that were harder to get, and I wouldn't go to India. The other option: although there are no ferries between Southeast Asia and India and almost no boat traffic, I could, nevertheless, try to find a way across the Indian Ocean.

The first option was more of a sure thing. I had just read in Internet forums that a few backpackers in Thailand had just tried option two and were not successful. To travel to India without flying, you have to have a visa in advance. It takes a few weeks to get one. So I had to apply and pay without even knowing if I would find a way to get there. Option two was "all or nothing."

If I go that route, I'll find a boat the way I always have in the past. A little more research revealed that, unfortunately, very few sailors stop in India due to the overwhelming amount of red tape. *Doesn't look good. When is the sailing season for the Indian Ocean, anyway?* That was easy to find out too. A couple of clicks and to my surprise, it was exactly . . . *now*!

Time for thinking had already run out. The Vietnamese embassy would close in a few minutes, and if I wanted my passport back to go looking for a boat, I had to cancel the visa for Vietnam right away. *Option one or option two?* I thought feverishly.

Option one made the most sense on a practical level. But when I asked God what I should do, I suddenly had the unexpected certainty that I should go for option two. This feeling is hard to describe: it's a little bit like an inner compass pointing the way. I'm usually more of a math-and-science kind of guy, and I'm suspicious of vague feelings. In this case, however, it was different. It felt as if someone was not just waving me toward a fence post but whacking me over the head with it so I would get the point—much like back in Spain, when I met the sailing teacher right before crossing the Atlantic, or when I almost had to fly home to reregister my residence, but a broken printer saved the day. During those times, I had this same "compass feeling." All arrows pointed toward go, and everything worked out. Same with the boat from the Philippines to Korea.

Let me be clear: this is not a feeling that I've had often. On the contrary, it's extremely rare. But very clear. *Just like now.*

I've never talked to anyone about the Myanmar route before. And just when I mention it, it happens to be the time to sail. I haven't rented an apartment in Vietnam yet; I haven't even gotten the visa. I'm still flexible. I'm traveling southwest right now anyway.

The decision was made. Having spent lots of time with sailors, I knew where to start: *Thailand, here I come!*

❖

From Vientiane I traveled to Bangkok and sent my passport and the necessary documents to Germany to request a visa for India. My family could also apply for a visa to Pakistan and Iran for me. It is not expressly forbidden to travel without identification in many countries. However, you still have to be able to prove who you are, which is why I would not recommend traveling without ID if you can avoid it.

It would take a couple of weeks for my passport to get to Germany and back. I planned to find a boat during this time. My starting point was the island of Phuket. Next to Langkawi in Malaysia, it has the most yacht traffic on that side of the Indian Ocean. The wiry Russian I had sailed to Korea with was living there, working with yachts. I had the perfect place to start.

When I arrived in Phuket, it turned out that the Russian captain with whom we had sailed was also working there at that exact time. Circumstances had brought all three of us back together. It was so great to see them again!

I helped them with their work. The wiry Russian treated me like a brother and let me sleep in his living room. He also introduced me to several key people to help me find a boat. He was so overwhelmingly kind! Thanks to him, in spite of the dire odds, it took only two weeks to find a boat planning to set sail at the beginning of March. This one even had a German skipper!

My passport completed its mission of securing visas and returned to me just days before my legal time in Thailand ran out. Had it taken a few more days, I would have had to pay a fine. But yet again, everything came together. Since I had a little time before the German skipper planned to depart, I planned to extend my visa for Thailand. So I took a detour down to Malaysia and Singapore. However, on the way back, just after crossing the border into Thailand on foot, I ran into some difficulties.

Reveling in the warm, pleasant evening, I walked along the main street of a border town looking for a good place to catch a ride. I had no idea how far I would have to go. The street flowed like waves over the hills, making it impossible to see very far. The paving stones turned from an ash-gray to clay-red beneath my flip-flops. Fans pumped the smell of fried chicken from food carts out into the street. The vendors sat on plastic chairs in the carts talking with friends and all who passed by. Packets of hot sauce and pieces of butcher paper were ready for customers to take their food to go. Along the street, scooters were parked under a tangle of electrical wires strung from one concrete pylon to the next.

After about fifteen minutes of walking, the shops and food carts were fewer and farther between. I still hadn't spotted a good place to catch a ride. *Would I be able to find one? I should have waited at the border.* But it was too late now.

"Excuse me just a moment." I waved to a married couple about to get in an olive-green compact car. They looked curiously at me. I got out my phone and showed them a message in Thai: "Could you drive me to the next major stoplight on a main road?"

"I can't read Thai," the man said in English. "We're from Malaysia. What do you want?"

Even better. I repeated the question in English.

"Of course we'll give you a lift," they agreed, and I squeezed into the back seat next to some shopping bags. The man started the car but just drove back and forth a little. Looking backward, I saw why: a scooter had blocked us in.

"We can do this," I swung the door open, picked up the scooter, and moved it back a little so the man could get out. When I hopped back in, they both thanked me. "Of course! No big deal," I said, shrugging it off. "Where are you going?"

"We're just looking for a pharmacy, so we can't take you far."

They dropped me off, in fact, less than a mile down the road next to a convenience store on a hill. *Better than nothing!* I set off on foot again, passing a nightclub where the police had pulled over a black SUV. A little ways down the road, I reached in my pocket for my phone to check my offline map. *Nothing.* I stuck my other hand in my other pocket, but it wasn't there. *This can't . . .* I frantically patted my pants pockets. *Empty. Where is my phone?!* I started to get nervous. The phone wasn't high-tech or anything, but it was still the most expensive piece of equipment I owned. And more importantly, its contents! *All my contacts, notes, pictures, communications—the telephone number of the German skipper.* Losing your phone is one of the biggest modern-day-luxury nightmares imaginable! Luxury aside, it *really* is a nightmare!

When did I use it last? I thought feverishly, holding my breath. *The compact car! It must have fallen out in the back seat.* I spun around and ran up the hill, backpack swinging wildly from side to side. My legs wore out quickly, and the weight felt heavier and heavier. I was out of breath but refused to stop. *You have to use the window of opportunity while it's still open!*

I pressed on, panting. Past the club, past the police car and the SUV. When I neared the store, I saw a small white car. *Is that it?* I couldn't quite remember the car's make or color. It was dark and I hadn't slept much, and I had ridden in so many cars that the details all blended together.

My heart skipped a beat when I looked through the window. No phone. Not even a back seat! *Wrong car. Noooo!* I looked around searching for clues. It didn't help. The car was gone and so was my cell phone. *I can't believe it!*

I rushed to the bar, where nothing had changed. I finally noticed that the SUV was a police car too.

"Excuse me," I gasped politely to the first available police-man. "TwopeopledrovemeandmyphonefelloutofmypocketandI

walkedawayandthennoticeditwasmissingandwhenIwentback
theyweregone!"

Even if the police had spoken English, they still wouldn't have understood me. I reached in my pocket to use my translator app, but my phone was gone!

The policeman knew that I wanted something. He gestured for me to get on his scooter with him to drive to the police station about two hundred yards away. *Maybe they can find the car on security cameras? And then stop them at the border to Malaysia? Or track them down sooner? There must be a way!*

The policeman took me to the precinct office where an officer who spoke a little English listened to my story. They asked me to wait for some of their colleagues, offering me a chair. I walked outside toward the entrance instead. The police obviously thought that was a little strange and waved for me to come back.

"I want to look at the street. Just in case they come back," I called over my shoulder. I was torn: the police were standing on one side, trying to convince me to come back in, but I couldn't help looking the other way at the cars driving by. I must have looked like someone having neck spasms.

"Can't we do this . . ." I suddenly interrupted myself. "There!"

A small, olive-green car drove by toward the store. *Could that be it?* The driver was in a shadow, bending over as if looking for something. My heart raced.

"I think I saw the car! I have to get to the convenience store! Quick!" I looked around expectantly. No one moved. I could see confusion written all over their faces. *They probably think I'm crazy. I can't blame them.* I hurried toward the entrance to go by foot.

"*Yoot!*" Someone yelled "stop" in Thai. "He'll drive you," said the English-speaking officer. Overjoyed, I jumped on the scooter, and we . . . didn't budge.

My driver exchanged a few words with the other officer. He

answered. And on and on. I don't know what they were saying. But I knew we weren't moving! After about thirty seconds, I jumped off the scooter and ran toward the entrance. *I don't have time for this. If the couple from Malaysia is looking for me, they won't look for long!*

"It's okay! He'll drive you!" the officer called out to me. While I was considering if I should believe him, the scooter caught up with me. I jumped on, and we took off, driving on the wrong side of the street. The median prevented us from getting over to the right side. *Are the police allowed to do this?* The thought sprung into my mind. *I don't care. Just as long as we get there fast!*

"Here, here, *yoot!*" I indicated that he should stop in front of the convenience store. There, in front of the entrance I saw . . . *the olive-green car!* I peeked through the window. *That's the right car!* But I didn't see my phone.

"Hey!" A street peddler called to me and pointed toward the club.

There, by the stoplight, stood the couple from Malaysia! They looked around, worried. "Thank you!" I called to the street peddler and ran off. "Over here! Hello!"

"We have your phone!" they called back.

When I reached them, I didn't say a word but gave them both a bear hug. It was awkward, and they did not seem to enjoy it. In Malaysia people probably do not go around gushing their emotions to total strangers. But I was just so happy! I had to show how grateful I was.

"We saw your phone when we were taking in the groceries, so we came right back," said the woman.

"I don't know how I can ever thank you!"

They repeated my words from earlier: "Of course! No big deal." After they drove away I shook my head. So much excitement to travel less than a mile!

Back in Phuket, the German skipper agreed to take me with him to the Andaman Islands, which belong to India. From there he planned to sail to Sri Lanka, and I would, in theory, catch a ferry to Calcutta.

Before taking on the Indian Ocean, we sailed to a cliff island belonging to Thailand. My new skipper was a hard-core adventurer of the Indiana Jones caliber. He was so rad!

The sight of the jungle island almost knocked me off my feet! The bay where we anchored was gigantic! The rocks had a grainy texture that ended up creating countless fissures and stalagmites, shooting up out of the water and opening up as gaping chasms. Monkeys hung from the steep cliffs, and in the background, the rugged landscape of the Phang Nga province rose up out of the water like the scales of an ancient dinosaur.

The skipper was excited: "It feels like a King Kong movie. We just need a giant gorilla up on the cliff, beating its chest!"

When the tide was out, we got the dinghy ready, grabbed some headlamps, and rowed to a cave across from where we had anchored. The ravages of time had dug deep into the cliff. Earlier in the day, the saltwater had hidden the cave's mouth, but now, low tide cleared the way to enter.

After a couple of turns, all daylight disappeared. The humid air was sticky and stagnate. Hosts of bats hung from the stalactites above. With their silky, brown pelts, shriveled-up little eyes, and flat snouts, they looked like pigs with wings. A variation of Homer Simpson's "Spider-pig" song started playing in my head: *Bat-pig, bat-pig, does whatever a bat-pig does.* I had to laugh. We rowed deeper and deeper inside until we reached a dead end. A wall blocked our way, but light shone from beneath the water.

"That must be a passageway!" the skipper concluded.

"I'll volunteer to be a test diver!"

"Go ahead!" he gave me the green light.

I slid into the water and swam about a hundred yards under the stalactites to where we thought there was an opening. I dove down, chasing the light. The passage felt small in comparison to the cave. About three feet wide, I guessed.

After just a few yards the hole opened up outside. I surfaced, wiped the saltwater out of my eyes, and was overwhelmed by the sight: *An enclosed lagoon in the middle of a mountain!* Cliffs shot up on all sides, rising up hundreds of feet like a giant kettle. To the north a branch of a river flowed to . . . *Where does it go? Maybe pirates hid their treasures here long ago!* It certainly fit the adventure-some atmosphere. I wanted to swim over to have a look, and then it dawned on me: *I have to find my way back!*

I restrained myself and turned to examine the gray, stone wall behind me. *Where the heck is the passage?* From the inside I had just followed the light. But from here I couldn't tell where the underwater entrance to the dark cave was located. The tide had already started to rise and the cave would soon be filled with water. If I didn't make it back fast, I would have to wait another ten hours for the next low tide. But even then there was no guarantee I would be able to find the tunnel. The skipper didn't even know if I had surfaced. *If I don't come back, he'll sound the alarm! I don't want to cause trouble.*

"Can you hear me?" I yelled at the top of my lungs and then listened. No answer. The water and cliffs made the area completely soundproof. I dove along the wall and felt the rough edges with my fingers. There were many massive holes big enough to dive in. The last thing I wanted was to choose the wrong underwater tunnel and drown! I surfaced, took a deep breathe, and thought about what to do. Waiting for low tide was not an option.

Wait a second! A few feet away a gentle eddy swirled in the water's surface. *It's flowing this way. If water is streaming in, then it must lead somewhere.* I dove down and felt along the wall, into the side of the mountain. The water was murky, and the farther I went, the darker it became. I was as blind as a bat. A burning in my lungs signaled that I was about to run out of air. I ignored it and swam on. *It has to lead up somewhere around here.*

My legs brushed against sharp edges. I reached up, hoping to find the cave so I could breath, but found only stone and water. I was about to panic. My heart raced, making me run out of air faster. I tried to calm myself down. Out of nowhere, a story told by Eric Thomas, a motivational speaker, came to mind. In the story a man longing for success went to see a wise man. The wise man led him to the sea and pushed him under the water. Afraid, he tried to defend himself, but the wise man just pushed him further under the water. Just before passing out, he allowed the wise man to lift him out. While he was still gasping for air, the wise man said, "If you want something as much as you wanted to breathe just now, you will get it."

Very motivating, but, to be honest, I'd rather breathe than find the stupid passageway! It's too dangerous. I turned back. Finding the way back was relatively easy. Just like the first time: *Follow the light!* But I had to go slowly to not hit my head on the stalactites.

Back outside I finally surfaced and gasped for air. I was over-joyed not to be wise enough to want the passageway more than breathing. When my pulse calmed down, I gave it another try. No success. It wasn't until the third time that I found my way back to the cave.

"What took you so long?" the skipper asked, relieved when he saw me swimming toward the dinghy.

"I almost couldn't find my way back!" I quickly described my dangerous experience and then started swooning about the lagoon. Hesitating, I let go of the boat. "I have to go back," I said. "Just three minutes."

"Be careful!" the skipper said, concerned. Then I dove down and reached the lagoon in a flash.

This time I memorized exactly where the tunnel was. I swam freestyle over to the river flowing out of the lagoon, just far enough to see that the river led to another lagoon. I was so excited that I stayed a lot longer than three minutes.

When I returned, the water level had risen, making the tunnel's entrance seem much lower. Luckily I knew exactly where I had to go.

"There are lots of lagoons. It's freaking amazing!" I sputtered right as I surfaced in the cave.

"We'll definitely have to come back again when the tide is out. Then I can dive and you can stay here!" said the skipper, delighted.

When we returned, we unfortunately did not find a hidden treasure chest full of gold. But we didn't need to either. *The real treasure is this phenomenally beautiful nature!*

<hr />

From Thailand we sailed to the Andaman Islands, which belong to India. Although they are far away from the mainland, the "exotic chaos and bustle" typical of India is present everywhere you look: honking, three-wheeled motorcycles; brightly painted, corrugated-metal houses; loud speakers screeching out competing Bollywood songs; the overwhelming smell of incense and spices; the even-more-overwhelming odor of the beggars; women in cheerful-colored saris; and, of course, numerous free-roaming cows scavenging for food among the mountains of trash.

Speaking of trash—it was everywhere! What would later be confirmed on the mainland was already obvious here: India has an enormous solid-waste problem. People throw plastic waste, packaging, really anything and everything simply everywhere. There is practically no trash service, and no one cares. It seems to be caused not just by poverty but, unfortunately, by the society and culture as well.

I have an Indian friend who spent a long time in Russia to complete part of his medical training. Upon returning home, he thought to himself, *India is like a giant zoo! The smells, the heat, the chaos, I couldn't help but think,* Where the hell am I?

When it comes to India, you either love it or you hate it. There's no in between. My first impression was: *I love it!* So much diversity and new, foreign things; it stole my heart in the blink of an eye. Nevertheless, I would soon witness the dark side of India.

Since he knew how ridiculously overblown the bureaucracy to enter and exit India is, the German skipper hired a travel agency to mitigate the process. When I disembarked, I had to pay a last-minute, forty-dollar "checkout" fee. *Probably for the Immigration Office because you have to have special permission to be on the Andaman Islands without a boat.*

The skipper set sail for Sri Lanka as planned, and I marched into the port office to buy a ferry ticket to go to the mainland. The piles of paperwork I had to wade through were inhumane! I needed two passport photos, several copies of my passport, copies of a special zone permission, and countless other forms that included questions about my chest measurement and how many liver spots I have! *Maybe important for models on a runway, but why do they need that information to sell you a boat ticket?*

They were sold out for the next few days. The earliest available ticket was for a ferry that departed in six days. *No problem. I'll just explore the island.* Now I just had to submit the ticket with the travel agency. At least that's what they told me to do. Then I'd be all set. Right?

I opened the door to the travel agency and went inside. The space was a cool, pleasant contrast to outside, with an air-conditioner maintaining a tolerable temperature. Several Indians appeared to be hard at work as they sat typing on computers.

"I'd like to speak with the boss," I said.

"I'll let him know. He'll be back soon," an employee told me, gesturing to a tattered couch. Advertisements for Air India hung on the wood-paneled walls, depicting an airplane and a flying carpet along with the words "Experience the difference."

Two hours later the boss came back and sat down on his leather chair behind the large end of a desk. *Soon* seemed to be a flexible term!

"What's up? Do you have your ticket?" he asked me.

I pulled the ticket out of my pocket and pushed it toward him. "Yep, all set. We leave in six days."

"What?! That won't do!" he cried. "You have to leave Andaman within three days! That was the only condition the immigration office had when you disembarked. Three-day transit time!"

Now they tell me! "Aren't my visa and all the forms I filled out enough?"

The boss shook his head. Confusingly, this can mean "yes" in India, but in this case it meant "no." "Andaman is a *restricted area*. Every visitor has to have special permission to be here. You can only apply for the permit on the mainland," he explained.

"Special permission in addition to the boat's 'special zone permission'?" I frowned.

"You got it."

I threw up my hands. "Then what was the checkout fee for?"

"For transportation to the hotel and airport."

"When was that supposed to happen?!" *The fact that I didn't want a hotel or flight was beside the point.* "And why do they call it a 'checkout' fee instead of 'transport'?"

"You didn't use the service, so I can refund 80 percent of the fee." The boss showed how generous he was.

But still. "And what," I came back to the point, "if I can't exchange my ticket and have to stay longer? The ferry that departs in two days is sold out."

"Then Immigration will put you on a plane at your expense," he concluded with a serious expression.

What? Would my plan to go "around the world without an airplane" go up in smoke so close to the finish line? This can't be happening! And I only have one day to do something about it.

I tried to get an earlier ferry ticket at the port terminal. Same answer: "Sold out."

Now I really need a miracle, I thought. It may not come as a big surprise, but I still had the feeling that things would work out despite my bleak prospects.

The first thing I did was to sit down in the sheltered waiting area and wrestle with the situation. Sweat rolled down my temples, and I was grateful for the fan blowing over my bench. A few paces away, dozens of Indians pushed and shoved in a line in front of the counter. When it comes to discipline in forming a line, they sure could learn a few things from German preschool kids.

"May I sit by you?" A rotund white man with wavy hair pointed at the empty place next to me. He was wearing gray shorts, sandals, and a purple argyle shirt.

"Of course," I nodded.

We started talking. He was from Belgium and had just come over to Andaman on the ferry. "What brings you here?" he asked.

I described my adventures up until that point and how I was facing another roadblock that could ruin everything.

"You'll figure it out," he tried to encourage me. "If there's one thing I know about you after our short talk, it's that you're the kind of guy who makes things possible."

"No, I don't think you understand," I contradicted him. "There have been countless times when I could have broken my back to work out a problem and it still wouldn't have changed anything. So much has happened that is totally beyond my control and everything worked out anyway. It has definitely *not* been because I am somehow special or did something extraordinary to make it happen."

"Well, a little luck never hurts," the Belgian said, shrugging it off.

"'A little luck' is a gross understatement," I replied, then laughed. "I've experienced so much by now that it would be ridiculous to believe it was just coincidences."

"So you believe in fate?" The Belgian raised an eyebrow.

"Actually, I believe in grace," I told him as I summed up my experiences and what they led me to believe. "I don't think these are normal occurrences nor coincidences, and I don't think that I am somehow more deserving than anyone else. I think they are gifts that should motivate me to search for the Giver."

Without pomp and circumstance I tried again the next day at the ticket office and—got the ticket I needed! If someone had canceled or something else happened, I'll never know. But I know that I can't take the credit!

15

KISS AND MACHINE GUNS

THE FERRY DOCKED in Calcutta three and a half days later after an entire day of sailing up a delta river. Smokestacks lined the shore. There must have been hundreds of brick factories.

In India I received a surprising message from Michal that made me a little nervous. We had been in contact for fifteen months and had been joking for quite some time about things that we would have to "talk about later over a cup of coffee." We actually agreed on a place for that coffee date: Mumbai. Sometimes it seemed like we were dead serious about it, but other times we were just kidding.

I let Michal pick the day. She decided on April 1. Unfortunately I didn't know how seriously I should take the proposal. I had already found out that Michal was notorious for extreme April Fool's jokes. I was, nevertheless, crazy excited over just the thought that it might not be a joke. If she were to come to India, then I would find out if

235

she thought of me as "just a friend." For me there was no denying how I felt. If she didn't show up, then the joke would definitely be on me. But at least I would know where we stood.

I had seven days to put the 1,300 miles from Calcutta to Mumbai behind me and pick up Michal at the airport. What takes one or two days on the German Autobahn takes *a little* longer in India.

To be clear: I crept along with various truck drivers at about twenty-five miles per hour along the *national highways*, sun beating down on the brightly painted, tin truck cabs, turning them into ovens. A heat wave bowled over India and Pakistan that March, with record temperatures up to 125 degrees Fahrenheit, sometimes even higher. It was the hottest spring since 1956.

In spite of how slow we were driving, the vehicle rocked violently every time the driver jerked the steering wheel to avoid a pothole or a cow. There were more of those two things than asphalt on the main road leading through the northern steppe. Massive semis overturned on the sides of the road served as reminders of the dangerous driving conditions.

To protect themselves from accidents, many truck drivers have little statues of Shiva, a Hindu god, on the dashboard, and they make a smoke offering of marijuana to the god every morning and night. This gives them a clear conscience and puts them in a good mood, too, which often flows effortlessly into a little spiritual song. At least that was my experience with the two truckers who picked me up.

The truck came rattling to a stop long past midnight. One of the two drivers was at the wheel, and his colleague slept beside me on the back seat.

"Do you have to go?" the driver asked me. I lifted my head in a sleepy haze.

"Yes, really bad," I drawled, still in a fog. Then I pulled myself up and climbed out. For some reason I was dizzy. We had stopped in a small town. The night stars twinkled above, and the dim outline of little houses far apart from each other could be seen on the dusky blue horizon. The distances made the town look empty and lonely.

I shuffled through the dust behind the semi over to a scraggly tree and undid my pants. There are not many proper toilets in India. Instead of digging a trench and laying sewage pipe, people just do their business outdoors out in the bush. Instead of using toilet paper, they use water from a bottle that they carry with them. There are villages with hundreds of inhabitants and not a single toilet!

Relieved, I let nature take its course—or at least, I tried to. Other than a few drops, nothing came out. I still felt an enormous pressure. I leaned against the smooth tree trunk and pushed harder. *Why won't it come?!* It felt like my urethra was blocked. *I must have a bladder stone*, I reasoned. I had never had bladder stones and didn't know what they feel like. But that seemed the only explanation. I tried again and was overcome by a dizzy spell. Everything went black, and hundreds of new stars joined in the twinkling. I took several deep breaths and dropped to my knees until some of the dizziness passed. *This won't do. I need a private place where I can push it out with all my might.* I had no idea what else to do. I didn't want my bladder to explode.

I felt my way back along the street to a larger building and went around the backside of a wall. It was pitch black and smelled like feces. *Clearly I'm not the first person to have this idea.* The leaves covering the ground rustled, along with shimmering pieces of plastic trash.

I stopped, stood still, and prepared myself for the pain. Then I tightened my stomach and pushed as hard as possible. A wave of nausea washed over me, and everything started to spin. I collapsed on a concrete median next to the wall.

Nasty. But still better than the grr . . . ouu . . . nnnd.

What smells so gross? I blinked. *Leaves? Where am I?* I felt something soft around my nose. *Thank goodness it's dark!* I clawed through the darkness and pulled myself up. *How much time has gone by? How long was I unconscious? Where is the truck?*

My legs wobbled underneath me as I fought to stand up, leaning against the wall. Dirt trickled out of my hair. There were big clumps of crud clinging all over me. *Well, at least it was a soft landing.* I carefully placed one foot in front of the other. The strength had spilled out of my body like from a sieve. I felt empty. Shaky. Weak. I staggered into the street like a zombie.

The Indian driver stood in the red glow of the taillights. He looked back and forth, searching for his lost hitchhiker.

"Over here," I croaked and stumbled toward him.

He nodded and said briskly, "Come on, we need to get going!" He was hurrying toward the cab. In the darkness he hadn't noticed how chalk-white and haggard I was.

I stumbled in confusion behind him. "No! Here!" Just those two words took everything out of me. "I . . . need . . . help," escaped my lips as I crumpled to my knees, hands hitting the dirt. Gasping, I fought the nausea. Everything flickered in front of my eyes.

A minute later two hands grabbed me under my armpits and pulled me to my feet. The Indian's back was toward me. "I . . . wanted to pee. And I fell down," I said, trembling. I had to focus on the ground so that I wouldn't puke.

The Indian dragged me to the truck. I wanted to help, so I flailed my legs, but it just made matters worse. *I'm so thankful I'm not alone!*

When we reached the cab, he put my hands on the running board so I could hold on. "We need to clean you up." When he reached in the truck for a bottle of water, I fell to my knees again. I felt so bad about it, but I was no longer in control of my body.

The Indian helped me get up again. He poured water over the clumps of dirt while I tried to scrub them off. Along with the dirt, some of my fogginess cleared, and I dragged myself back into the cab. I stunk to high heaven, and filth was clinging in my hair. *Please let it be dirt!*

We rattled forward. The other driver still slept on a wool blanket in the back seat. *I'm lucky that Indians aren't very picky about hygiene. The seat's not all that clean either.*

"Drink!" He threw a water bottle in my lap.

Without thinking, I took a couple of greedy gulps. Then I held back. "I shouldn't drink anymore. My bladder will explode!"

The Indian smiled and stuck some chew in his mouth. "Nothing will explode. You are dehydrated. Your body is playing tricks on you."

It took me a minute to understand what he meant. *So the feeling in my bladder isn't real?* I had to smile too. In fact, when I thought about it, it was really funny. *I was trying to pee like an idiot when I just needed to drink something!* And I ended up falling full length into—I won't say what—in the midst of this noble attempt. *Pranked!*

Later that morning the driver gave me a two-liter bottle of soda, and I put two teaspoons of salt in it. By that afternoon I felt much better.

I had learned how important it is to drink enough water. I also found out that being there for each other can be a matter of life and death, especially if someone gets sick. Those truck drivers could have left me lying on the ground and driven off with my backpack. Instead, they took care of me. It's hard to express how thankful I was and am for them!

We all want others to stand by us and sacrifice for us when we are having hard times. But are we ready to stand by someone else and make sacrifices for them? In their entire lives, those two truck drivers will never have as much money as most Germans, and yet they, like many others I met on my journey, didn't think twice before investing in friends, family, and even a stranger like me. In the end, it makes them happier than most Germans.

One Harvard study followed hundreds of men from different social backgrounds over a period of seventy-five years. The results showed the following: the happiest and healthiest people are not the most successful, the richest, or the most famous. They are not the best looking, most talented, or the most educated. On the contrary, these factors contribute little satisfaction to a person's life, despite what magazines, TV shows, and Internet sites tell us. The happiest people are the ones with good relationships!

This is so extremely important that I want to say it again: the happiest people are the ones with good relationships! Those with friends and family they can count on in hard times—and the reverse too. Very little in life makes a person happier than helping other people.

This is kindergarten-level wisdom. Everyone knows it's true. But right now, in the richest nations, we are seeing more and more lonely people. We seem to have trouble applying this logic. I tend to take on too many tasks and not have enough time for the people around me. And yet I want to make them a top priority!

It's not a one-time deal. We have to commit to this anew every day. My goal is far more important than career, financial security, looks, or popularity: nurture good relationships, treasure the people in my life, and serve them.

In Mumbai I found a place to stay with a member of the couch-surfing network. Luckily I had the opportunity to take a thorough shower and wash my stuff. My host treated me to a delicious curry dinner too. *What a nice guy!*

Michal's flight was supposed to arrive the next day. I got up and left the house long before sunrise to make it to the airport on time. First impressions are very important! The traffic lights weren't on yet, and the streets looked lonely and deserted. A sleeping dog on the side of the road was startled when I walked by, and it sprung to all fours.

Surprisingly the chaotic Indian train system worked exactly as planned. I reached the airport long before her flight was due to arrive and stood with hundreds of Indians in the waiting area. *Impressive!* The building's architecture was like a giant, organic spaceship. Glowing pillars docked like enormous fuel lines on the ceiling, reminding me of a larger-than-life network of tree roots. The waiting area had tropical plants and fountains like an upscale mall. Hidden speakers pumped in relaxing lounge music, creating a contrast to the teeming crowds.

After what felt like an eternity, Michal finally came through the revolving doors. She walked toward the stainless-steel barrier. She hadn't spotted me in the throng of people, so I walked right up to her without her noticing. *Wow, she's prettier than I thought*, was the first thing that came to mind. The second was, *I'm just a little bit taller than she is.*

Just before greeting each other with a hug, our eyes met for the first time. Her hazel eyes were beaming. It was like someone had stopped time just as the camera snapped a picture, as if everything stood still for a few seconds before returning to normal.

I was somehow very serene, but during that moment, a wave of emotions hit me. *Maybe this really is the woman I will spend my life with!*

Michal and I spent ten days together in Mumbai. It was strange at first: On the one hand, we knew each other through and through from our countless e-mails and conversations. But on the other hand, standing right there next to each other, we were complete strangers. That feeling melted away as the week went on. We let the chaos of the city sweep us along and had deep conversations, confirming how similar our views are. But we still hadn't answered the question about what was going on between us.

"What do you get most excited about?" Michal asked as we walked through the streets on the second night.

I wanted to say "*You!*" but suppressed the urge. Not knowing if it would make matters better or worse, I decided to finally take the plunge. "Is it okay if I kiss you?" I asked, completely changing the subject.

"What—uh . . . okay?" she said, visibly startled.

I gave her the kiss I had long been waiting for. *Not very smooth, but hey, it worked!*

We had taken the first step! Since Michal and I are both the type to be very careful about starting something so important, we thought a lot about what our brand-new relationship should look like. Some people may say we were overthinking, but if you want to drive a car, you get a driver's license first and equip yourself to avoid having an accident. To me, driving is a lot easier than having a healthy relationship.

For my twenty-three years of age, I didn't have much relationship experience. But I saw lots of happy and well-functioning marriages during my travels. Curious, I always asked these couples, "What's your secret?" The answers were as varied as the people, but most ended up something like this: the most important thing is to be honest and discuss solutions to problems right away. *Everyone knows that*, I kept thinking. But I'm pretty sure a lot of people forget when it's most crucial.

"You shouldn't expect good communication to happen by chance," a Filipino friend told me a few months earlier. "You should take time for each other regularly and address everything that is important and weighing on you. In my opinion the main thing is not to hide anything from each other."

Another piece of advice that caught my attention is that both people need to be happy independently of each other. They shouldn't seek fulfillment in their partner, expecting them to satisfy their desires and needs. Sooner or later we'll all come up short. You shouldn't burden another person with the responsibility of making you happy.

The third key factor is to understand that people express and perceive love in different ways. Some feel love through gifts, whereas others need compliments and affirmation. Gary Chapman wrote a book called *The 5 Love Languages*. He refers to a particular way of showing love as a language. And we all know that you have to practice a language! If two people have very different love languages, this can lead to grave misunderstandings. One person may be going all-out with compliments, whereas their partner is waiting for the physical nearness they actually need. So it's important to know the other person's love language!

"How do I know what my love language is?" Michal asked me.

"What did your parents do to show that they loved you when you were little? How do you show other people that you care about them? That's usually what makes you feel loved too."

We resolved to pay attention to these details right from the start of our new relationship in hopes that it would flourish like a well-tended garden.

One day we planned to catch the bus downtown to go to Goa. We had to take the train to get downtown and almost missed it. Huffing and puffing, we jumped in just before the doors closed and sat down with the cold drink-boxes our couch-surfing host had given us. We stuck the little straws through the plastic holes and sat slurping our Nesquik macchiatos.

I was about to plan our route when Michal started laughing.

"What?" I asked, confused.

She pointed to our drinks. "I didn't picture it quite like this, but I'm glad we finally get to have a coffee together!"

"I've always hoped that my husband would be much taller than I am because I love wearing high heels," said Michal on the way up the escalator in the airport. Her last day in Mumbai had come all too soon. I had to stand one step higher than her for my head to be much higher than hers. She teased me: "Some people would be worth going barefoot for your whole life. I like wearing high heels, but it's nice to be the same height when you kiss."

"You can wear heels anytime you want. I think we can make it work even if your shoes make you taller than me. If not, I'll put on heels too!" I grinned.

But then the happy mood disappeared, and Michal voiced her concerns. "What if you change during the rest of your trip, and you're not the same when you get back?"

"My sister asked that, too, before I started traveling. She was afraid I would be somehow different. I told her, 'I hope I won't be the same! I want the experiences to change me for the better!'" Then I turned the tables. "What if *you* are the one who changes?" I asked Michal.

After all, I was taking a risk too. Life is a process. There are no guarantees. Everything that happens—our thoughts, feelings, and decisions—determines who we will become. As John C. Maxwell teaches, what we decide today determines who we will become tomorrow.

"We will hopefully keep changing as long as we live," I said. We were approaching the entry to Gate 5, where Michal had to check in. "If we grow together and not apart, everything will be okay," I continued, and Michal agreed with me.

After one last kiss I gave Michal her bag. "I'm not going to turn around!" she assured me as she started off. About ten steps away she looked back. After ten more paces she did it again. And again. *I love this woman!*

April 2017

After Michal's departure, I stayed in India for two months to finish my book, since I didn't get the chance to do it in Vietnam. Two sisters whom I had met in Korea generously offered to let me stay with their affluent family in Nagaland. The tribal people of this rainy, mountainous region have a distinct appearance and are culturally different from the population in central India. They look more like Mongolians than Indians. Originally, their culture centered on hunting and collecting the heads of their enemies as trophies. This practice continued all the way into the 1960s. Since then they have become a notably peace-loving, friendly people.

Much of this book was penned in that relaxing atmosphere, surrounded by mountains, thick forests, and fabulous friends. How wonderful it is when people believe in each other and offer help, even when they don't know how things will turn out. I was about to cross through the Middle East, one of the most dangerous regions on earth. As close as I was to the end of my travels, I wasn't there yet. Anything could happen.

The time had come for me to continue my travels. From New Delhi I took a bus to Lahore in Pakistan. Due to a violent attack on the border, our bus was escorted by soldiers and a police car with lights flashing and sirens sounding. We had to keep the curtains closed. A big Indian with a machine gun guarded us from the back seat.

Pakistan looks like India but is more heavily influenced by Arabs. Not surprising, since it is a Muslim country, but on the other hand, it belonged to India just seventy years ago. My impression was that Pakistan is more traditional than India. For example, most marriages are arranged by the parents, and newcomers are pelted with flower petals as a sign of respect. The men in Pakistan wear long, single-colored robes called *shalwar kameez*, giving the area an oriental flair. In India, most traditional clothing has been replaced by pants, shirts, and polos.

I spent a considerable amount of time near Lahore with friends whom I had met in Fiji. Over and over people offered me a place to stay in Pakistan for my honeymoon someday. It may not sound like a romantic dream vacation to most Westerners, but to be honest, I thought the idea wasn't half bad. After all, Pakistan is very affordable and the culture is so diverse and exotic, you just can't get enough! But I was also in a relatively safe area at the time. That changed after my departure for Balochistan.

The desert region of Balochistan stretches across the eastern side of Iran, the southern side of Afghanistan, and then southwest into Pakistan. The province is occupied by territorial tribes and paramilitary fighters who have taken control from the governments in some areas. Very little is known about Balochistan, due to general disinterest shown by some of the media along with multiple murders of the reporters who have dared to go there. Limitless opportunities for trafficking illegal drugs and weapons!

If the armed gangs aren't firing at you, then the Taliban, Al-Qaeda, or separatist fighters are always there, ready to take over. Limitless opportunities for terrorists and extremists as well!

July 2017

The train that took me toward Quetta, the capital of Balochistan, could hardly have been more uncomfortable. The fiery desert sun heated up the metal walls so mercilessly that you felt like you were in an oven being roasted alive. The wind whistled through the open windows like air from an old hair dryer, and a fine cloud of sand penetrated through every little crack, covering anything and everything with a thick layer of dust: the benches, the walls, the fans, and even our clothes and faces.

What's more, I had a ticket but no seat. The bench assigned to me was occupied by a dozen people. I don't know if they boarded without a ticket, or if the train station just sells more tickets than they have seats. I was the only foreigner on the whole train, so instead of arguing over it, I befriended a group of soldiers dressed in civilian clothes. I was able to find a seat in their train car because they got more respect than the others.

The train suddenly began to shake and squeak loudly. I peered through the dirty metal window frames and saw that we were slowing down. Sparse, dry thornbushes were growing in the stony ground. Some reddish mountains were barely visible in the distance.

A small settlement stood in front of us. It looked like a movie set for a war scene in the Middle East. Figures wrapped in strips of cloth holding AK-47s squatted on the roofs. Their weapons were shaded by tarps that had been stretched tight above them. The

air seemed to swirl in the shimmering heat, blurring the edges of
the town.

The train hissed to a stop. I had seen a blue sign a little ways
back that read, "Mushkaf." *Is that a warlord's headquarters?*

One of the plainclothes soldiers looked out as well. He wore
a dark-blue shalwar kameez and had short hair and a three-day
beard. There was a scar under his left eye, a gap between his front
teeth, and his sharp chin and hairy arms added to his masculine
appearance.

"Shower?" he said out of nowhere, looking quizzically at me.

I stared at him, confused. At that moment there was nothing I wanted more than a shower, but I didn't know why he was
asking that question then and there. *What about this scene makes
him think of a shower? There's no water for miles around!* I nodded,
still unsure.

"Come!" he said, gesturing for me to follow him. We jumped
out of the train with two other soldiers and approached the wall surrounding the town. Alarmed, a man on a roof ordered us to stand
still. Behind him stood a little shelter equipped with a machine
gun on a tripod. My escorts began a discussion with the man on
the roof, and two more people came out of the house. I don't know
what they said, but finally he indicated that we should proceed.
Inside the settlement the dust continued to crackle under our feet
and between our teeth.

We reached a little square with a well in it. We looked inside
expectantly but saw only a muddy puddle about sixty feet down.
"Keep going," called the soldier with the scar.

At the edge of the village, about three hundred feet from the
train tracks, we found another, smaller well enclosed by a short,
stone wall. We pushed the wooden covering aside and threw a stone
in. A big *plop!* signaled that we had found the right place. One of
the soldiers grabbed the rope that hung around the crossbar and

loosened it. He tossed the bucket tied to the rope inside and started turning a lever on the crossbar. When the bucket came up, full to the brim, he gave it to the man with the scar.

He eagerly poured the water over his head, and we quickly filled it up again. I got to dump the glorious liquid on my head next. We pulled the bucket up a third time, and then the train whistle sounded. *Time to go!*

Startled, we let the bucket splash into the well and ran to the train. It was already moving. We ran faster to jump onto the platform of the last car. Quite literally at the last second, we jumped on the train and turned the door handle. *Locked!*

This can't be happening! Since half of the compartments were used for freight, our chances that someone would let us in were pretty slim. Behind the door was nothing but luggage.

"Other side!" I gasped, and we jumped off and ran behind the train to the other side. *This is freakin' crazy!* The locomotive had picked up speed, and we had to sprint to keep up with it. The mixture of dirt and water made my sandals slippery, and I was afraid I would either lose them or sprain an ankle.

We ran as fast as we could and were barely able to jump on the running board. I jumped first, then the man with the scar, and then the other two. The door on that side was unlocked. We smiled at each other, relieved.

Wow! That was just like a stunt from an Indiana Jones or a Wild West movie!

There was only one hotel in Quetta that accepted foreigners. The other hotels thought outsiders were too sketchy. The monopoly took advantage of the situation and charged three times as much as a normal hotel or youth hostel. But, in this case, I had no other choice if I wanted to stay alive. And I was still planning on living another eighty years or so.

In an effort to blend in a little, I wore a black shalwar kameez, a turban to cover up my blond hair, and sunglasses. My getup made me look kind of like a member of the Taliban. Of course, that was my goal. *When I get home, I'll be ready for Karneval!*

On my first morning in Quetta, three policemen armed with machine guns picked me up from the hotel. I was not allowed to go anywhere without them. Even with their supervision I could go only three places: the office where I could apply for permission to continue my travels, a bus terminal to do so, and the police station.

I spent the overwhelming majority of my time in Quetta at the third location. The station was built like a fort with a concrete courtyard surrounded by thick walls and barbed wire. Plain, flat-roofed buildings covered in crumbling plaster stood round about. In the back of the facility, prisoners could be seen through bulky, metal bars. When the police were thirsty, they ladled water out of fat, clay jugs they kept in the shady entrance leading up to a narrow watchtower.

While I waited, the iron gates suddenly opened, and a silver Toyota Mark X 250G drove in. The windshield was splattered with blood. Both windows on the right side were smashed, and there were four bullet holes through the back window. The door on the left had several dents, apparently from shots fired at the vehicle.

While I stood there in shock, staring at the car, someone opened the driver's-side door. It took a minute to process what I saw: the driver's seat, the gearshift, and the console were all soaked with blood.

A successful assassination had occurred just fifteen minutes ago, one of the officers explained matter-of-factly. The driver was an important member of a political party.

The wet blood shimmered on the console. I felt the urge to

vomit rising up inside me. I had gotten used to a lot of things, but this was completely different. Even though the body wasn't in the car, I felt like I had seen the whole thing play out in my mind's eye. The window exploding. The passengers' screams. Massive, deafening rounds tearing through the driver's body in a fraction of a second. Then the shrill ring of a telephone. The call to his wife, informing her that her husband would not be coming home that night. Children growing up without a father. Life ripped away.

While I struggled to compose myself, a man in a white shalwar kameez walked up and looked through the passenger window. A suppressed cry escaped his lips and he pounded his fist on the roof of the car. Tears ran down his cheeks and into his beard. It broke my heart. *His brother, perhaps?* I wondered. I, too, wiped tears from my eyes. *Why would anyone do such a thing?*

The chief police officer came up to me and elbowed me in the ribs. He pointed to the car and said, "We have worry for us, for you." I think he meant to say that the same thing could happen to me too.

I gulped. *Way to make a guy feel better!* Reality can't hit you in the face much harder than that. This wasn't a movie. It was real. Not Disneyland, but a war zone.

❖

Soon after, an SUV reinforced with steel plating drove me to the bus-station terminal. They maneuvered me into an empty bus so that I wouldn't have to shove my way through a crowd of Pakistanis to get on board. I hadn't eaten since breakfast, but it was too late now. I was not allowed to exit the bus until I reached my destination.

The bustling began. Every seat filled up and men were also standing in the aisles. The bus driver was fearless. A combination of sharp curves and poorly stowed luggage resulted in objects continually toppling from the overhead bins into my lap. As far as I could see, the bus didn't have an escort. No one inside had a weapon either. Very different from the border between India and Pakistan. *Probably the best protection here is to not attract attention.* So I kept the window curtain closed, all but a sliver.

The picture of the blood-drenched car was still vivid in my mind, and I considered the possibility that a burst of gunfire could shatter through our windows at any minute. Or they could stop the bus, and I might be kidnapped for ransom money. That kind of thing happened in this region. Then it occurred to me: I had read that attacks on buses are usually carried out with bombs that just blow the whole thing up. *Not too comforting either.*

I don't have to mention that I was the only foreigner on the bus, do I? Of course not.

We had just left the city when the bus stopped in the middle of the road. The door swung open. Someone was talking to the people in the front of the bus. There was a little commotion. *What's going on?* I strained my neck to see what was up. Just then everything went silent and all eyes stared straight at me. I was the only one who didn't understand what was going on. My heart pounded. *I have a very bad feeling about this.*

"Come! Out!" the driver called in a serious tone. I cowered back. *This is what I was afraid of! Why am I the only one?!* I reached for my bag, but the driver shook his head. "No. You—come!"

My mouth went dry. I nervously bit my lip and walked hesitantly down the aisle, pushing past the people blocking my way.

When I got close enough to the front, I saw two men in the entrance dressed in black, each holding a machine gun. I feverishly reviewed my options. There were none. The windows were solidly built and blocked by passengers. Escape from those weapons would be impossible anyway. *I have no other choice.* The only thing I could do was to get on their good side as much as possible.

"*As-salāmu 'alaykum,*" I greeted the men politely, according to custom. *Peace be with you!*

"Country?" they asked harshly, rather than wishing me peace as well.

"Germany."

The men nodded and led me a few yards away to a shelter made of boards and plastic sheeting. Might I say, the landscape in Balochistan is gorgeous! Sunset had immersed the desert in dramatic lighting. Rocky mountains stretched upward, thrusting their jagged peaks into the sky. It felt rugged, untamed. But, unfortunately, I just couldn't enjoy the view for some reason.

One of the men said, "Name?"

"Christopher."

"Mustafa? Islamic name! You are Muslim?"

I almost assented to gain favor with them, but that would have been a lie and would go against my principles.

"No. Not Mustafa, Christopher. I am Christian. Christopher—Christian. Mustafa—Muslim." That's how people could usually remember my name.

Obviously disappointed, the man grabbed a book from a nearby stool. "Passport?"

I quickly pulled it out of my pocket and handed it over. He scribbled my information in smeared pen on a blank page. Then he gave my passport back.

"Sign!" he pointed to an empty space.

I did him the favor.

With a loud bang, he shut the book and threw it back on the stool. Then he waved toward the bus and jerked his chin.

I can go? I thought, incredulously.

The man clicked his tongue in confirmation. I didn't wait to be told a third time! I hurried back on the bus and slipped into my seat.

Thank God! It was just a security check!

Most people don't like to think about death even though it will get us all sooner or later. We think it's something unpleasant that happens far away in hospitals, battlefields, or hospices.

At least that's how it is in Germany. Many countries that I visited view death differently. For them, death is painful, of course, but it is a familiar visitor that they encounter frequently. The death rate is higher, and people there do not die in institutions but with their families because many generations live together under one roof. The daily presence of death is not only negative but positive. Dealing with death helps us to focus on what is important in life. What really matters.

If a person has only one week to live, they don't spend their time bickering over little things. At least that's how I felt on the bus ride in Balochistan, not knowing if I would survive the trip. I thought about my family, about Michal, about all the good things that had happened to me, and what life is really about.

We drove all night long, and I was hauled out of the bus over a dozen times for security checks. A "service" provided by the paramilitary. If I were to go missing, they would know where I was last seen. After the sixth check, a Pakistani with a Kalashnikov rifle got on the bus and introduced himself as my personal bodyguard. Another "service" to show hospitality. As it turned out, my seatmate was his best friend. That fact loosened things up and made the rest of the journey more relaxed and personable. To be honest, we got along so fabulously that I was tempted to go back for another visit. (Mom, please forget I said that!)

The border crossing to Iran went without a hitch. On the other side, the soldiers took my passport and escorted me to a military base. We rode on the back of a flatbed truck protected by a man with a heavy machine gun on the roof. *I've never seen masses of weapons like this anywhere but in Balochistan!* There, they loaded me into another vehicle just like the first, drove me to a checkpoint, and handed me off again.

By the time I reached the bus station at Zanhedan, I had been passed between military personnel and the police eight times. They had kept my passport during all that time. I finally got it back before boarding the bus and was allowed to continue straight on my way.

I took the next bus to Tehran, the capital of Iran. I hadn't showered or shaved in three days, and I was still wearing the black shalwar kameez I had donned as a disguise to fit in. I stuck out like a sore thumb in the capital city. People there wear modern clothes: jeans, polished leather shoes, shiny belts, and fitted shirts.

"You look like an extremist!" a man in the subway informed me after I asked for directions. To me, it was somehow humorous! *A German terrorist in Iran!*

It seemed that the majority of the city's inhabitants were more advanced than the government. Although headscarves were required, the women wore so much makeup that the original purpose of the modest dress code was completely sidestepped. Female students often "forgot" to put it on. Suggestive music videos by artists such as Rihanna played constantly on TVs and cell phones. Although homosexuality is punishable by death, men greeted each other with a kiss on the cheek. Many wanted to kiss me right on the mouth. They made no secret of their sexual orientation.

In contrast, the villages in the country adhere to a much stricter form of Islam. When an Iranian software developer invited me to meet his family in a remote settlement, I made the mistake of reaching out to shake his sister's hand. Terrified, she opened her eyes wide and stepped back to avoid touching me. With good reason, women make sure not to be in a room alone with a man. If a man rapes her under such circumstances, she doesn't stand a chance in court, and the family's dishonor is so overwhelming that most women remain silent, taking their secret to the grave. Many blame themselves for the assault. The man's responsibility is downplayed, as if he were a victim of his urges.

An Iranian woman told me about her cousin who said point-blank, "If my husband cheated on me, I'd forgive him. He can't help it. The woman who seduced him is to blame!" I had traveled the entire globe and was so close to Europe again, and yet stories like these made European culture seem light-years away.

The last country I had to get through was Turkey. I wanted to travel as quickly as possible so that I could spend the last couple of weeks of Michal's year abroad in Italy with her. Plus, I missed my family so much! It was obviously time to go home.

In less than ten days my father was going to chaperone a youth group traveling to South Tyrol in northern Italy. I was planning to surprise him there! If you can call it that. My parents only like surprises when they don't come as a surprise.

I caught a ride with two Iranian truckers bringing a load to Istanbul. We passed the famous Mount Ararat on the way. The landscape transformed from the arid desert of Iran to Mediterranean hill country full of green meadows, fields of blooming flowers, and cyprus and olive trees. Shepherds tended their flocks while insects hummed in the gentle breeze.

The first Turkish ice cream I tried was simply unforgettable! It was so sticky that the vendor did funny tricks with it. (Warning! Placement advertisement: The world's best ice cream, I later discovered, is found in Michal's parents' Eiscafé Alfredo in Pirna, Germany. Really! My flavor tip: mango and coconut with *milchreis* [German rice pudding].)

Past Istanbul, I found myself on European soil again. I picked up the pace even more, "heading for the barn door," as they say! My galloping gait took me through Eastern Europe, and in just three days I arrived in the sunny village of Raas in South Tyrol, beating my father by a day.

This is exactly how I pictured the Alps. White houses with dark wooden balconies covered with magnificent potted flowers in full bloom. Paved streets leading to lush apple orchards, and spectacular, snow-peaked mountains in the background. *Just like on the milk cartons.* It was almost embarrassing. *I'm a German who has traveled around the whole world and never even been to the Alps!*

It felt so weird to chat with people on the street in my own language again. It had been a long time. I quickly found the pension that my father's youth group had booked. Lucky for me, there was a group that left a day ahead of time, and I was allowed to stay in their room. The owners did not charge me, since the room had already been paid for. *A soft mattress, a shower, soap—now there's nothing standing in the way of a happy reunion!*

I showered yet again the next morning, just to make sure. I didn't want my father to think that I was a mess. Scrubbing myself with a hand towel, I left the bathroom to get dressed. Sunlight flooded my room as water dripped from my hair onto the cork floor. *There's no hair dryer,* I realized. I sat on the bed and pulled on my socks. Outside, I heard the dull thud of a car door closing. *They can't be here already!*

I went to the window and pulled the drapes slightly to the side.

There was a white minibus in the parking lot and . . . *MY PAPA!!!*
Tears sprang to my eyes unexpectedly. He looked the same as ever!
His kind expression. The grocery-store reading glasses. The only
thing that had changed was his hair, which had more gray than
before.

What am I doing? I jumped back so as not to be discovered,
threw on a light-blue shirt, and checked myself in the mirror once
more to see if I was presentable. *A-OK.* At least on the outside. My
heart pounded. It felt like a heavy stone was lying on my chest,
making it hard to breath. *We haven't seen each other for four years!*

I scurried out the door in my socks and hurried over the sand-
colored tiles. Pictures of youth groups that had spent their vacations
in the hostel hung on the walls. Upon reaching the entryway, I
stopped and peeked around the corner. On the other side stood
my father, his back partially turned toward me. He was wearing a
comfortable gray sweatshirt, jeans, and tennis shoes. He was looking in the kitchen, and by his gestures, it seemed like he was talking
to someone.

I snuck up behind him quietly, joyfully anticipating what
would happen next. I heard the words, "Your son's already here!"
At that moment, I covered his eyes with my hands, but then I didn't
know how to continue the surprise. *If I say anything, he'll know right
away that it's me! But that's probably already pretty obvious.*

While I thought about it, he turned around and looked into
my eyes. Then he gave me a wild bear hug and kissed me. I felt
like a balloon that was being pumped up with an air compres-
sor, filling me so full that I might burst at any moment. All the
emotions of all those years came tumbling down on me like an
avalanche. It felt as if my veins were full of carbonated water, not
blood. So overwhelming. *Papa! My role model! My childhood hero!*
The stone that had been pressing on my chest was gone. I was
light as a feather.

After a long time we loosened our hug and looked at each other. He raised his hand to touch my face. Then we hugged again. This time tears ran down our cheeks. "It's nice to see you again!" I sobbed.

At some point we each took a deep breath and pulled ourselves together. The owner of the pension was standing next to us, and a caretaker had come in too. *I wish they wouldn't bother us right now!* My father introduced me to the caretaker, and some of the youth came in.

"How are you now?" asked the owner, excited.

"I have to go to the bathroom." My father laughed. "It was a long trip!"

Thank the Lord! "You can go in my room. I'll show him back," I offered, happy to have some time alone with him.

In my room we fell into a long discussion about God and the world. It was unbelievably wonderful to talk to him again!

"You have the exact same mannerisms as your brother," he noticed with satisfaction. "I'm glad there is still a little barnyard smell on you."

We talked a blue streak until late that afternoon, when he finally wore out. He was exhausted since he hadn't slept the night before. We took a half-hour nap together in the double bed.

"It's weird," my father contemplated, head on the pillow. "You are so familiar and yet somehow like a stranger."

While I was considering his words, he had already started to snore.

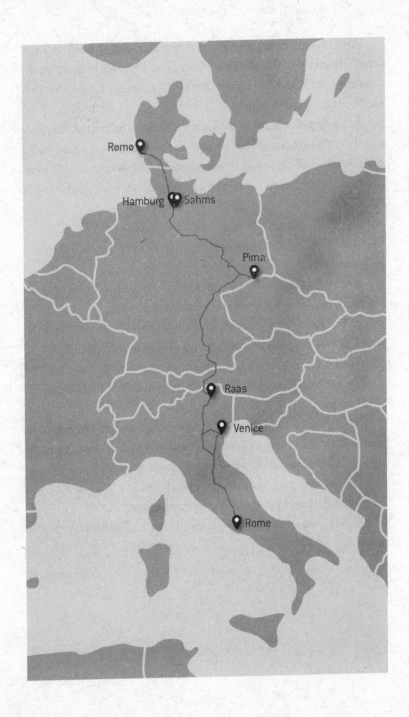

16

BACK HOME

SEEING MY FATHER AGAIN left such a deep impression on me that I still get teary-eyed thinking about it. Nevertheless, I did not stick around for long in Tyrol. I was too excited to get home and wrap my arms around my twin brother, younger sister, and mother.

But before seeing my family in Germany, I picked Michal up in Rome. Her year abroad in Italy was coming to a close, and we wanted to travel back home together. In the evenings we had picnics at the Colosseum, we got lost in the winding alleys of Venice, camped by candlelight in a Tuscan olive grove with a view of an ancient fortress—the days spent road tripping with Michal were so beyond imagination, they belong at the end of a romance novel. Who knows? Maybe we'll write one together someday.

261

Crossing the border to Germany was exactly as I imagined it would be: we rolled down the windows and drove slowly, while policemen in neon yellow jackets looked at us suspiciously. A cold summer wind blew fine raindrops in our faces and on the dashboard. A mass of gray clouds billowed in the gloomy sky. *Oh, Germany! I missed you.* I had to smile. *But not your weather!*

Michal stayed in Pirna with her family, and I hitchhiked on to Northern Germany; my sister was waiting for me in Hamburg. My parents and brother had gone ahead to Denmark for vacation—to the exact same summer cabin where we had spent our vacations since I was a kid.

A TV crew filmed my reunion with my sister. At first we worried that it might bother us, but luckily we didn't even notice the cameras; we were so overjoyed to see each other again. My sister and I are so close that, aside from my mother, she probably had the roughest time with my prolonged absence. *My little sister! Back in my arms.*

We drove to our vacation home in Denmark that same day. Finally, we were all reunited! Even my twin brother, who almost never cries, couldn't help but get a little teary-eyed. *How wonderful to have people who are so happy when you come home!*

Sometimes I ask myself what it would have been like if my reunion with my family hadn't been spread out—first my father, then my sister, then everyone together—but rather all in one place at one time. I'm actually happy that it turned out the way it did. Stretching it out over time helped me get a feeling of closure. I had time to arrive. Plus, the profound joy of reuniting not just once but three times! You know what they say: "Good things come in threes!"

My parents smiled constantly for the next few days. My dad said he was getting muscle spasms in his cheeks.

I found it both funny and frightening that everything was just like it used to be. The roles we played as siblings, the jokes, the gestures. It often felt like I had never been gone. *What a priceless treasure of a family I have!*

The house I grew up in won't be around for long. My family moved while I was away. The insulation was so bad that in spite of having the heat on, we used to have to wear ski coats in the house just to survive. It will probably be demolished. I drove past it one last time. It looked overgrown and abandoned. Not a pretty picture. But that was not important to me. Home is not a building. Home is where the people you love are. That's why I never felt lonely on the road. People met me with such kindness and made me feel at home. Just like I am now—at home!

The odd sensation that I had never left home came over me more and more frequently. Especially when I saw people or places that seemed like they hadn't changed at all. Like my old school or my awesome neighbors.

It was a different story with my friends—most of them had been trained for a profession, were in college, or were in the workforce. And me? I'm already twenty-four years old with no training, no education, and no job. Did I waste four years of my life? That's an easy question to answer: no!

My world travels are and will remain my education. I basically had one internship after another for four years: as a gardener, ship crew member, tour guide, gas jockey, plumber, actor, cook, model, guinea pig, stall-mucker, tutor, party guide, speaker, cleaning man, canal line handler, construction worker, charcoal maker, helmsman, salesman, translator, cargo loader, carpenter, gold prospector, author, harvest helper, fisherman, babysitter, waiter—the list goes on and on. I've acquired so many skills in a variety of fields. I can navigate a boat now, repair pipes, start a fire with my bare hands, gut fish, and much more. I left speaking German, and along the way I learned Spanish, Portuguese, English, Italian, and halfway-passable Korean.

But above and beyond all of these things are the priceless treasures that cannot be measured. I can now see the world through other people's eyes. To some extent, I've made new discoveries in myself as well. My own strengths and hidden weaknesses have been revealed. I questioned my reasoning behind old convictions. I got to know God in a very personal way that I didn't even think was possible.

I learned to be happy with practically no possessions. Not just happy, but thoroughly content. I discovered what it means to be thankful. Not just the polite "thank you" that you mumble when someone blesses you after you sneeze. No, I mean true, deep, profound gratitude for the big and small gifts in my life. A good meal, a warm shower, a loving family, a peaceful homeland.

No institution can compare to the living school I had the honor of attending. I saw things of which I had never even dared to dream! No course of study could have communicated such personal stories about people and cultures like the experiences of these four years. And the gifts just keep giving! The countless friendships have truly created a worldwide network. Many visits back and forth have already been planned.

Last but not least, and by far the biggest surprise a hitchhiker could imagine: I got a girlfriend! Or should I say, a wife.

December 2017

Michal and I went back to her favorite place in Rome, Trajan's Column, and I proposed. Surrounded by candles, on one knee, playing the guitar, and singing a song I had written for her. Sometimes you just have to be super cheesy! She said yes. We made our wedding rings ourselves out of the gold I had mined in Guiana. I can't wait to go through thick and thin with this amazing woman!

Soon after my return I started studying theology near Darmstadt. Yes, "Bowels City"! If you are wondering if someone is still college material after such a long break, the answer is yes. For me, it's no problem. Maybe that's because I constantly read and studied during my travels: languages, how to do various jobs—I spent time researching fascinating histories, regions, and cultures, and read piles of books that somehow fell in my lap.

Getting used to a daily routine wasn't hard either. Along the way I had many strict, organized procedures to follow, like sailing in shifts. In spite of everything I truly enjoy how productive I can be when my days are well structured.

The small amount of free time I have is spent on mini-adventures with my bride-to-be and making videos to answer the loads of questions that travel-hungry people are asking me. I believe it is extremely important to help people achieve their dreams. After all, my accomplishments were only possible due to all the people who stood by my side, giving me advice, aid, hospitality, encouragement, experience, and time.

Thanks to their support, I was successful in what I set out to do: I struck out on a journey with fifty bucks in my pocket and returned a rich man.

How we live our lives is, for the most part, up to us. "I've always wanted to . . ." So many people carry a sentence like this in their hearts. The second half of the sentence is different for everyone, and that's a good thing. For me, it was a journey around the world. For someone else, it might be something completely different. The main thing is to make sure that it's not a wish but a resolution: "I will . . . !" Maybe my book can nudge someone in this direction. That would make me so happy!

Adventure isn't putting yourself in danger but allowing yourself to experience the unexpected. The same attitude that I cherished on my trip, I will take with me into the next stage of life: "Don't worry. The best things always happen when you least expect it!"

My next adventure starts . . . now!

ACKNOWLEDGMENTS

IT MAY BE MY NAME under the title, but this book is the product of many participants who made it possible.

First and foremost, I thank God Himself, to whom I owe all my gratitude for everything.

I cannot express with words all that my parents have done for me. Thank you for the love you give us every day. Thank you for the encouragement and comfort. Thank you for your prayers and support, for your help with no strings attached, and for believing in us. Thank you for all you have taught us about values and attitudes toward life.

Without all of this, my trip would not have been possible.

Thank you to my sister, Annedore, and my brother, Benedict, for preparing and training me since I was a child for the adventures and dangers of this world.

Thank you, Michal, my dream girl, helper when I'm in need, soul mate, chapatti, best friend, and joy of my life! The genius behind my insanity.

Thank you, Grandma Greta and Grandpa Hans Heinrich, as well as Grandma Inge and Grandpa Rudi, for all the time and energy that you invested in us as a family. You are my inspiration and role models for what it means to be generous, give lovingly, and live life. Thank you for your prayers, your support, and your love and caring that made our family what it is.

Thank you, Yanbemo Lotha, Mhasivonow, Areni, Christina, and Longshio Humtsoe, for all your hospitality, generosity, and kindness. You contributed a gigantic part to make this book a reality! I can hardly thank you enough for all your help and this precious friendship! Also thank you, Nzan, Chumbem, Lijan, Lijan's parents, Akhrieo, and Lotha Tribe!

To Karoline Kuhn for dedicating your untiring devotion to the text and making the best of it. Thank you for sharing your talent with us all.

Thank you, Janet Gesme, for all the laughter we had during the translation process. Somehow you did the impossible by becoming the American version of me.

Thank you to Juli, as well, for the patience you had when your mom came home much later than expected.

Thank you, Felipe Monteiro Vazami, for gracing the cover with your photo.

Thank you, Tina Teucher, for believing in me right from the start and supporting me! You truly made things possible!

Thank you, Jochen and Claudia Hofmann, for your unbeatable ice cream, for standing by my side, for incomparable hospitality, and a million thanks for your daughter!

Thanks go to Mini, as well, for incredible inspiration and self-lessness, neighborly love, self-sacrifice, and spunk.

Thank you, David and Jeschi Holey, for telling Michal that I'm the right one for her and for all your prayers. You are a wonderful example of how to live one's faith!

And thanks to Noah, Grandpa Hofmann, Uschi, and the Alfredo team.

I'd like to thank the BHA: Hannes Fuchs, Hendrik Reinke,

Robin Wegener, Leonard Rehfeld, Ole Werner, and Eric Wohlgetan—you are an example of what true friendship is!

To many other friends and acquaintances as well!

Thank you, Adam Yalcinöz and Sammy Frey, two fabulous roommates. Thank you for your support, encouragement, and everything that I learned from you day by day. You guys are the best!

The list of people that I would like to write a personal dedication to is so long that there's just not enough room. (You more than deserve it though!) At the very least, I would like to express my heartfelt thanks to:

GERMANY
Tino Schumann
Jörg and Dorothea Eymann
Willi Lanek
Peter Sutter
Gabi Meier
Frank Heinke
Milan Langer
Phileman Schott
Thorben Kreienbring
Jan Nickel
Jakob Justus
Micha Bührle
Markus Schäfer
Florian Tschapek
Finn Lucas Van der Velde
Sorush Ghods
Cynthia Sieber
Gideon Aßmus
Sabrina Buss
Misgana Gebremichael

Luisa Kolb
Paul Pfister
Miriam Dominique Popp
Manuel Rose
Jeremy Seelinger
Dominic Zimmerli
Marco Bergelt
Michael Schweitzer
Esther Koch
Doris Müller
Christina Kunz
Mirjam Schmidt
Duygu Aygül
Everyone who prayed for me

HOLLAND
Peter Hikspoors
Leon Strikwerda

BELGIUM
Christophe Sepot

FRANCE
Wilfried Texier
Arpage Lagaffe
M. Jaque B.

SPAIN
Enrique Pavés Jiménez
Sonia and Sebastian Castaño
Jorge and Jodie

ITALY
Stefano Dagonoli
Roberto and Nok Gaziello
Fabrizio and Sergio
Matteo Chiarelli
Timoteo Pancin
Fabrizio and Tanja
Sonnenhof in Raas

ENGLAND
The crew of the *Te Natura*

IRELAND
Gerry (from the *Justin's Odyssey II*)

VENEZUELA
Piter, Adela, Thais, and Bisley Jimenez
Eleazar and Any Gamardo
Pastor Juan
Omar and Romeo's family in Curiapo
Jose Armando
Arature Dorf

GUYANA
Roy Gooding
Melissa and Manella Ramkaran
Marwin, Eugene, and Dave in Aranca
William in St. Martin
Marc (on the way to Kaikan)
Arau Dorf

BRAZIL
Jeronimo, Elyziane, and family
Manoel Andrade and family
Igrej Batista Bíblica Renovada
Felipe and the Vazami family
Filipe Faraon and family
Camila Costa
Mario Sérgio Guimarães
Deivid Mineiro
Eliane Lemos
Francisco Alferes Thesco
Paulo Ivan de Oliveira

PERU
Armanda Cornejo
Berto from Arequipa
Carla Perrein, Yadira, and the Taipe family
Golber Alan Acosta Saldaña
Pedro Pablo and father
Fredy Ramos Barrios

BOLIVIA
Mariana and Juliane Chavez
The family of Abiel in La Paz
Arco Iris in Uyuni

ARGENTINA
Sebastian, Flo, and Facundo Ponce

ECUADOR
Daniel Quevedo
Juan Francisco Ledergerber

COLOMBIA
Nadya Stephy
Nancy, Juan Alejandra Guasca
Mariluz Fuquen and family

COSTA RICA
Daniel Foulkes

PANAMA
Susy Rios
South Africa
Cedric Brown

QUEBEC
Ray

USA
Daniel Gann
Tony and Keith (Citylight)
Lauren Kish
Josh Rios

SWITZERLAND
The Kaiser family

SWEDEN
Goeran Persson

NORWAY
Tor Dahl
Idunn and family
Greta and Tom (Raratonga)

FIJI
Apisai Domolailai

VANUATU
Chief Isaac Wan
Repacksvir Village
Kevin in Ouere

PHILIPPINES
Henry, Adelina Fe, Fort, Henadel, and Dominic Remigio
Albert, Lisa, Gilda, Cherissa, and Alyssa Yap
Jane and James Matriano
Elvin and Kaye Villar
Pat and Crisina Catubig
Mark Esperancilla
Dioshame Cruzada
Therese and family from Manila

KOREA
최용문 and his wife
Doyoon Kim
Inhong Kim, family, and congregation
Young Joon Chun
Nayul Lina Kim
이미래 and 황호영
희즌 and 박승혼
Yun Sup Park
Gyung Tak Sung
Hyungjin Jacob Cho
Leo Rhee
Yeasl and Chris Rowe

JAPAN
The Kawamoto family
Shintaro Kondo
Yumi Tabaru and family
Mitsumasa Uchigaki
A couple from Fukuoka
Kisuke Nishikawa and his friend
Yadoya Guest House in Tokyo

CHINA
Suzy and Peng Bo Li
A couple from Baoding
Lorin

VIETNAM
An Nguyen, Trung đạo, Toan, Hân

THAILAND
Jame, Pe Nyng, Pe Po, Kookkai

KUWAIT
Mohammed

MALAYSIA
Aj Anthony

NEPAL
Nepels

RUSSIA
Alexander Nekrasov
Andrey Yakushev
Alexandr (North of Phuket)

INDIA
Mr. "Bikash Nandi Maunder"
Jimmy Naliyath and family
Arnie Rumberfield and his mother
Bankas and Sodid
Pramod Saha, Titu, Mantas, Sanji

PAKISTAN
Bishop Aher Khan, family, and congregation

IRAN
Farhad and Tara Toosi
Hossein from the area of Nazarabad
Vahid and Hassan from Tabris

POLAND
Adam and Asia Dzielicki
Marcin Sky Lanc

TURKEY
Merve Akarsu

AUSTRIA
Mathias Brugger

APPENDIX

55 Tips for a Backpacker on a Budget

Preparation

1. Apply for your passport far enough ahead, and make sure that it is valid for the required amount of time. Most countries demand that the passport be valid for a minimum of six months after your exit date.

2. Find out at least three months before entering a country if they require a visa. If you can't have the visa authorized abroad, you can apply by sending your passport to your homeland to the embassy of the country you want to visit. The website http://travel.state.gov gives the basic requirements for each country. For details, visit the embassy's website. **Warning:** Make sure to research using the embassy in your homeland (e.g., "Consulate General of India, Chicago").

3. Get any needed vaccinations ahead of time. Ask your doctor what you need for each country.

4. Open an account with Couch Surfing (www.couchsurfing.com) and host travelers before your trip. The more good ratings you have, the more likely others are to take you in later. Plus, you get to know people from all over the world, and you can find out about their countries and collect helpful travel tips.

5. Get travel medical insurance if you are adventurous and want to travel without a lot of money. For this, you should seek the advice of an expert. It is also important that it includes emergency evacuation. This feature pays for your trip home if the country you are in cannot offer the medical care you need.

6. Pack light. Almost every backpacker tends to pack too much stuff. If at all possible, hold to this rule of thumb: if you don't use it at least once a week, you can probably leave it at home. Detailed packing lists are easy to find on the Internet, so this is just a small list that has served me well:
   a. Roll of electrical tape, a pocket knife, and a thin, strong rope.
   b. Sharpies for making hitchhiking signs.
   c. Half roll of toilet paper, for obvious reasons (you can take the cardboard out of the middle to save room).
   d. Hammock with a mosquito net. It's more comfortable than a tent, especially in the tropics. If you sleep on a diagonal across the fabric, then your back won't hang down.
   e. Camping mat.
   f. Tent with plenty of extra tent pegs.
   g. Quality shoes and a good backpack (worth the price).
   h. Clothes: seven pairs of underwear, seven pairs of socks, three T-shirts, three pairs of pants (for warm climates, pack two pairs of shorts and one

pair of pants), one sweatshirt, and one jacket. You can bring more clothes to do laundry less often, but you'll pay for it by carrying extra weight. Your clothes take the most space and constitute the heaviest part of your load.

i. Bottle of water. In the city sixteen to thirty-two ounces is enough. Outside of cities, it's better to bring one-half to one gallon of water. Find out if the tap water is potable where you plan to travel. I drank the water almost everywhere and had no problems. If you're not sure, bring water purification tablets, boil the water for three minutes, or use a filter.

7. Take a trial trip with your equipment to find out what its weaknesses are. You might figure out what else you need to bring or what you can leave at home. Get a little practice hitchhiking. That way you'll know if the reality matches what you had in mind.

Housing

8. The least-expensive option is sleeping in a tent or hammock, or couch surfing.

9. If you plan to sleep outside, don't ever sleep in dark, isolated corners! You are better off in high-traffic areas, such as next to a gas station, hospital, police station, or building that has night watchmen. If you are a woman traveling alone, it may be best not to sleep outside, depending on the country and culture. If you play an instrument, can perform circus tricks, or make jewelry (like bracelets), you may be able to earn a few dollars to sleep in a youth hostel.

Mobility

10. Hitchhike to save money or, if you have the time and are seaworthy, become a crew member on a yacht or work on a boat. The latter is easier to arrange on-site than online.

11. Use public transportation in the countries where it is inexpensive and makes sense to use it.

12. If you have a smartphone, download helpful apps (e.g., the ÖV app and offline maps). I recommend Maps.Me (https://maps.me/).

Hitchhiking

13. Be patient. It can easily take five hours to find a ride.

14. Don't drink too much before long drives. You never know when you'll find the next available toilet.

15. Pick a spot where cars can easily stop and where drivers have time to think about if they want to offer you a ride or not. The best places are gas stations, stop lights, or parking lots. If you can exchange some personal words, your chances are better.

16. Look for cardboard boxes for signs behind gas stations, rest stops, restaurants, or businesses. Don't forget your Sharpie!

17. Write the direction and the next biggest cities on your sign. For example, instead of "Boston," write "I-95 North: Philadelphia–New York–Boston." If the people driving by see their own destination, you have a better chance of getting picked up.

18. Let people drive you from one rest stop to the next. Don't get off the highway unless someone is taking you to the city where you want to go. Otherwise, it takes a ton of time to

get back to the highway. It's better to get out one rest stop too soon than one too late.

19. Try to dress in clean, unobtrusive, and modest clothing. Don't wear sunglasses. Make sure people can see your eyes. Straw hats have a nice effect. Smile! The more harmless you seem, the more likely drivers are to pick you up.

20. When you find a ride, use the time well and ask the driver friendly and interesting questions. Knowing more about other people's lives definitely broadens your horizons.

21. Plan a route using your maps app ahead of time. Be sure to charge your phone so that you can call for help if necessary. It's a good idea to have a power bank for recharging your phone as well as a paper map, just in case your phone gives up the ghost.

22. Stock up on plenty to eat and drink so that you won't have to buy marked-up goods at convenience stores.

For Women (from Michal, who hitchhiked alone around Europe)

23. Carry pepper spray.

24. Don't travel at night, and make sure to be in areas with plenty of people.

25. Wear long sleeves and pants, even if it's warm. The more skin you show, the more likely you are to get a ride with someone who is not respectable.

26. Text a friend the license-plate number before you get in any car.

27. Ask your driver about their family, friends, and job. If you don't get a straight answer, then get out of the car as soon as possible.

28. Don't tell anyone if your phone is dead.

29. Be aware of the country's culture and how women are treated. There are some countries where you should absolutely never hitchhike alone.

Food

30. Eat local food that the inhabitants eat—it is always the most affordable. What this food is differs from country to country, but it should be easy to find by checking the prices. Oatmeal, rice, couscous, bread, bananas, potatoes, corn, and the like are often affordable staples.

31. Go dumpster diving. If you can handle the thought of it, the trash cans in highly developed countries often have a lot to offer (behind supermarkets, restaurants, and so forth).

32. Work for food. Many restaurants will exchange food for labor, if you ask.

Safety

33. Leave your expensive jewelry, watches, or other luxury items at home. The best protection against theft is to look like you don't have anything to steal.

34. Hide important items and documents. In many countries, it is inexpensive to have a pocket sewn into your underwear or bras: the perfect hiding place.

35. Read up on travel conditions in each country. Many regions have several travel blogs that can help you to be well informed.

36. If you plan to be in an area with no cell service or places to

charge your phone, have a good GPS tracker. SPOT Gen worked well for me. Your family will be happy to receive signs of life from you now and then.

37. Don't ever be in a hurry to go with someone. Ask a lot of questions first, including various details. Liars hate details and try to give only vague information. Trust your gut. You can usually sense if someone is authentic or not very quickly.

38. Be suspicious if someone refers to you as "my friend." Eighty percent of the time, these people have an ulterior motive. Be even more suspicious if they keep emphasizing that you are safe and have nothing to fear.

Health Precautions

39. If you go into the wilderness, bring a disinfectant, antibiotic ointment, bandages, and oral antibiotics.

40. Protect against the most common and unpleasant tropical illnesses with the best tools: a mosquito net, long clothing, and insect spray. Do not underestimate the importance of these precautions!

41. As trivial as it may sound, take good care of your teeth. Toothaches are bothersome, and it can be difficult to find a qualified dentist abroad.

42. Drink enough water and have sufficient supplies on hand. You need a gallon of water every day—more or less depending on the climate and your level of physical exertion. In many mountainous regions it is safe to drink water from the streams. It should be clean, flowing, pleasant-smelling water, ideally with no civilizations upstream. If it's cold, all the better!

43. Bring Band-Aids for blisters if you are hiking a lot. If you

don't have any, layering several pairs of socks can help with cushioning.

44. Take extra underwear with you. When hiking for long periods of time, it is essential to change your underwear often and wash yourself thoroughly. Otherwise bacteria will irritate certain skin surfaces that have been rubbed raw by friction, making every step painful.

Internet

45. Find Internet in many countries at public squares, rest stops, or cafés with free Wi-Fi.

46. In big cities you can use the Internet for free while trying out devices at Apple Stores or other technology sales centers.

47. Use apps that give you the Wi-Fi passwords for certain places. These passwords are shared by other people who have used the app. For example, the Wi-Fi Master Key or Wi-Fi Map apps. **Warning:** You need an Internet connection to use them! With Wi-Fi Map you can save the key ahead of time.

Communication

48. Download offline translators, such as Google Translate, ahead of time. It is definitely worth it. English is the best language to use for these apps. Install the country's keyboard, so that the person you are talking to can type in their response. If people want to understand each other, it usually works out somehow.

49. If you are planning an extended stay in a country, it is well worth your time to learn some of the most important phrases in the local language. When residents see that you have taken the time and trouble to learn their language, it opens many doors. Download an app for this, too, so that you can keep learning while you are waiting or on the road. I recommend Memrise (https://www.memrise.com/). Vocabulary is much more important than grammar. Don't be shy! Just start talking!

Work

50. In developed countries find jobs on Craigslist (www.craigslist.org).
51. Wherever you are, ask around and talk to people. You can almost always find a job through acquaintances and relationships—assuming you're not picky.
52. References are practically useless for odd jobs. No one ever asked me for a reference. However, a well-written résumé can open many doors.

Basics

53. Always be friendly and nice. People are the key to everything: work, fun, information, and so on. Try to figure out the country's customs and rituals as quickly as possible to avoid doing anything they might perceive as negative.
54. Use the best icebreaker: a smile and a question. Ask for directions, a recommendation, and so forth. If you are open and positive, others will most often return the favor.

55. Take time to talk. In many countries people are curious and want to find out about those from other countries. In lesser-developed nations, the people have a lot of time for conversations. Enjoy it!

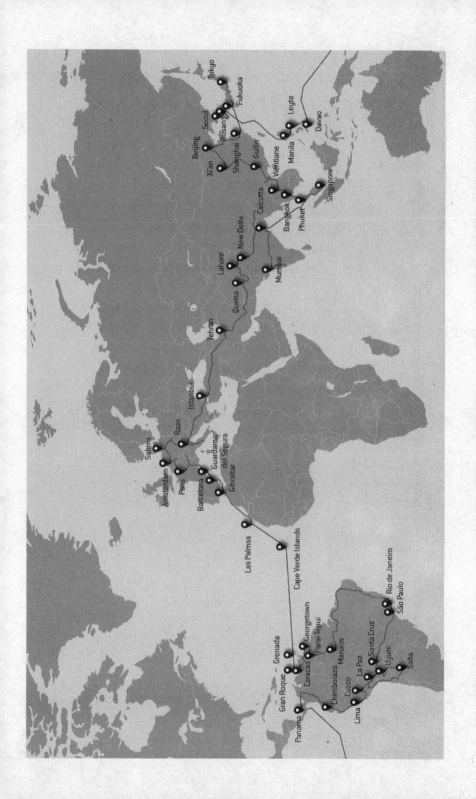

ABOUT THE AUTHOR

Christopher Schacht, born in 1993, grew up in the village of Sahms, near Hamburg in Northern Germany. Over a four-year period he traveled to more than forty-five countries and covered more than sixty thousand miles, walking and hitchhiking, and not once using a plane. (Who knew you can hitchhike across oceans?) His only provisions were an adventurous spirit, a positive attitude, a bright smile, and the willingness to embrace what lay ahead—whatever people, traditions, cuisine, and work opportunities came his way.

In his travels Christopher encountered many different cultures, fascinating landscapes, dangerous adventures, great hospitality—*and* the Maker of all the greatness. He also met the love of his life, Michal. Returning to Germany in September 2017, Christopher began to study theology, and in June 2018, he and Michal were married.

Christopher's father is a Lutheran minister, and he also has two siblings—a twin brother (who is his exact opposite!) and a younger sister. After graduation Christopher had a full college scholarship in computer science waiting for him, but he decided instead to embark on a trip around with world with only fifty euros in his pocket, no credit cards, no backup plan, and no schedule or itinerary. *Around the World on 50 Bucks* is his story about his unusual journey, and it was an instant success in Germany.

Christopher and Michal are now ready to face whatever new adventure life has in store for them.